All the best,
Elizabeth Kay

Fresh from Elizabeth's Kitchen

Gluten-Free, Allergy-Free Recipes for Healthy, Delicious Meals

by Elizabeth Kaplan
Founder of The Pure Pantry

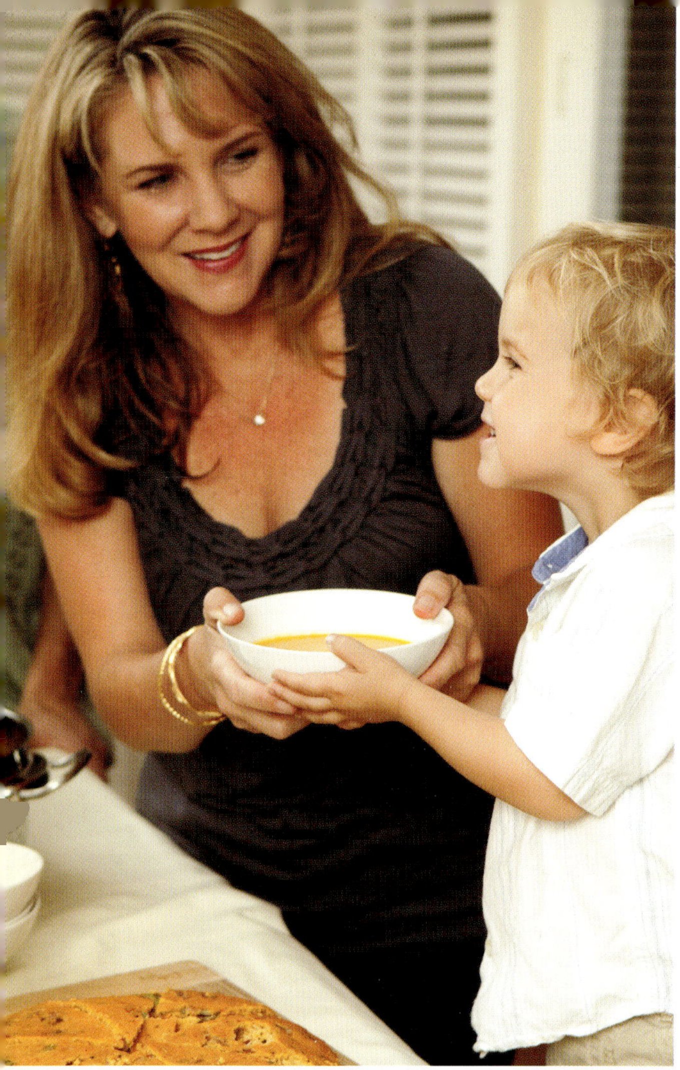
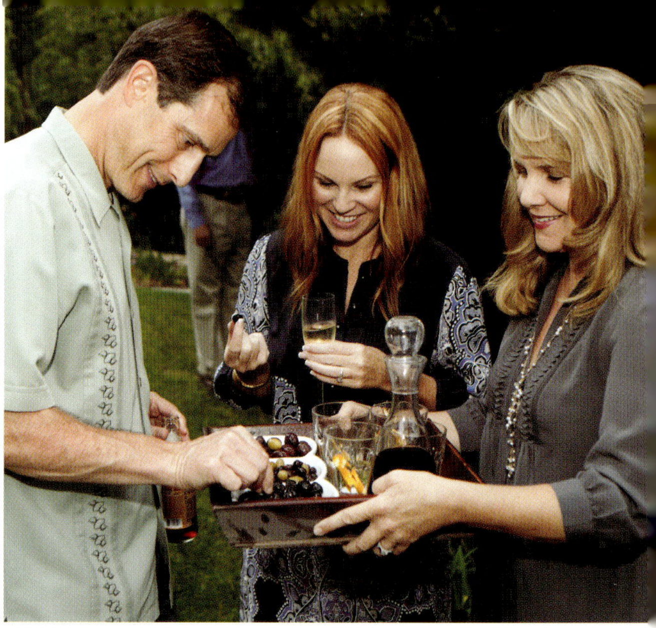
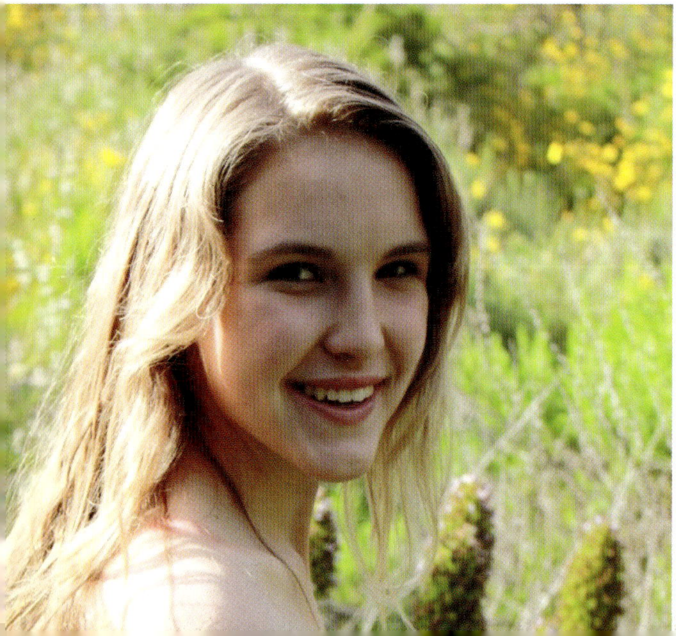
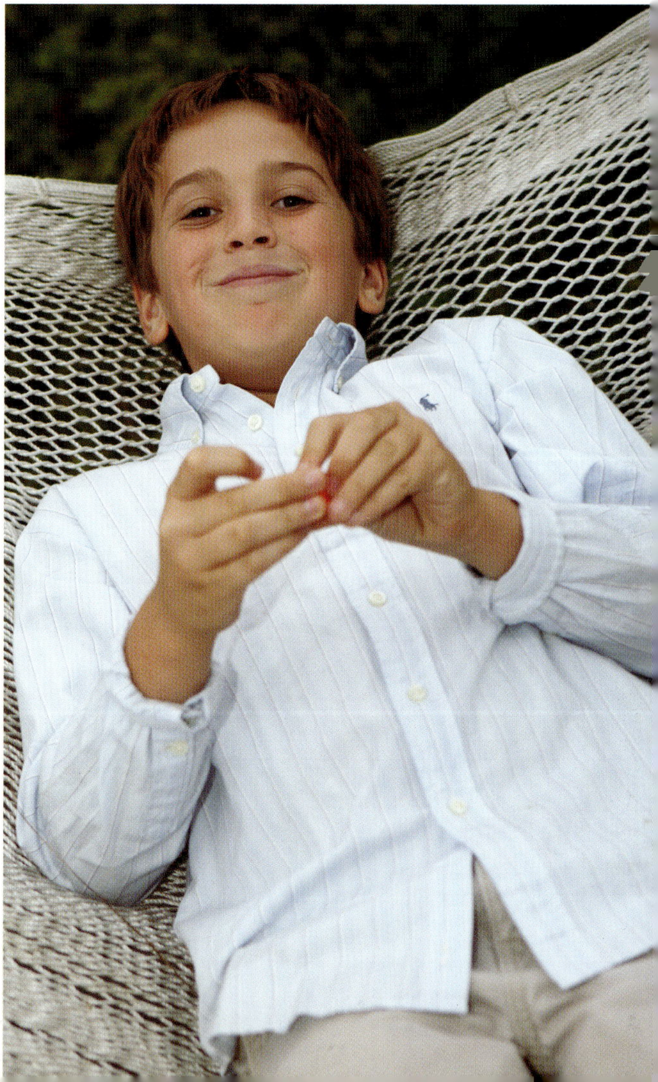

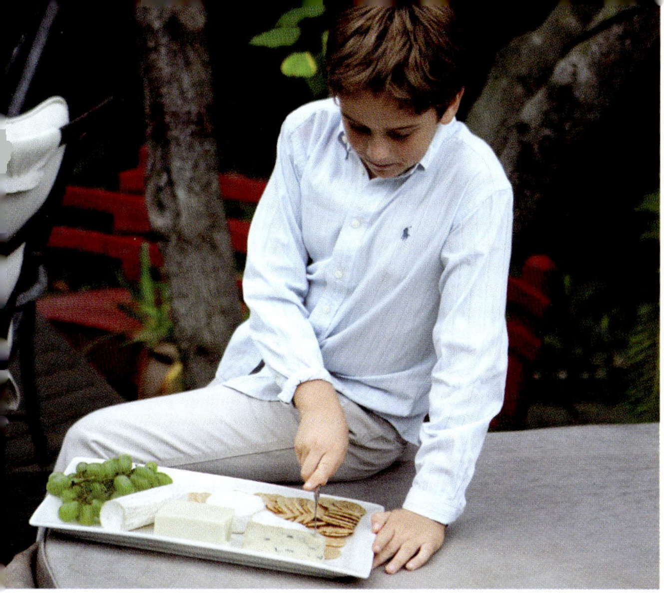
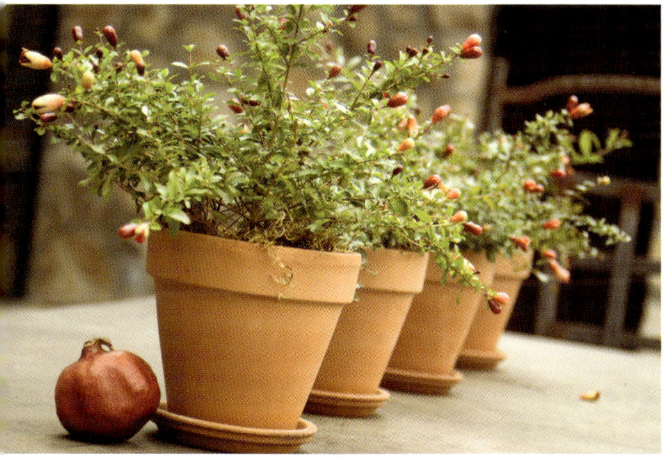
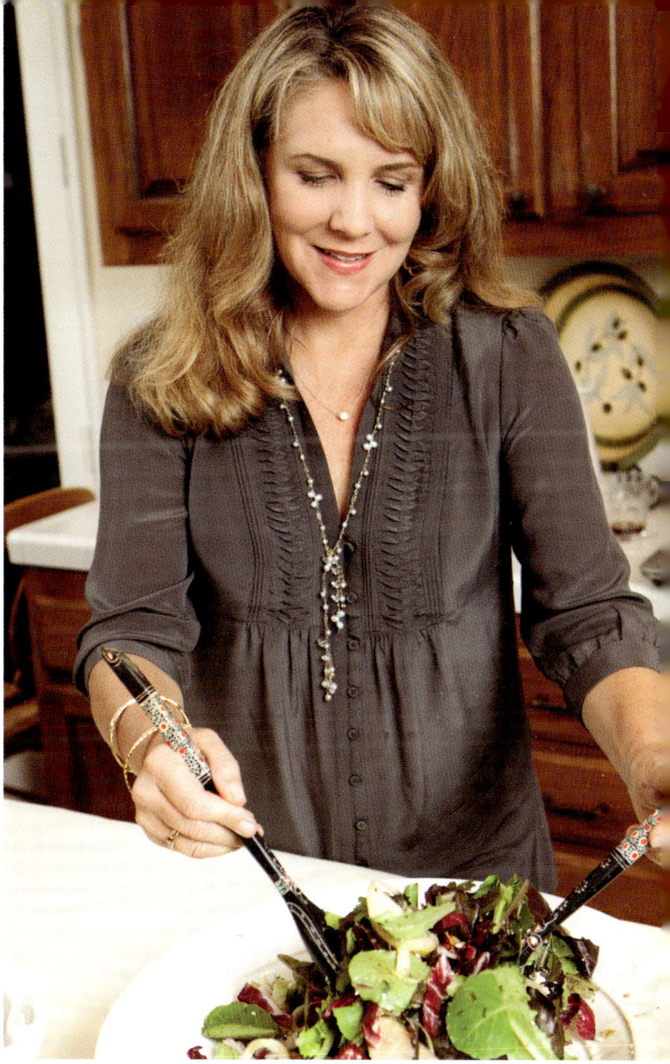
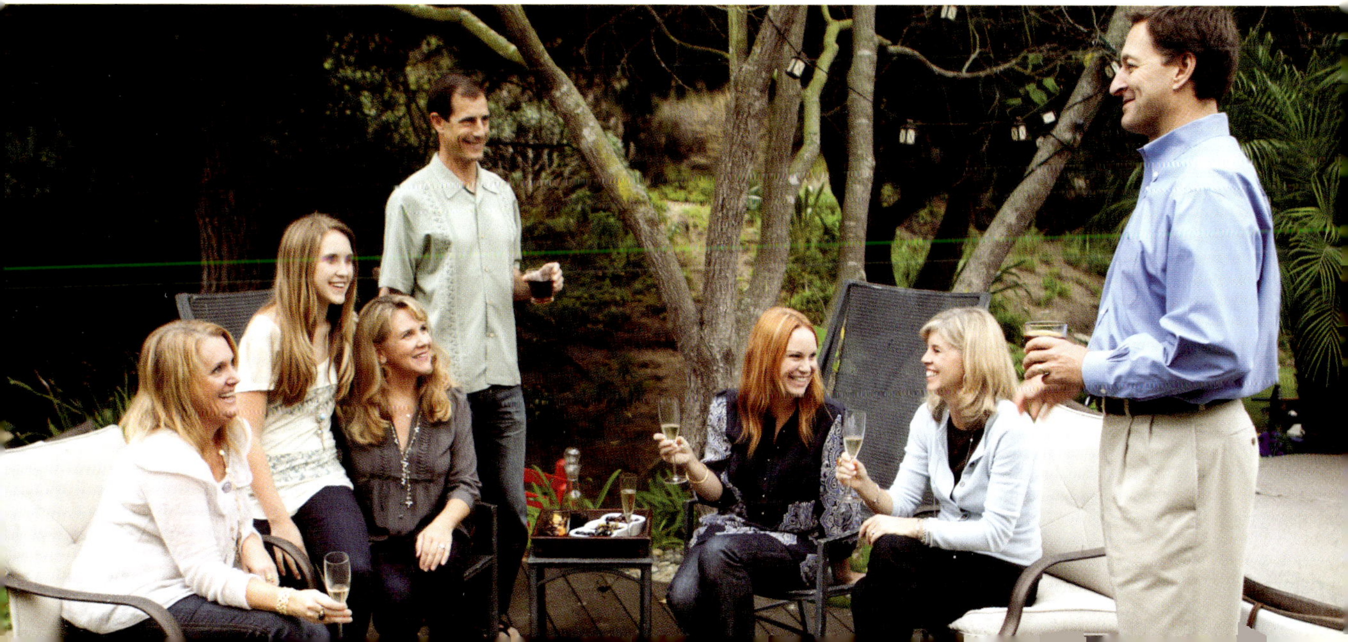

Copyright © 2011 by Elizabeth Kaplan

Food and Lifestyle Photography by Mark Whitehouse © 2011
Cover image of author by Stephen Kahn Photography © 2011
Editors: Karla Olson and Louise Julig
Designers: Molly Gumner and Susan Duffy

All rights reserved. No part of this book may be reproduced, stored in a retrieval system, or transmitted, in any form, or by any means, electronic or mechanical, including photocopying and recording, without prior written consent form the publisher.

Published in the United States by Pennington Press Publishing Group,
119 North El Camino Real, Suite E146, Encinitas, CA, 92024, USA.

Library of Congress Cataloging-in-Publication Data
Kaplan, Elizabeth.
Fresh from Elizabeth's Kitchen / Elizabeth Kaplan. -- 2nd ed. -- San Diego : Pennington Press Publishing Group, c2011.
   p. ; cm.
   ISBN: 978-0-578-07307-1
   Subtitle on cover: Gluten-free & allergy-free recipes for healthy, delicious meals.
   Includes index.

   1. Gluten-free diet--Recipes. 2. Food allergy--Diet therapy--Recipes. I. Title.

RC588.D53 K36 2011
616.97/50654--dc22   1101

ISBN 978-0-578-07307-1

This book is available at special sales discounts for bulk purchases.
For more information, contact info@thepurepantry.com or 760-479-2339.

Second edition
Printed in San Diego, California.

To my loving husband, David,
and my darling children Isabelle, Ryan and Dolan.

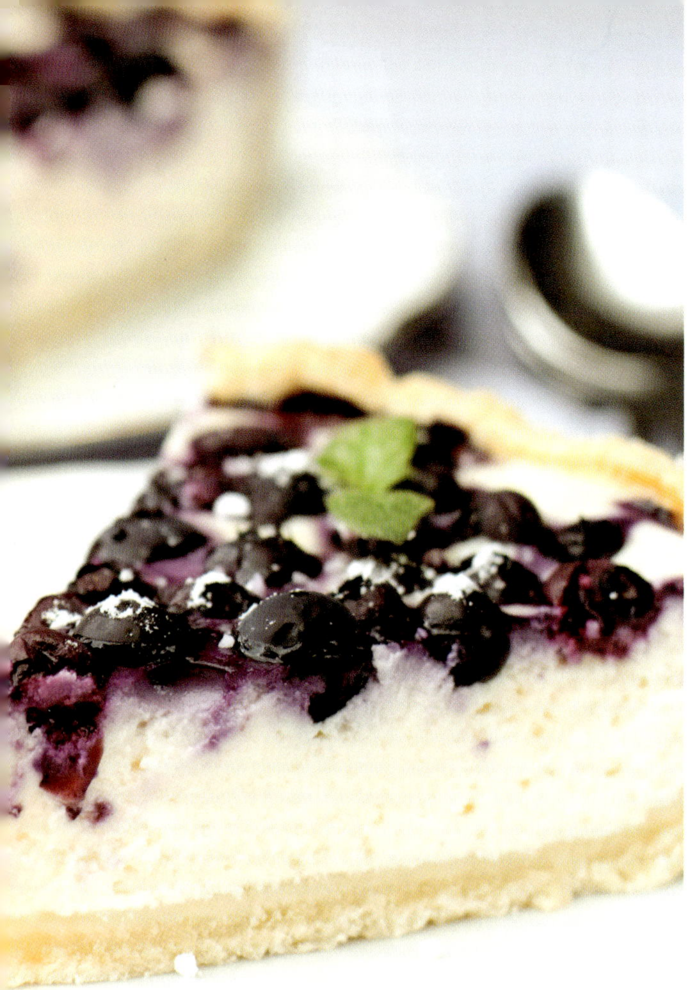
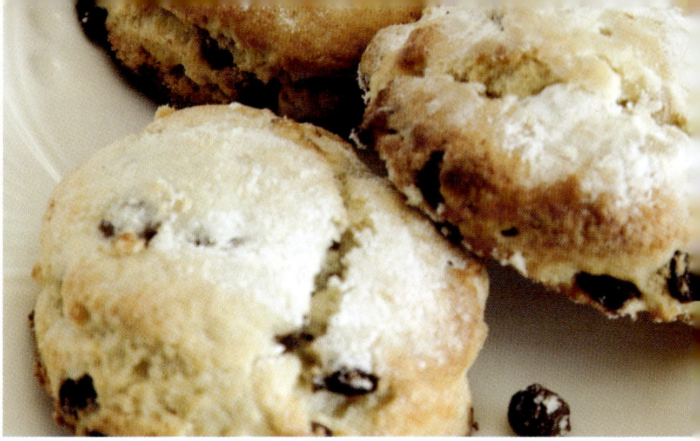
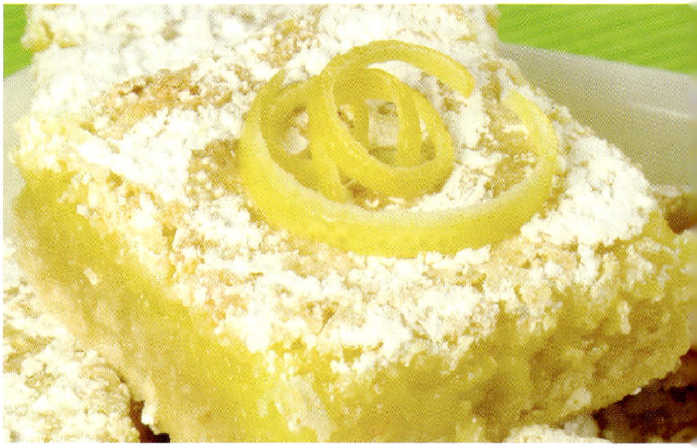
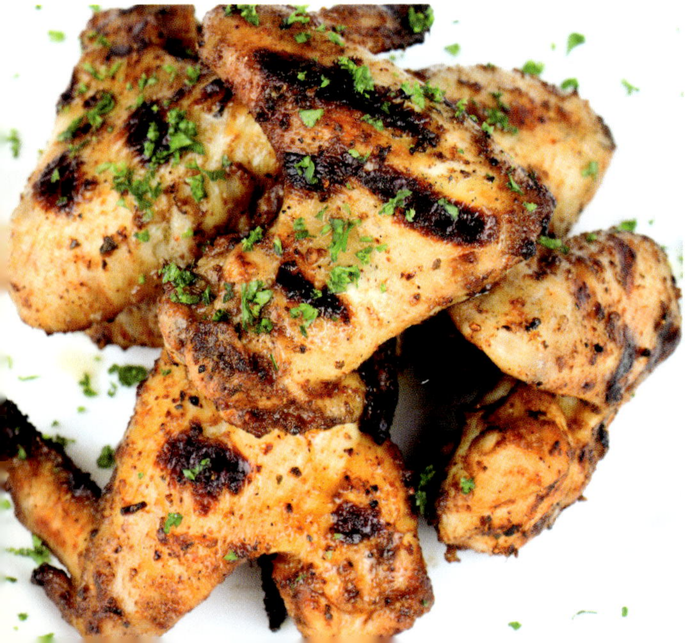
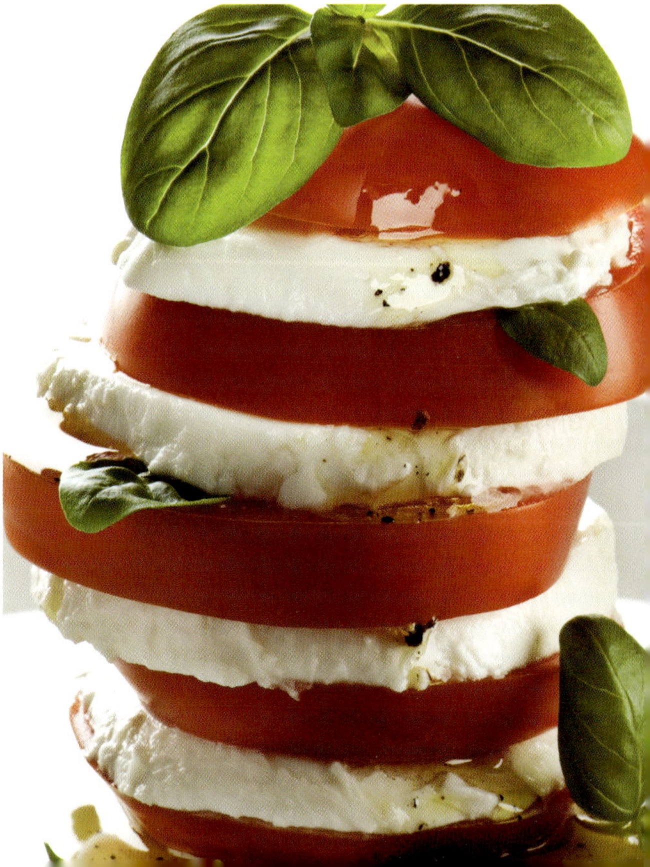

Table of Contents

Foreword 1

Introduction 2

Stocking Your Gluten-free Pantry 16

Family Breakfasts 20

Breads, Muffins, Scones & Biscuits 44

Soups & Salads 66

Family Dinners 90

Divine Desserts 120

The Allergy-free Cookie Jar 150

Menu Ideas 166

Index 170

Foreword

by Dr. Joni Labbe DC, CCN, DCCN

Both my clinical experience and the scientific literature show that gluten is at the core of so many health maladies common today. Research links 55 diseases to gluten, among them osteoporosis, irritable bowel disease, anemia, cancer, fatigue, rheumatoid arthritis, canker sores, lupus, multiple sclerosis, and almost all autoimmune diseases. I treat many patients with Hashimoto's, an autoimmune disease responsible for 90 percent of cases of hypothyroidism in this country. The links between gluten and Hashimoto's are so well established that a gluten-free diet is one of the first things I prescribe to my patients, often with miraculous results.

Gluten is also linked to many neurological disorders, including anxiety, depression, dementia, mental illnesses, migraines, and autism. Many of my patients have seen their brain fog, poor memory, fuzzy thinking, depression and symptoms of autism subside or disappear when they adopted a gluten-free diet.

A gluten-free diet can lengthen your life as well as improve it. A 2009 study found that those with gluten sensitivity had up to a 72 percent increased risk of death. The saddest part of this news is how many people don't even know they are sensitive to gluten.

You would think the prospect of a life half-lived and an early death would have everyone kicking the stuff. Yet the idea of gluten-free seems to be worse than actually doing it. My patients always report that being gluten-free is easier than they thought it would be, and it is even fun as they to discover new products and recipes.

Which is why I am so grateful to Elizabeth Kaplan, founder of The Pure Pantry, for her new book *Fresh from*

Elizabeth's Kitchen: Gluten-Free & Allergy-Free Recipes. With a pleasing color palette and gorgeous photos, *Fresh from Elizabeth's Kitchen* envelops you in the possibilities. The book opens with creative twists on a breakfast standby, the pancake—blueberry oat, nutmeg pumpkin, strawberry pecan. You quickly discover Elizabeth's recipes put a whimsical touch on healthy eating.

In fact, it is Elizabeth's emphasis on nutrition that impressed me. Most gluten-free cookbooks seem to have abandoned good nutrition in favor of copying wheat-based recipes. To improve health it's imperative you not only banish gluten, but also repair the damage it has inflicted on the lining of the digestive tract and elsewhere in the body. Elizabeth also includes many recipes that are dairy-free, egg-free and free of other common food allergens.

Parents will appreciate the attention Elizabeth, a mother of three, gives to kid-friendly recipes. Your child will unwittingly eat her vegetables for breakfast with the Veggie Frittata, in Lentil and Root Vegetable Soup for lunch, and Spaghetti with Turkey Meatballs for dinner. More mature palates will take pleasure in a gluten-free French Onion Soup or Grilled Salmon on Edamame Pesto Hummus with Zucchini "Pasta."

A gluten-free diet is neither a fad nor a clever marketing ploy. It is a new way of life to ensure our wellness in a world that requires more attention than ever to health. But that doesn't mean drudgery or an unpleasant sacrifice. As Fresh from Elizabeth's Kitchen so beautifully and scrumptiously illustrates, a gluten-free diet is a joyous celebration of good health.

Dr. Joni Labbe DC, CCN, DCCN, is a San Diego-based Chiropractor and Board Certified Nutritionist specializing in science-based nutrition with a focus on women's health issues. She uses clinically proven nutraceuticals, dietary modifications, and other tools of natural medicine to address the true cause of dysfunction and disease. http://thyroid-dr.com & www.labbehealthcenter.com

Introduction

It all started with ear infections. Our son Ryan got his first one at six months and continued to get them every three to four months for several years. Being a new mom, I followed the advice of our pediatrician and administered antibiotics, month after month. When baby Ryan tried his first foods, he developed odd rashes, bumpy breakouts and watery eyes. Our pediatrician did not advocate allergy testing but instead told us to do a very careful study of his reactions to each baby food.

We patiently tried food after food, writing down reactions on a chart. In many baby pictures Ryan has a red rash on his cheeks and swollen eyes. As time went on, we began to understand that his food allergies were significant — a couple of scary trips to the emergency room with asthma attacks and we knew we really had to get to the bottom of his allergies.

His ear infections were reduced dramatically when he had surgery at age three to put tubes in his ears. At the time, this was the age pediatricians recommended for children to have this surgery, and although it did help, his immune system was very fragile after years of antibiotics.

Later I read a study that reported that children who had received antibiotics in their first year were significantly more likely to develop asthma, particularly those who had received more than four courses. "No wonder," I thought — Ryan had had at least eight courses of antibiotics in his first three years.

Unfortunately, we were not in the clear yet. At the age of six Ryan began to have grand mal seizures. His first seizure was the scariest experience I had been through yet as a mother, and a diagnosis of epilepsy sent us into a tailspin.

> **After many visits with specialists who wanted to put Ryan on drugs that have dangerous side effects, I decided that a gluten-free diet was the key to solving his seizures and his asthma.**

We researched as much as we could about the causes of childhood epilepsy. After many visits with specialists who wanted to put Ryan on drugs that have dangerous side effects, I decided that a gluten-free diet was the key to solving his seizures and his asthma. Although the pediatric neurologist did not agree that there could be a link between his diet and the seizures, my own intuition, my own struggles with food sensitivities, and extensive research led me to follow a natural healing path.

I had extensive allergy tests done on Ryan to discover all of his allergies: eggs, peanuts, beans, peas, legumes, olive oil, gluten and soy. His test for celiac disease proved positive and explained many of his symptoms. I put him on a gluten-free, allergy-free organic diet. This is where my adventure with allergy-free baking and cooking began.

introduction 13

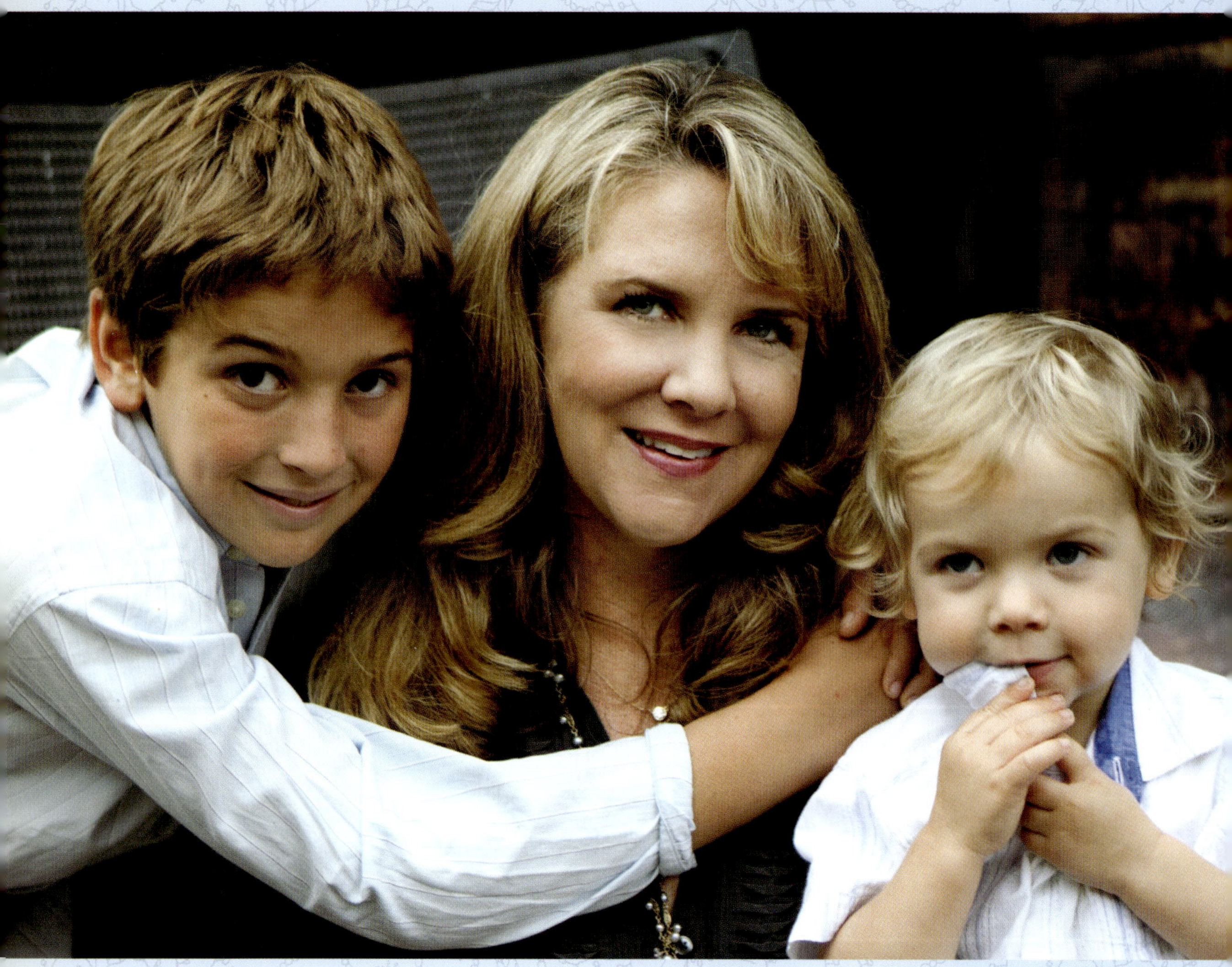

During this time, some symptoms I had while growing up worsened. I was now trying to care for two small children while dealing with achy joints, inflammation, migraine headaches and stomach distress. I visited six different specialists and was tested for cancer, diabetes and a myriad of other diseases and was finally diagnosed with "chronic fatigue," which really didn't tell me anything I didn't already know. It wasn't until I visited a naturopathic doctor that I was told my symptoms were synonymous with celiac disease.

Once I was diagnosed with celiac and began a gluten-free diet, I felt amazingly better. At last, I was so grateful to finally have found help and to be able to use my newfound knowledge to identify that Ryan also had celiac disease. This helped solve much of the mystery behind his many health problems.

Today, our whole family is gluten-free. All three of our children must eat a strict gluten-free diet and our youngest, Dolan, is also dairy-free. Luckily we are all healthy and thriving. Ryan has not had a seizure in five years and only rarely experiences asthma. My children are my

> "Once I was diagnosed with celiac and began a gluten-free diet, I felt amazingly better."

inspiration and my "chief taste testers." It has been exciting to work with them on recipes for this book, which are truly "kid-approved."

While living gluten-free and allergy-free can be challenging, it is worth every bit of effort; allergies can cause many health problems that are often overlooked by medical practitioners, and celiac disease can be life-threatening if not attended to.

While our journey with allergies has been a rocky one, I feel blessed that there is a supportive community of people dealing with the same issues who can share their stories to help others. I hope that sharing the recipes in this book will bring happiness and healthiness to you, your family and friends.

Stocking Your Gluten-free Pantry

What can I eat? Where do I start?

That is often the first thought of people newly diagnosed with food allergies or intolerances. There are many books, magazine articles and websites that focus on what to avoid that contains gluten, dairy and other allergens. My goal in this book is not to focus on what to avoid or deprive yourself of but rather what you can enjoy! Living a gluten-free and/or dairy-free lifestyle does not mean you have to live without delicious, gourmet foods. There are so many creative choices and alternatives for cooking sumptuous meals and desserts – no one needs to feel left out.

You may be wondering where to start. If you have food allergies or, like me, celiac disease, your immune system is compromised. What our bodies need is foods that support healing and don't make us sick. Unfortunately, there are many packaged gluten-free/allergy-free foods on the market that are filled with poor nutrients, such as white rice flour and sugar, which do not help promote healing in our body.

Remember what Hippocrates said, "Let food be thy medicine, and medicine be thy food." With that in mind, fill your plate with fresh, organic produce, lean organic meat, poultry and fish, whole grains and healthy dairy-free alternatives or organic dairy products. Avoid processed foods, fast foods and as much as possible, packaged foods. Set up your pantry with the right gluten-free and dairy-free alternatives so that you can prepare healthy and safe meals that everyone will enjoy.

Stocking Your Gluten-Free Pantry

Here is a list of ingredients that are used in recipes in this cookbook. I recommend using organic ingredients as much as your budget allows.

Gluten-Free Grains and Flours:

Gluten-free rice: Brown rice, brown basmati rice, Arborio rice

Gluten-free brown rice pasta: Tinkyada has the best texture and taste, www.tinkyada.com

Gluten-free oats: Gluten-free Oats, LLC, sells various package sizes and gf oat products, www.glutenfreeoats.com

Gluten-free instant oats: Gluten Freeda makes instant packages for a quick breakfast, www.glutenfreeda.com

Quinoa: A nutritionally dense whole grain, providing a complete protein, quinoa is similar to couscous and comes in red, yellow and black varieties.

Gluten-free flours: There are a variety of healthy, whole grain flours to experiment with including almond flour, amaranth flour, brown rice flour, buckwheat flour, millet flour and sorghum flour.

Gluten-free flour blends and baking mixes: Keeping an already prepared baking mix on hand makes gluten-free baking a breeze. A combination of special flours and xanthan gum is needed in gluten-free baking in order to replace the gluten that helps bind baked goods together. The Pure Pantry's Organic All-Purpose baking mix will work in all the recipes in this cookbook and already combines the necessary binders and leavening agents needed. If you wish to create your own baking mix, the recipe for Elizabeth's Gluten-Free Flour Blend can be stored in an airtight container for up to four months. All recipes in this book using the flour blend will detail the recommended baking powder and/or soda needed. See Elizabeth's Gluten-Free Flour Blend recipe on page 18.

Beans and Lentils:

Organic soy beans: "edamame"

Lentils: Puy French lentils, available from Goldmine Natural Food Company

White beans: cannelli or white northern beans, available from Goldmine Natural Food Company

Protein:

Organic: lean fish, meat, poultry and turkey sausage

Vegetables, Fruits and Herbs:

Fresh vegetables and fruits: all varieties

Nuts and Seeds:

If you are not allergic to nuts and seeds, they should be a part of your daily diet as they provide valuable, nutritionally dense omega-3 fatty acids and fiber.

Nuts - Almonds, walnuts, pinenuts, pumpkin seeds, sesame seeds

Flax seeds and chia seeds – excellent egg replacers in baked goods (see egg replacers below)

Elizabeth's Gluten-Free Flour Blend

Ingredients	4 cups mix	8 cups mix
Organic brown rice flour	1 ½ cups	3 cups
Organic white rice flour	1 ¼ cups	2 ½ cups
Organic sorghum, millet or amaranth*	½ cup	1 cup
Organic potato starch flour	½ cup	1 cup
Organic tapioca flour	¼ cup	½ cup
Xanthan gum	2 teaspoons	1 tablespoon

Mix all ingredients together and place in air-tight container.
Makes 4 cups mix.

*When choosing which flour combination to use, consider that sorghum will give you the lightest result in baking. Millet and amaranth will give you a heavier result. For cakes and cookies, I recommend using sorghum. For breads, scones, and biscuits, millet or amaranth are good choices.

Dairy: If Tolerant

Organic dairy products: milk, yogurt with pro-biotics, cream (for occasional desserts), cream cheese and sour cream.

Hard cheeses: parmesan, cheddar, gruyere.

Soft cheeses: goat feta, goat cheddar - easier to digest than cow's milk.

Dairy-Free Alternatives:

Coconut milk: refrigerated, So-Delicious brand, www.turtlemountain.com or canned, light and regular coconut milk.

Coconut yogurt: So-Delicious brand.

Cream cheese alternative: Tofutti brand, www.tofutti.com.

Sour cream alternative: Tofutti brand.

Cheese alternatives: Daiya mozzarella and cheddar cheese, www.daiyafoods.com.

Dairy-free ice cream: Coconut Bliss Ice Cream, www.coconutbliss.com.

Butter Alternatives:

Non-hydrogenated palm fruit oil or shortening: Spectrum organics, www.spectrumorganics.com.

Coconut oil: Spectrum organics.

Non-hydrogenated margarine: Earth Balance Buttery Sticks, www.EarthBalanceNatural.com.

Organic Eggs or Egg Alternatives:

Egg Replacers: Ener-G Foods makes an egg replacer that works well in most baked goods. In the recipes in this book, I indicate if an egg replacer can be used in place of eggs. www.ener-g.com.

Flax gel or chia gel egg replacer: To replace one egg, mix one tablespoon ground flax meal or chia seeds with 3 tablespoons hot water. Let sit for 5 minutes or until thick and stir again.

Sweeteners:

Whenever I can, I prefer to use unrefined sugar or other healthy sweeteners. You will see that in many recipes I replace sugar with agave nectar or use a combination of the two.

Agave nectar – makes a great sugar replacement because it is naturally sweeter than sugar, saving calories, and it has a low glycemic index which does not spike blood sugar levels. There are many agave nectars available but I prefer Nature's Agave because they have three varieties, raw, amber and clear, that work for different outcomes. Nature's Agave is available at many natural food stores or on-line at www.naturesagave.com.

Maple sugar – both the taste and the nutritional benefits make it a great sugar substitute. It can be used in place of brown sugar in most recipes.

Coconut sugar – a distinctive taste, it can be used to replace brown sugar.

stocking your pantry

Chapter One

Family Breakfasts

Homemade Gluten-Free Pancakes

Blueberry-Oat Pancakes with Blueberry-Agave Syrup

Isabelle's Strawberry Pecan Pancakes with Strawberry-Agave Butter

Nutmeg Pumpkin Pancakes

Gingerbread Waffles with Pecan-Agave Butter and Cinnamon Poached Pears

Homemade Gluten-Free Crêpes

Apple-Cinnamon Crêpes

Raspberry Chocolate Crêpes

Ryan's Berry Blintzes

Quick Cranberry Nut Coffee Cake

Chocolate Chip Espresso Coffee Cake

Tomato-Pesto Breakfast Strata

Maui Onion and Chèvre Tart

Veggie Frittata

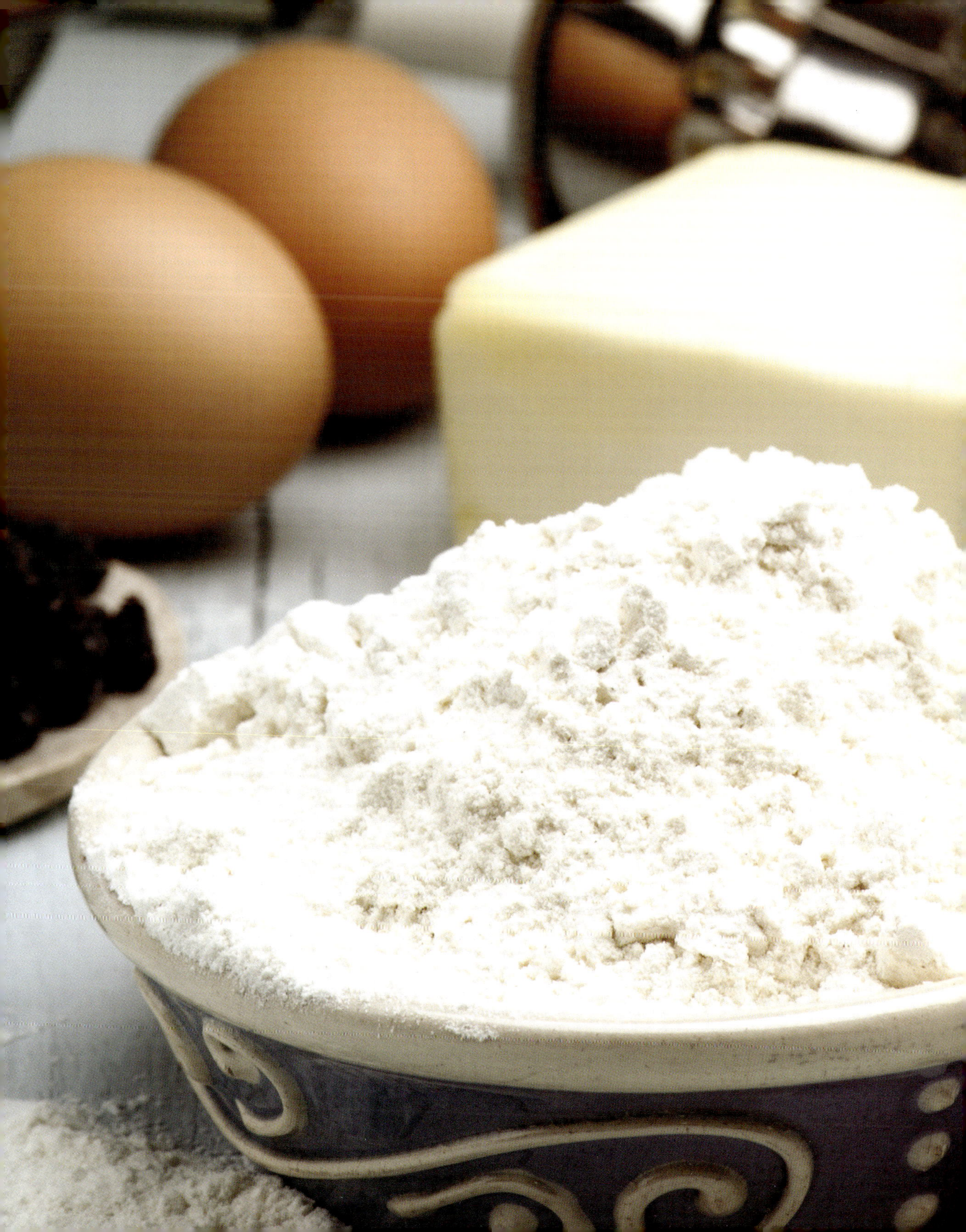

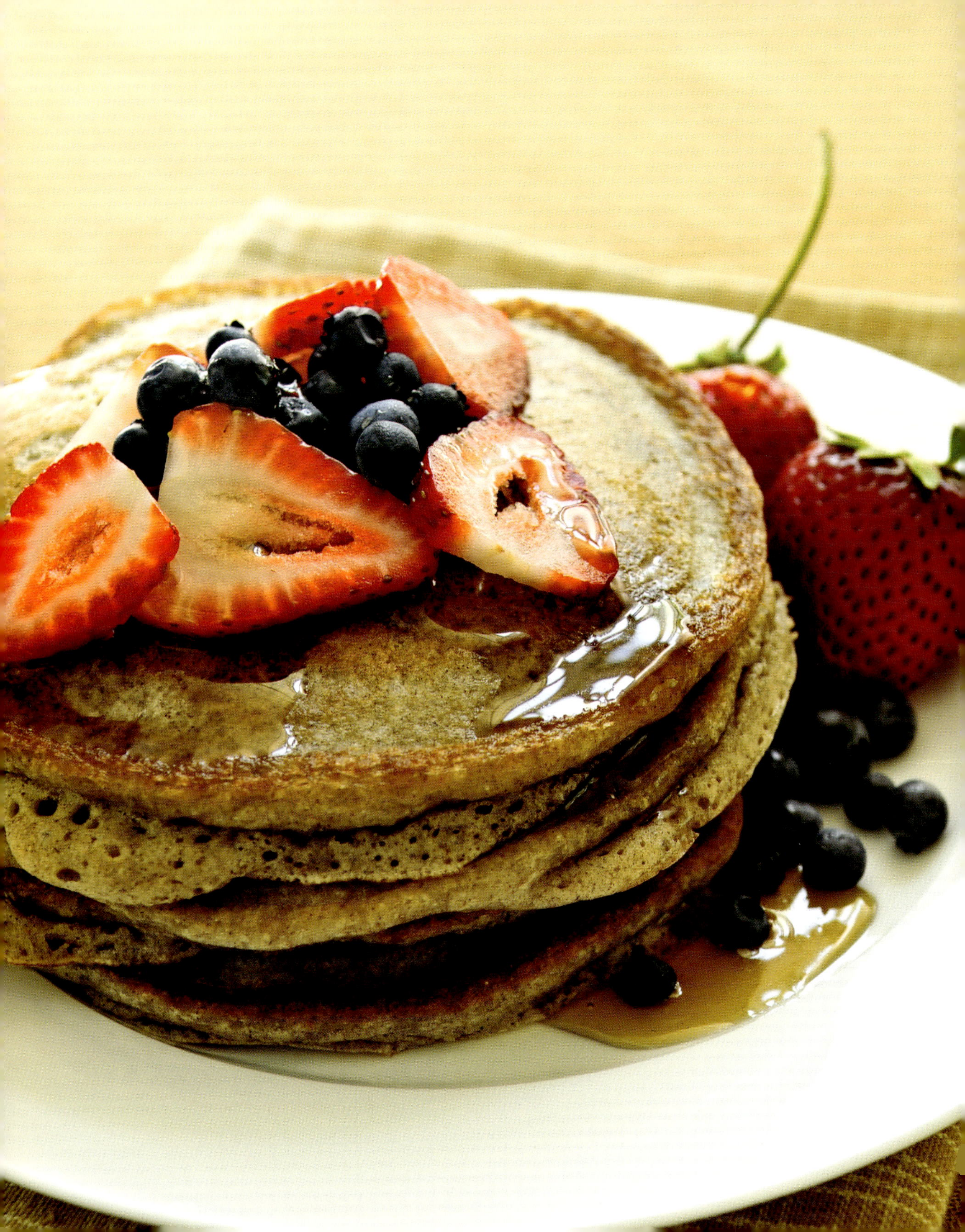

Homemade Gluten-Free Pancakes

Gluten-Free/Dairy-Free Option

Makes 8-10 pancakes

1 1/3 cups Elizabeth's Gluten-Free Flour Blend (see Index)

1 teaspoon baking soda

1 teaspoon baking powder

1/2 teaspoon salt

1 1/3 cups milk of choice (regular, rice milk or coconut milk)

1 egg

1 tablespoon safflower oil

1 tablespoon agave nectar, preferably Nature's Agave, Amber variety

1. In a large bowl, place flour blend, baking soda, baking powder and salt. Whisk to combine. Make a well in the center of the dry ingredients.

2. In a medium bowl, whisk together milk with egg, oil and agave nectar. Pour milk mixture into well in dry mixture and blend together.

3. Grease pancake griddle and place on medium heat. Using ladle or 1/4-cup size measuring cup, pour batter onto pancake griddle to form pancakes. Cook for 2-3 minutes or until bubbles pop. Flip pancakes over and cook for one minute or until golden brown.

Blueberry Oat Pancakes with Blueberry-Agave Syrup

Gluten-Free/Dairy-Free

Makes 8-10 pancakes

Pancakes

1 batch Homemade Gluten-Free Pancake batter (see Index) or 1 batch pancake batter using The Pure Pantry Gluten-Free Organic Old Fashioned Pancake and Baking Mix

½ cup gluten-free quick-cook oats, preferably Legacy Valley brand

½ cup vanilla yogurt or coconut-vanilla yogurt (dairy-free)

1 cup fresh or frozen blueberries

Blueberry-Agave Syrup

¼ cup blueberry spread, preferably Crofter's Organic

1 cup agave nectar, preferably Nature's Agave, Clear variety

1. Prepare pancake batter as specified in Homemade Gluten-Free Pancakes (see Index) or prepare batter using The Pure Pantry mix. Add gluten-free quick cook oats, yogurt and blueberries. Stir to combine. Refrigerate for 30 minutes.

2. Place blueberry spread in small saucepan over low heat and stir until melted. Add agave nectar. Bring to low boil for 2 minutes, stirring constantly. Pour into serving pitcher.

3. Stir pancake mix again before preparing pancakes. Grease pancake griddle and place on medium heat. Using ladle or ¼-cup size measuring cup, pour batter onto pancake griddle to form pancakes. Cook for 2-3 minutes or until bubbles pop. Flip pancakes over and cook for 1 minute or until golden brown. Serve with Blueberry-Agave Syrup.

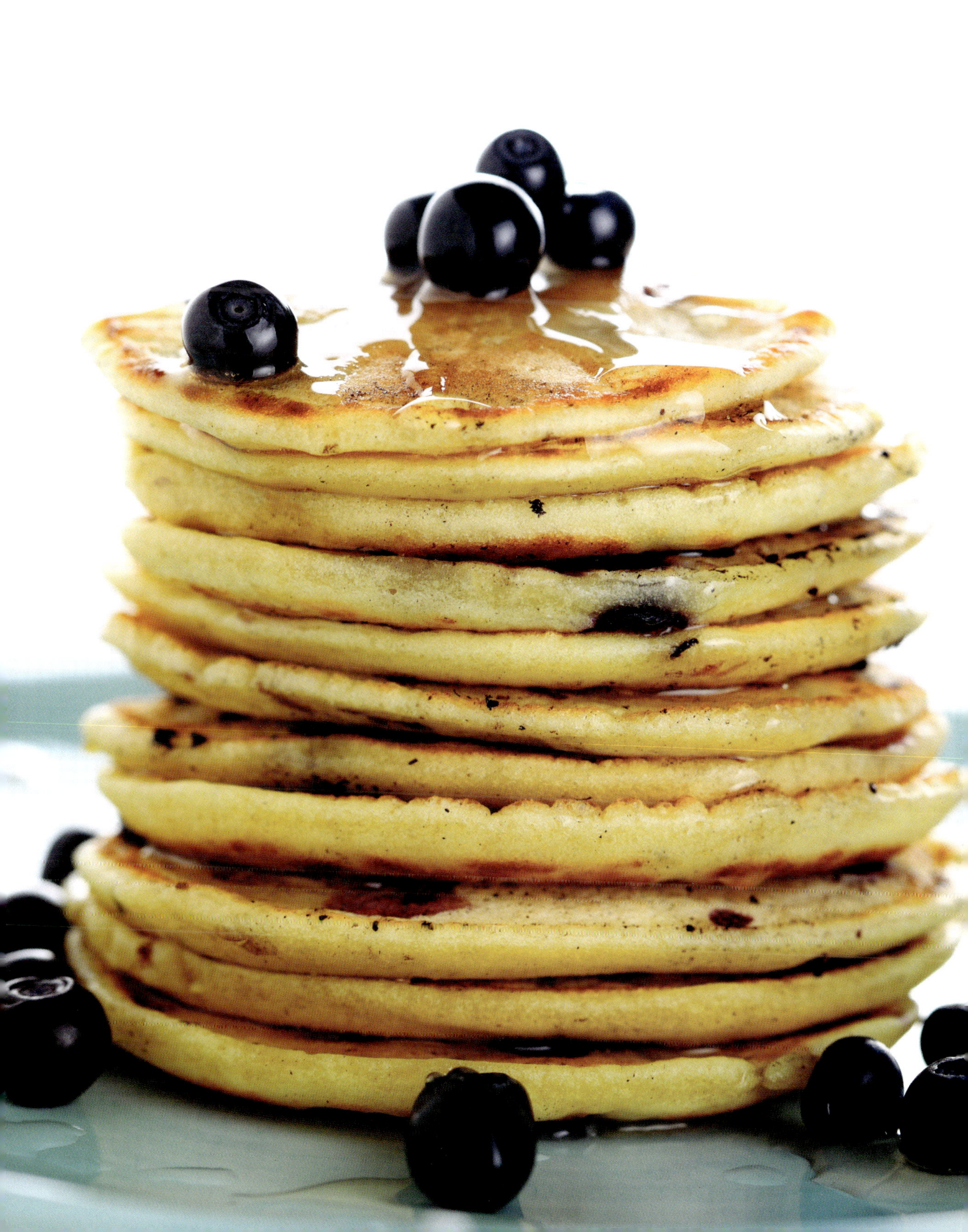

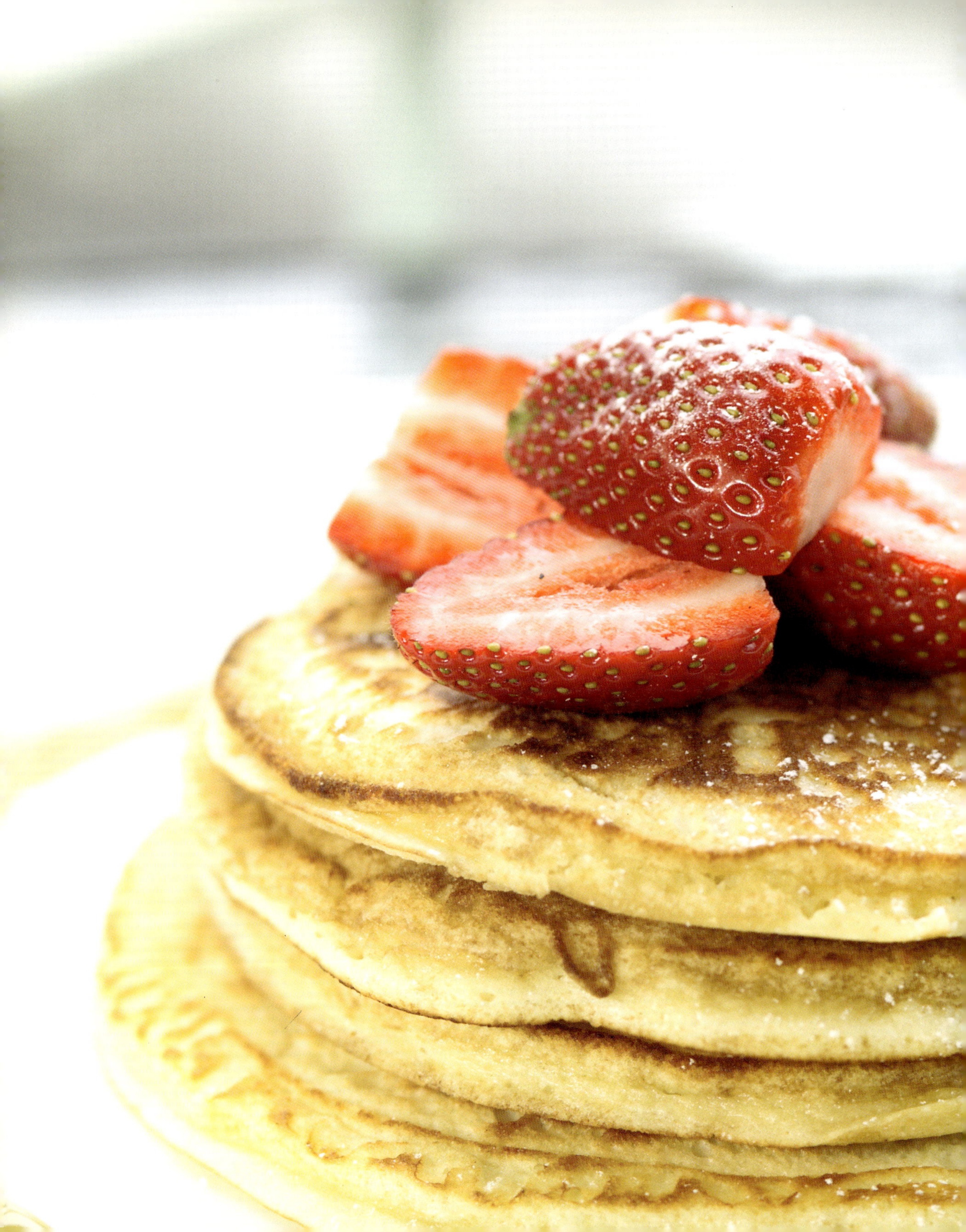

Isabelle's Strawberry-Pecan Pancakes with Strawberry-Agave Butter

Gluten-Free/Dairy-Free Options

Makes 8-10 pancakes

Pancakes

1 batch Homemade Gluten-Free Pancakes (see Index) or 1 batch pancake batter using The Pure Pantry Gluten-Free Organic Old Fashioned Pancake and Baking Mix

½ cup chopped pecans (optional)

¾ cup diced fresh strawberries, plus more for garnish

½ cup vanilla yogurt or coconut vanilla yogurt (dairy free)

Strawberry-Agave Butter

½ cup butter or Earth Balance Buttery Spread

¼ cup fresh strawberries, diced

¼ cup agave nectar, preferably Nature's Agave, Clear variety

1. In large bowl prepare pancake batter as specified in Homemade Gluten-Free Pancakes or prepare batter using The Pure Pantry mix. Add pecans, strawberries and yogurt. Stir to combine.

2. Using ladle or ¼-cup measuring cup, pour batter onto pancake griddle to form pancakes. Cook for 2-3 minutes or until bubbles pop. Flip pancakes over and cook for 1 minute or until golden brown.

3. For Strawberry-Agave Butter: Place butter in bowl of electric mixer and blend until smooth. Add diced strawberries and agave nectar and mix until blended. Top stack of pancakes with one generous scoop of Strawberry-Agave Butter and garnish with fresh strawberries. Drizzle with agave nectar.

Nutmeg Pumpkin Pancakes with Pecan-Agave Butter

Gluten-Free/Dairy-Free

Makes 8-10 pancakes

These are a special Halloween morning treat in our house. We decorate the pancakes to look like Jack O'Lanterns using triangles and wedges of melon for the eyes, nose and mouth.

Pancakes
- 1 batch Homemade Gluten-free Pancakes (see Index) or 1 batch pancake batter using The Pure Pantry Gluten-Free Organic Old Fashioned Pancake and Baking Mix
- 1 large egg
- 1 cup canned pumpkin
- ¼ cup agave nectar, preferably Nature's Agave, Amber variety
- 1 teaspoon cinnamon
- ½ teaspoon nutmeg

Pecan-Agave Butter
- ¼ cup butter
- ¼ cup agave nectar, preferably Nature's Agave, Amber variety
- 1 teaspoon cinnamon
- 1 tablespoon brown sugar
- ½ cup finely chopped pecans or walnuts (optional)

1. In a large bowl, prepare pancake mix as instructed for Homemade Gluten-free Pancakes, or prepare batter using The Pure Pantry mix. In a small bowl, blend egg, pumpkin, agave nectar, cinnamon and nutmeg. Combine pancake mix with pumpkin mixture and whisk until blended.

2. Heat nonstick griddle to medium heat. Grease griddle. Using a ladle or ¼-cup measure, scoop portions of pancake mix onto griddle. Cook pancakes until bubbles pop. Turn over and cook for one minute or until edges are golden.

3. For Pecan-Agave Butter: With fork, combine butter, agave nectar, cinnamon, brown sugar and chopped nuts. Place 1 tablespoon on top of each pancake stack. Serve with agave nectar.

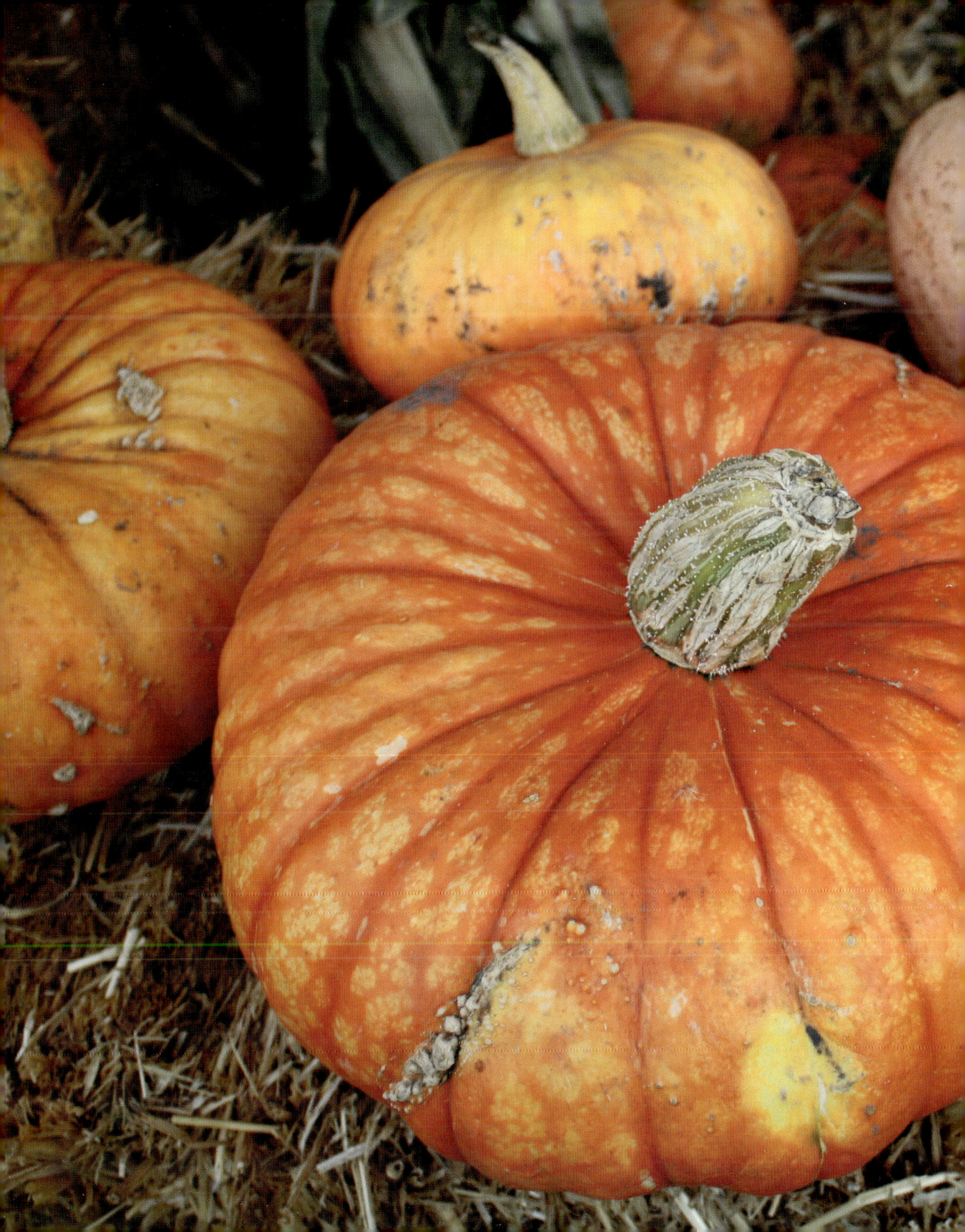

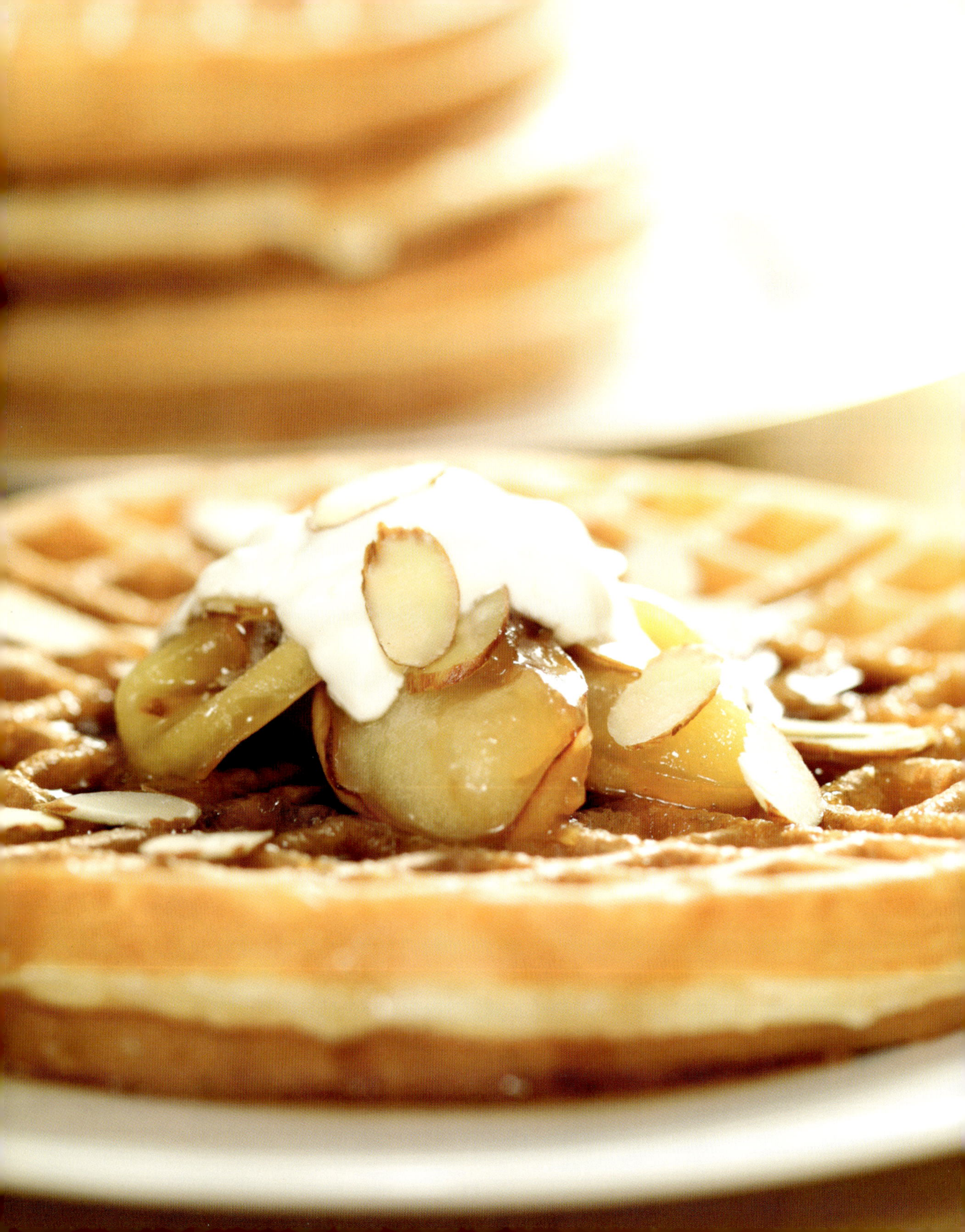

Gingerbread Waffles
with Pecan-Agave Butter and Cinnamon-Poached Pears

Gluten-Free/Dairy-Free Options

Serves 4 - 6

Waffles
1 recipe Homemade Gluten-Free Pancake Mix (see Index) or 1 batch of The Pure Pantry Old Fashioned Pancake Mix

¼ cup blackstrap molasses

1 teaspoon cinnamon

1 teaspoon ground cloves

1 teaspoon ground nutmeg

1 tablespoon ginger

1 teaspoon vanilla

1 recipe Pecan-Agave Butter (see Index)

Cinnamon Poached Pears
2 tablespoons agave nectar, preferably Nature's Agave, Clear variety

2 tablespoons brown sugar

¼ cup butter or coconut oil

2 D'Anjou Pears, core removed, cut into quarters

2 tablespoons slivered almonds, (optional)

1. Prepare pancake batter in large bowl. Add molasses, cinnamon, cloves, nutmeg, ginger and vanilla. Prepare waffles as indicated by waffle iron manufacturer.

2. Prepare Pecan-Agave Butter recipe (see Index).

3. Combine the agave nectar, brown sugar and butter or coconut oil in sauté pan over medium heat. Let cook, stirring constantly, for 2 minutes. Add pears and gently toss while sautéing the fruit. When pears are soft, about 3 minutes, serve over hot waffles and top with 1 tablespoon of Pecan-Agave Butter or slivered almonds.

Homemade Gluten-Free Crêpes

Gluten-Free/Dairy-Free

Makes 8-10 large crêpes

1½ cups Elizabeth's Gluten-Free Flour Blend (see Index)

2 teaspoons baking powder

2½ cups milk of choice (regular, rice milk or coconut milk)

2 eggs

1 teaspoon safflower oil

1 teaspoon vanilla

1. Whisk together flour blend and baking powder in a large bowl. Make a well in the center of the flour mixture.

2. In a separate bowl, whisk together milk, eggs, oil and vanilla. Pour wet ingredients into the well in the flour mixture. Mix together until smooth. Batter can also be made in a blender. Refrigerate for 20 minutes.

3. Grease crêpe pan with cooking spray. Preheat pan over medium-low heat. Using a ¼-cup measure or ladle, pour crêpe mix into crêpe pan and rotate in circular motion to spread the batter out to the edge of the pan. If batter does not spread easily, add 1-2 tablespoons of rice milk to batter. Once tiny bubbles have popped, lift edges of crêpe with spatula and flip over. Cook for additional minute. Place cooked crêpes on platter with waxed paper in between each crêpe. Fill with favorite filling.

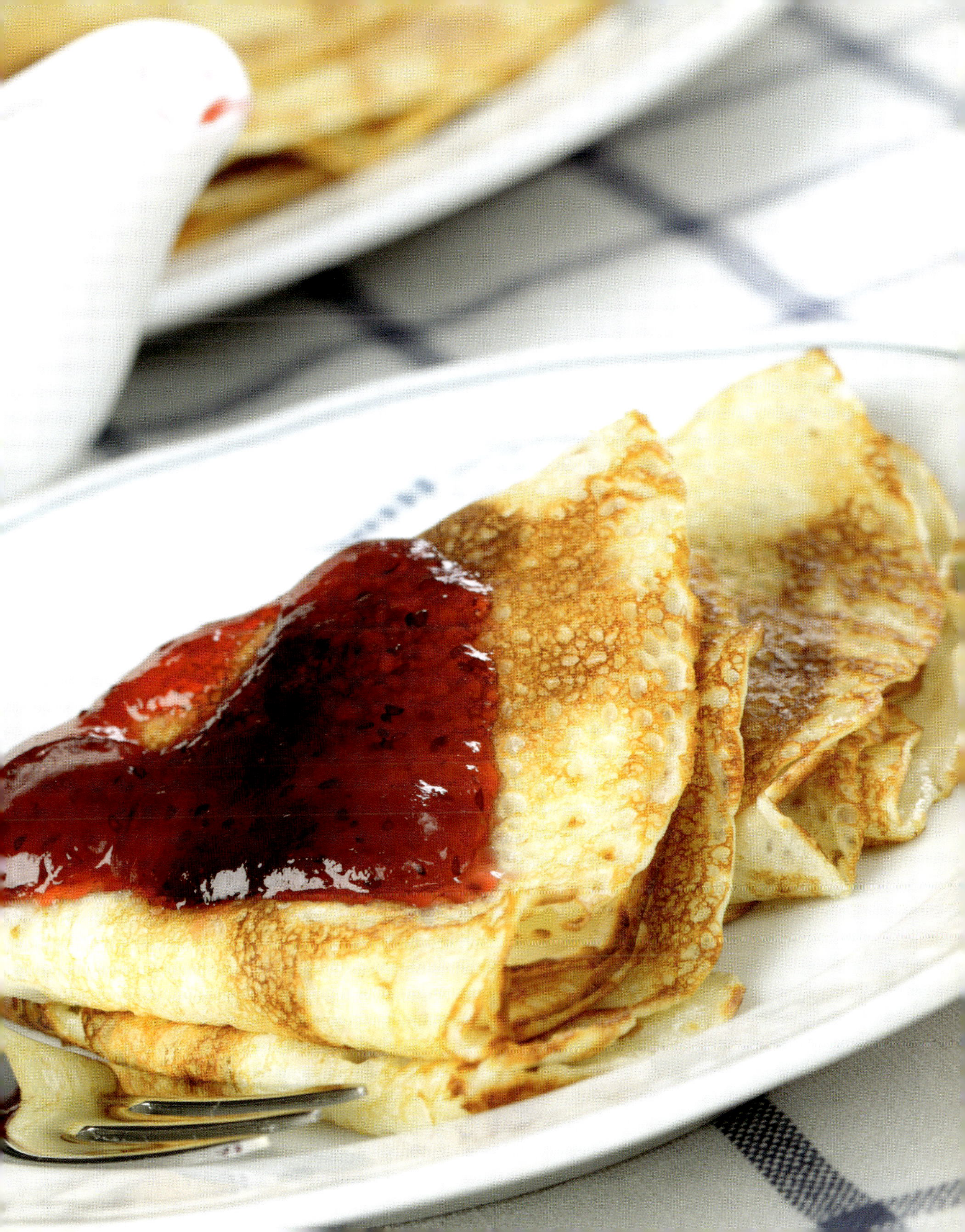

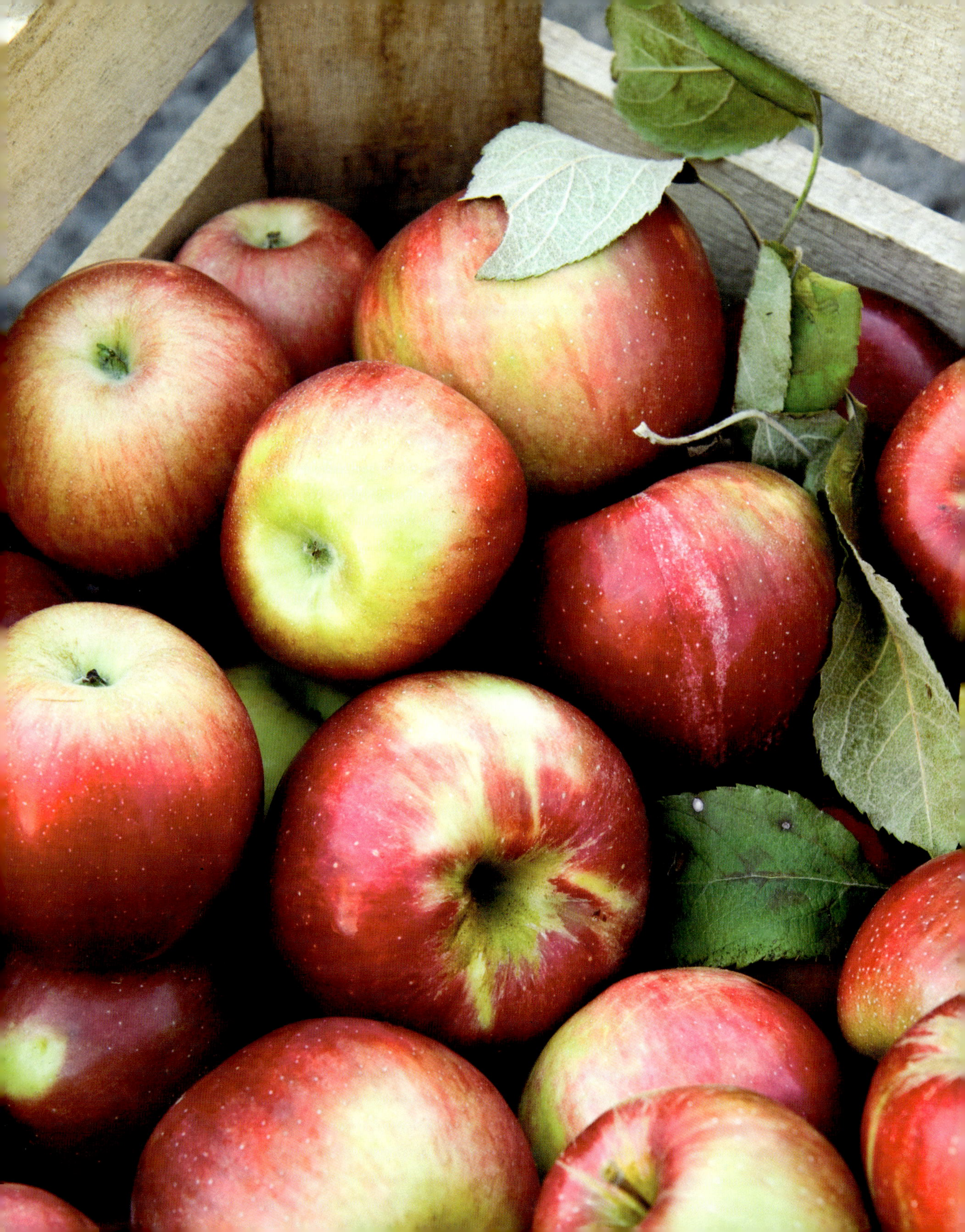

Apple-Cinnamon Crêpes

Gluten-Free/Dairy-Free

Makes 10-12 crêpes

Crêpes
1 batch Homemade Gluten-free Crêpes (see Index) or 1 batch crêpe batter using The Pure Pantry Gluten-Free Organic Old Fashioned Pancake and Baking Mix

1 teaspoon cinnamon

1 tablespoon agave nectar, preferably Nature's Agave, Amber variety

Filling
¼ cup butter or coconut oil

4 Fuji or Honey Crisp apples, peeled, cored and thinly sliced to ¼ inch thickness

3 tablespoons agave nectar, preferably Nature's Agave, Amber variety

3 tablespoons brown sugar

1½ teaspoons cinnamon

1. Prepare crêpe batter as specified in Homemade Gluten-Free Crêpes or use The Pure Pantry mix. Add cinnamon and agave nectar to batter. Make crêpes and layer between waxed paper.

2. For filling: Melt butter or coconut oil in medium sauté pan over low heat. Add agave nectar, brown sugar and cinnamon. Cook until mixture begins to bubble, then add apple slices. Sauté apples in butter mixture until slightly softened, about 3-4 minutes.

3. Fill each crepe with 3 or 4 apple slices and roll up. Place on plate. Drizzle with agave nectar and sprinkle with cinnamon.

Raspberry Chocolate Crêpes

Gluten-Free/Dairy-Free

Makes 10-12 crêpes

Crêpes
1 batch Homemade Gluten-free Crêpes (see Index) or 1 batch crêpe batter using The Pure Pantry Gluten-Free Organic Old Fashioned Pancake and Baking Mix

1 pint fresh raspberries

1½ cups raspberry or any berry fruit spread, such as Crofter's Organic Premium Spread

1½ cups Chocolate-Agave Sauce (see Index)

1. Prepare crêpe batter as specified in Homemade Gluten-Free Crêpes or use The Pure Pantry mix. Layer between waxed paper.

2. Spread 1 tablespoon fruit spread on crêpe and roll up. Place two crêpes on each serving plate. Top with 6-8 fresh raspberries. Drizzle with Chocolate Agave Sauce. For dessert, add vanilla ice cream, coconut ice cream (dairy-free) or freshly whipped cream.

breakfast 35

Ryan's Berry Blintzes
Gluten-Free with Dairy-Free Options

Makes 8 blintzes

Ryan is the crêpe-maker in our household. Together we enjoy preparing these blintzes (rolled, filled crêpes) for special holiday morning breakfasts. To save time, these blintzes can be prepared the day before and refrigerated. In the morning, remove from the refrigerator, bake and add the berry topping.

Crêpes
1 batch Homemade Gluten-Free Crêpe batter (see Index) or 1 batch crêpe batter using The Pure Pantry Gluten-Free Organic Old Fashioned Pancake and Baking Mix

1 teaspoon freshly grated orange peel

Filling
½ cup cottage cheese (for dairy-free, omit cottage cheese)

½ cup vanilla non-fat yogurt (or coconut vanilla yogurt)

½ cup whipped cream cheese (for dairy-free, increase to 1 cup Tofutti cream cheese substitute)

½ teaspoon grated orange peel

1 cup strawberry fruit spread, preferably Crofter's Organic

Topping
1 cup fresh blueberries

1 cup fresh strawberries

½ cup vanilla yogurt (or coconut vanilla yogurt)

1. Prepare crêpe batter as specified in Homemade Gluten-Free Crêpes and add grated orange peel. Make crêpes and layer between waxed paper.

2. Prepare filling by mixing cream cheese (or Tofutti cream cheese) with electric mixer until creamy. Add vanilla yogurt (or coconut vanilla yogurt) and cottage cheese (omit cottage cheese for dairy-free and increase Tofutti cream cheese to 1 cup) and blend. Mix in ½ teaspoon grated orange peel.

3. Preheat oven to 350°F. Grease a 9 x 12-inch baking pan with butter or vegetable shortening. Place a crêpe on work surface. Place 1 tablespoon strawberry fruit spread in center of crêpe and spread toward the outside edges of the crêpe leaving a 2-inch border. Place 2 tablespoons cream cheese mixture in the center of the crêpe. Fold in opposite edges of each side of the crêpe then roll one side up to make a packet (like a burrito). Place side by side in baking pan. Once all blintzes are complete, bake for 10 minutes.

4. Remove blintzes from oven. Stir remaining ½ cup vanilla yogurt until smooth. Pour ribbon of yogurt over blintzes and bake for 3 more minutes with pan on top shelf of oven

5. Place two blintzes on each plate. Top with blueberries and strawberries and serve.

Quick Cranberry Nut Coffee Cake

Gluten-Free/Dairy-Free Options

Serves 8

¼ cup brown sugar

½ cup chopped walnuts or pecans

½ teaspoon cinnamon

⅔ cup whole berry cranberry sauce

2 cups Elizabeth's Gluten-Free Flour Blend (see Index) plus 1 teaspoon baking powder and 1 teaspoon baking soda or 2 cups plus 2 teaspoons The Pure Pantry Gluten-Free Organic All-Purpose Baking Mix

2 tablespoons sugar

½ teaspoon cinnamon

1 egg

⅔ cup milk (regular, rice milk or coconut milk)

1. Preheat oven to 350°F. Generously grease bottom and sides of square 8 x 8-inch baking pan or small 4-cup bundt pan with 1 tablespoon butter or margarine.

2. In a small bowl, mix together brown sugar, chopped walnuts or pecans and cinnamon. Sprinkle nut mixture in bottom of pan. Spread cranberry sauce over nut mixture.

3. In a large bowl, combine baking mix (if using Elizabeth's Gluten-Free Flour Blend, add 1 teaspoon baking powder and 1 teaspoon baking soda) with sugar, cinnamon, egg and milk. Stir until well blended. Pour over cranberry sauce.

4. Bake 25 minutes. Cool cake for 15 minutes. Run knife along edge of pan to loosen sides. Invert pan onto plate. Dust with powdered sugar, if desired.

Chocolate Chip Espresso Coffee Cake
Gluten-Free

Makes one 12-cup bundt cake

Streusel Topping

¼ cup butter or coconut oil, melted

1 cup brown sugar

¼ cup Elizabeth's Gluten-Free Flour Blend (see Index) plus ½ teaspoon baking powder, or ¼ cup The Pure Pantry Gluten-Free Organic All-Purpose Baking Mix

1 tablespoon instant espresso (optional)

½ cup gluten-free, dairy-free chocolate chips, preferably Enjoy Life brand

Cake

½ cup butter or coconut oil

¼ cup agave nectar, preferably Nature's Agave, Clear variety

1 teaspoon vanilla

2 eggs

⅔ cup rice or coconut milk

2 cups Elizabeth's Gluten-Free Flour Blend (see Index) plus 1 teaspoon baking powder and 1 teaspoon baking soda, or 2 cups plus 2 teaspoons The Pure Pantry Gluten-Free Organic All-Purpose Baking Mix

½ cup gluten-free, dairy-free chocolate chips, preferably Enjoy Life brand

1. Preheat oven to 350°F. Generously grease 12-cup bundt pan, with butter or margarine and dust with gluten-free flour blend.

2. Prepare streusel topping: Using a knife, cut butter into small pieces and place in small bowl. Add brown sugar, flour blend and espresso. Using pastry blender or fork, combine ingredients until pea-sized lumps form. Do not overmix. Toss in chocolate chips and set mixture aside.

3. Prepare cake: In large mixing bowl, cream together butter or oil, agave nectar and vanilla until fluffy. Add eggs one at a time. Add half the milk and half the flour blend, and mix on low speed until combined. Add remaining milk and flour blend, and mix together. Fold in chocolate chips.

4. Place half the streusel mixture in the bottom of the bundt pan. Spread half the cake batter on top. Sprinkle the remaining streusel mixture on top of the cake batter. Spread the remaining cake batter over the streusel mixture. Bake for 45 minutes or until a wooden toothpick inserted in the center of the cake comes out clean. Cool for one hour. Do not attempt to remove cake until it is cooled. Loosen the sides of the bundt pan with a knife. Turn over onto cake plate and serve.

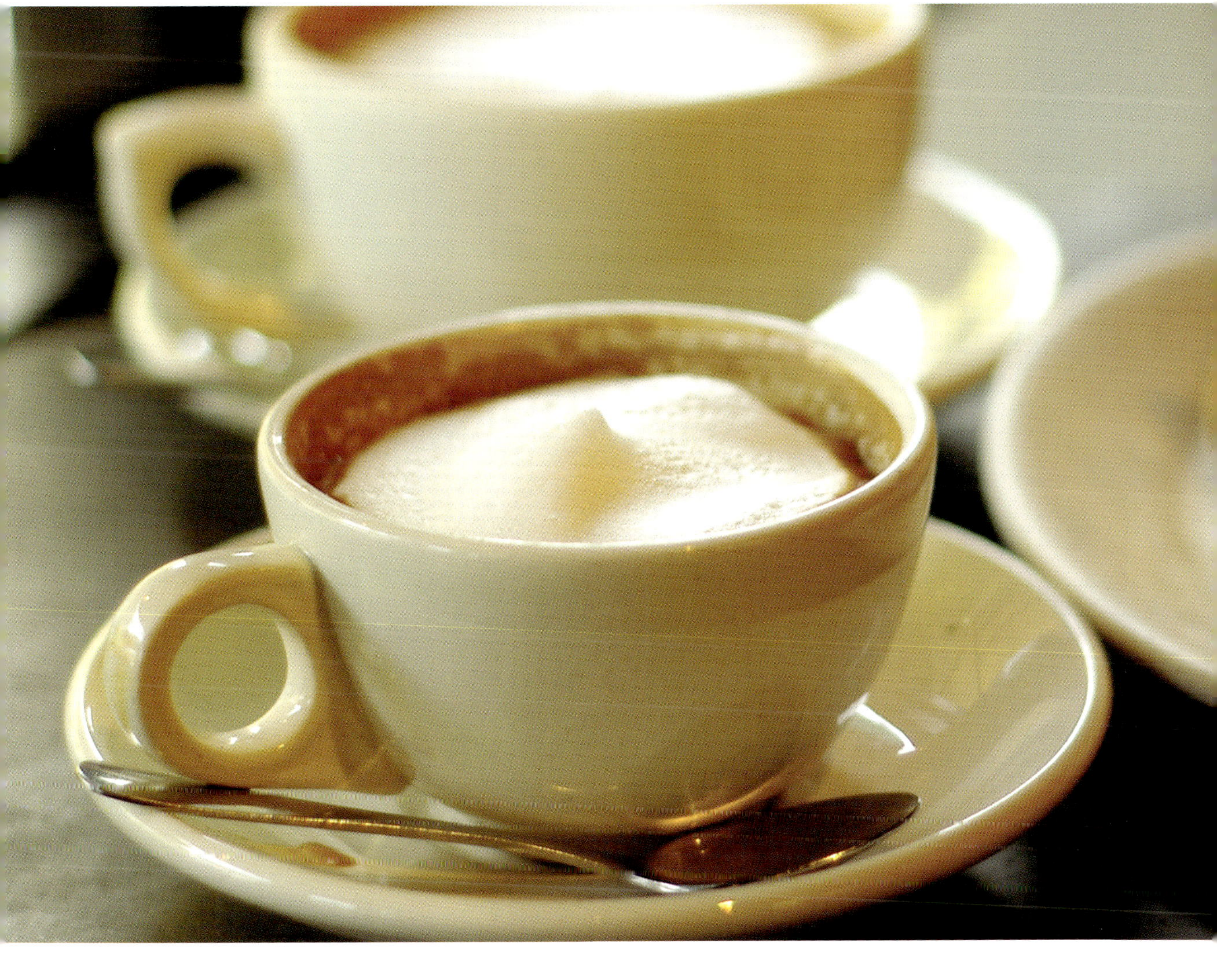

Tomato-Pesto Breakfast Strata

Gluten-Free/Dairy-Free Options

Serves 8-10

1 loaf gluten-free bread (about 10 slices)

1 cup Spinach Pesto Sauce (see Index)

6-7 ripe Italian plum tomatoes, sliced thin

2 cups shredded skim-milk mozzarella cheese (or Daiya cheese substitute)

8 eggs, beaten (or 5 whole eggs and 4 egg whites)

3 cups milk of choice (regular, rice milk or coconut milk, no vanilla flavoring)

1 teaspoon sea salt

1 teaspoon freshly ground pepper

2 tablespoons fresh basil, chopped, for garnish

1. Cut the crusts off the bread slices and save for making bread crumbs. Tear bread into 2-inch pieces. Coat the sides of a 9 x 13-inch baking dish with olive oil. Layer half the bread pieces on the bottom of the dish. Spread a thin layer of pesto sauce over the bread. Layer tomatoes on top of pesto. Sprinkle with 1 cup mozzarella cheese. Repeat layers with bread, pesto and tomatoes.

2. Beat eggs with milk until combined. Add salt and pepper. Pour egg mixture over layers. Top with remaining cheese. Place in refrigerator overnight or for at least 6 hours.

3. Preheat oven to 350°F. Bake strata for 1 hour or until puffy and golden brown. Remove from oven and let stand for 10 minutes. Garnish with freshly chopped basil before cutting with sharp knife.

Spinach Pesto Sauce

Gluten-Free

Full of omega-3s, antioxidants & iron, this pesto sauce is a staple in our kitchen.

1 cup loosely packed fresh spinach leaves, rinsed and patted dry

¾ cup loosely packed fresh Italian parsley

¾ cup loosely packed fresh basil leaves

2 cloves garlic, crushed

¼ cup olive oil

¼ cup walnuts or pine nuts

½ cup freshly grated Parmesan cheese

1. Combine spinach, parsley, basil and garlic in the bowl of a food processor fitted with chopping blade. With the food processing running, slowly drizzle the olive oil through the top and continue processing until smooth.

2. Add walnuts and Parmesan and pulse 4-5 times until pesto is smooth. To make a thinner pesto sauce, add 2-3 tablespoons more olive oil.

Maui Onion and Chèvre Tart
Gluten-Free

Serves 8

---

1 Gluten-Free Pastry Crust (see Index)

10 ounces mild goat cheese, such as Chèvre or Montrachet

8 ounces light cream cheese or Tofutti cream cheese

2 eggs, lightly beaten

¼ cup Elizabeth's Gluten-Free Flour Blend (see Index) or ¼ cup The Pure Pantry Gluten-Free Organic All-Purpose Baking Mix

1 teaspoon fresh thyme leaves, finely chopped, or ½ teaspoon dried

1 teaspoon sea salt

2 tablespoons butter or Earth Balance Buttery Spread

1 tablespoon sugar

1 Maui or yellow onion, halved and sliced thin

1. Preheat oven to 350°F. Prepare Gluten-Free Pastry Crust (see Index) in a 10-inch tart pan with removable bottom. Bake in middle of oven for 10 minutes. Remove from oven and set aside.

2. In a food processor, blend goat cheese with cream cheese. Add eggs, flour blend, thyme, and salt. Process until smooth. Using a spatula, remove goat cheese mixture into a medium bowl.

3. In a skillet, melt butter on low heat. Add sugar to butter and stir. Add onion slices. Cook onions for 3-4 minutes until soft and caramelized. Remove from heat and let cool for 5 minutes. Fold onions into goat cheese mixture. Pour into prepared pastry shell and smooth top.

4. Bake for 20 minutes or until filling is set and tart is slightly golden brown. Remove from oven and let cool for 10 minutes. Remove from pan by pushing up on the bottom until the fluted side part separates. Slice and serve with small organic greens salad.

Veggie Frittata
Gluten-Free

Serves 8

This is one of the recipes I always feel good about making for my kids because I can "hide" a ton of vegetables in the frittata and they gobble it up! Also, it's high in protein and even kids who don't like eggs love this dish!

2 tablespoons olive oil

¾ cup red bell peppers, finely chopped, or ¾ cup tomatoes, finely chopped, juice drained off

¾ cup onion, finely chopped

1 large zucchini, grated

1 garlic clove, minced

5 large eggs, or 5 egg whites and 2 whole eggs, beaten

1 cup ricotta cheese or low-fat cottage cheese

⅓ cup Elizabeth's Gluten-Free Flour Blend or ⅓ cup The Pure Pantry Gluten-Free Organic All-Purpose Baking Mix

1 tablespoon fresh basil, chopped

1- 10 ounce pkg. frozen chopped spinach, thawed, squeezed dry

½ teaspoon sea salt

½ teaspoon pepper

1 cup feta cheese, crumbled

1. Preheat oven to 350°F. Spray 9-inch spring-form pan with cooking spray. Place olive oil in large skillet and heat over medium heat. Add red bell pepper, onion, zucchini and garlic and sauté until tender for about 2 minutes. Remove from heat, drain and cool.

2. In a mixing bowl combine beaten eggs, ricotta and baking mix until well blended. Add basil, chopped spinach, salt, pepper, cooked vegetables and crumbled feta cheese.

3. Pour mixture into prepared spring-form pan and place pan on baking sheet. Bake for 45-50 minutes. Let cool 5 minutes before removing sides of pan to cut.

breakfast 43

Chapter Two

Breads, Muffins, Scones and Biscuits

Blueberry Millet Scones

High-Fiber Date Nut Scones

Maple Nut Scones

Apricot Amaranth Muffins

Banana Bread or Muffins

Lemon Tea Bread

Pumpkin Streusel Bread or Muffins

Cornbread or Cornbread Muffins

Peach Cobbler Muffins

Savory Polenta Bread

Cheddar Drop Biscuits

breads, muffins & scones

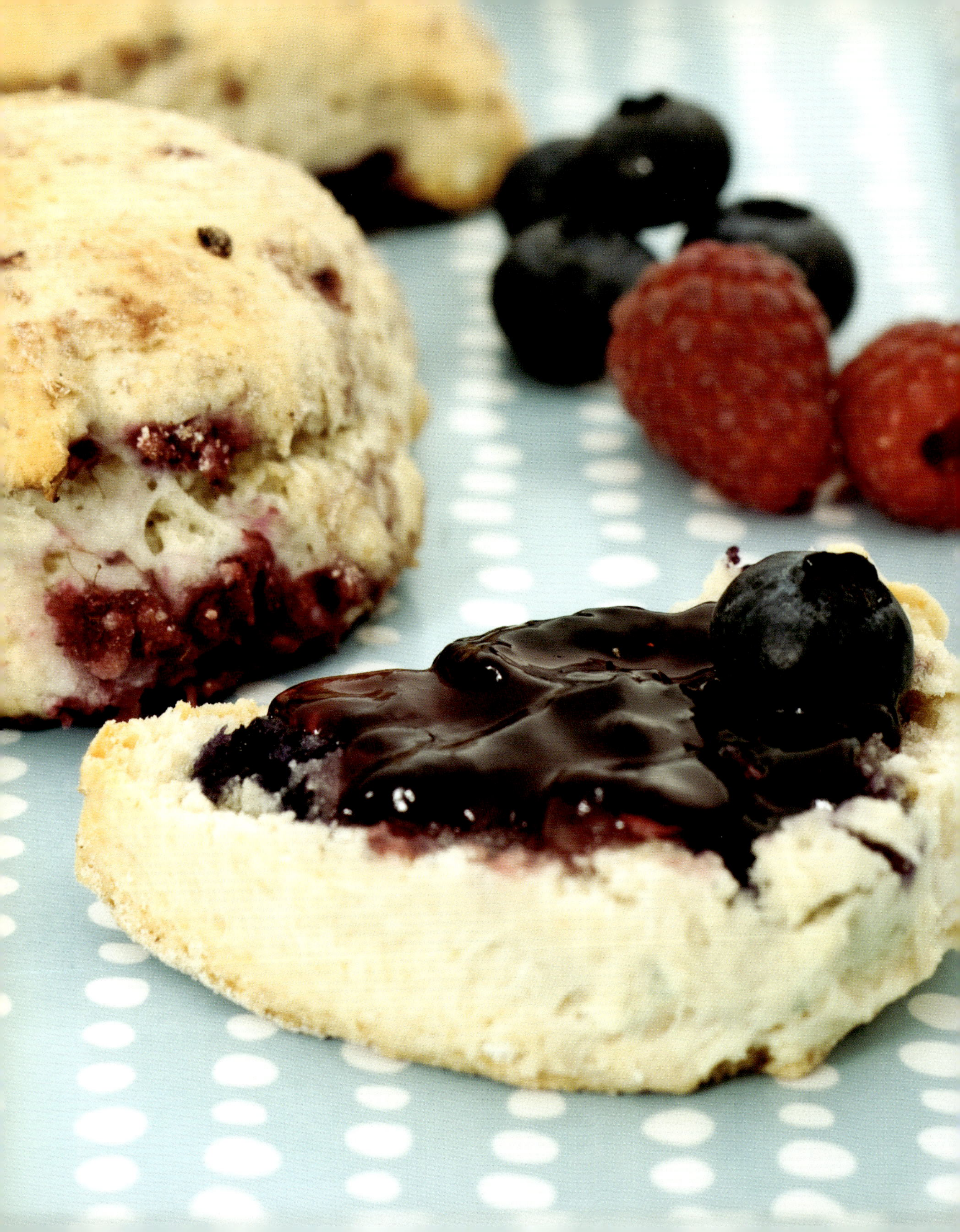

Blueberry Millet Scones

Gluten-Free/Dairy-Free Option

Makes 8-10 scones

2 cups Elizabeth's Gluten-Free Flour Blend (see Index) plus 2 teaspoons baking powder, or 2 cups The Pure Pantry Gluten-Free Organic All Purpose Baking Mix

½ cup millet flour or almond flour

¾ cup butter, chilled, or butter alternative (See Index)

2 eggs or egg replacer (see Index)

2 tablespoons agave nectar, preferably Nature's Agave, Amber variety

¾ cup fresh or frozen blueberries

½ cup So-Delicious brand Coconut Milk Creamer or regular cream

Raw sugar, for topping

1. Preheat over to 375°F. Grease baking sheet and lightly dust with baking mix or rice flour.

2. In a large bowl, combine baking mix (add baking powder if using Elizabeth's Flour Blend) and millet or almond flour.

3. Cut butter into small pieces with knife. Add to flour mixture. Blend butter with a fork or your fingers until it resembles coarse meal. Add eggs, or egg replacer, and agave nectar, stirring just until dry ingredients are moistened. Wash and drain fresh blueberries, or if using frozen, place blueberries in colander and run under water for a few minutes. Drain. Stir in blueberries. Dough will be sticky.

4. Lightly dust a work surface and hands with rice flour or baking mix. Turn dough out onto work surface. Knead lightly and pat dough into an 8-inch circle and place on parchment paper on a baking sheet. Score top of circle with knife, creating 10 wedges but not cutting all the way through dough. Or, using a large spoon drop dough ¼ cup at a time, 3 inches apart, onto greased baking sheet.

5. Place coconut milk creamer or regular cream in small bowl. Using a pastry brush, generously brush cream on top of scones. Sprinkle with raw sugar. Bake for 25 minutes or until scones are golden brown. Cool completely. If you created the 8-inch circle, cut into 10 scones and serve.

High-Fiber Date Nut Scones

Gluten-Free/Dairy-Free Option

Makes 10 scones

These scones are easy to make and low in calories (only 186 per scone) and high in fiber (4.6 grams per scone). This may be just the breakfast or snack you've been looking for!

2¼ cups The Pure Pantry Gluten-Free Organic Buckwheat Flax Pancake and Baking Mix

¼ cup brown sugar

2 teaspoons ground cinnamon

3 tablespoons chilled butter or butter alternative (see Index)

⅓ cup pitted dates, chopped

⅓ cup chopped pecans or walnuts

⅔ cup vanilla low-fat yogurt, or soy or coconut yogurt

2 egg whites, lightly beaten, or egg replacer (see Index)

1. Preheat oven to 375°F. Grease a baking sheet with cooking spray. Combine baking mix, brown sugar and cinnamon in a large mixing bowl. Cut butter or butter alternative into small pieces with a knife. Blend butter into dry ingredients with a fork or your fingers until it resembles coarse meal. Add dates and pecans or walnuts, yogurt and egg whites, stirring just until dry ingredients are moistened. Dough will be sticky.

2. Lightly dust a work surface and hands with gluten-free baking mix or rice flour. Turn dough out onto work surface. Knead lightly and pat dough into an 8-inch circle and place on parchment paper on a baking sheet. Score top of circle with knife, creating 10 wedges but not cutting all the way through dough. Or, using a large spoon drop dough ¼ cup at a time, 3 inches apart, onto a greased baking sheet.

3. Bake for 25 minutes or until scones are golden brown. Cool completely. If you created the 8-inch circle, cut into 10 scones and serve.

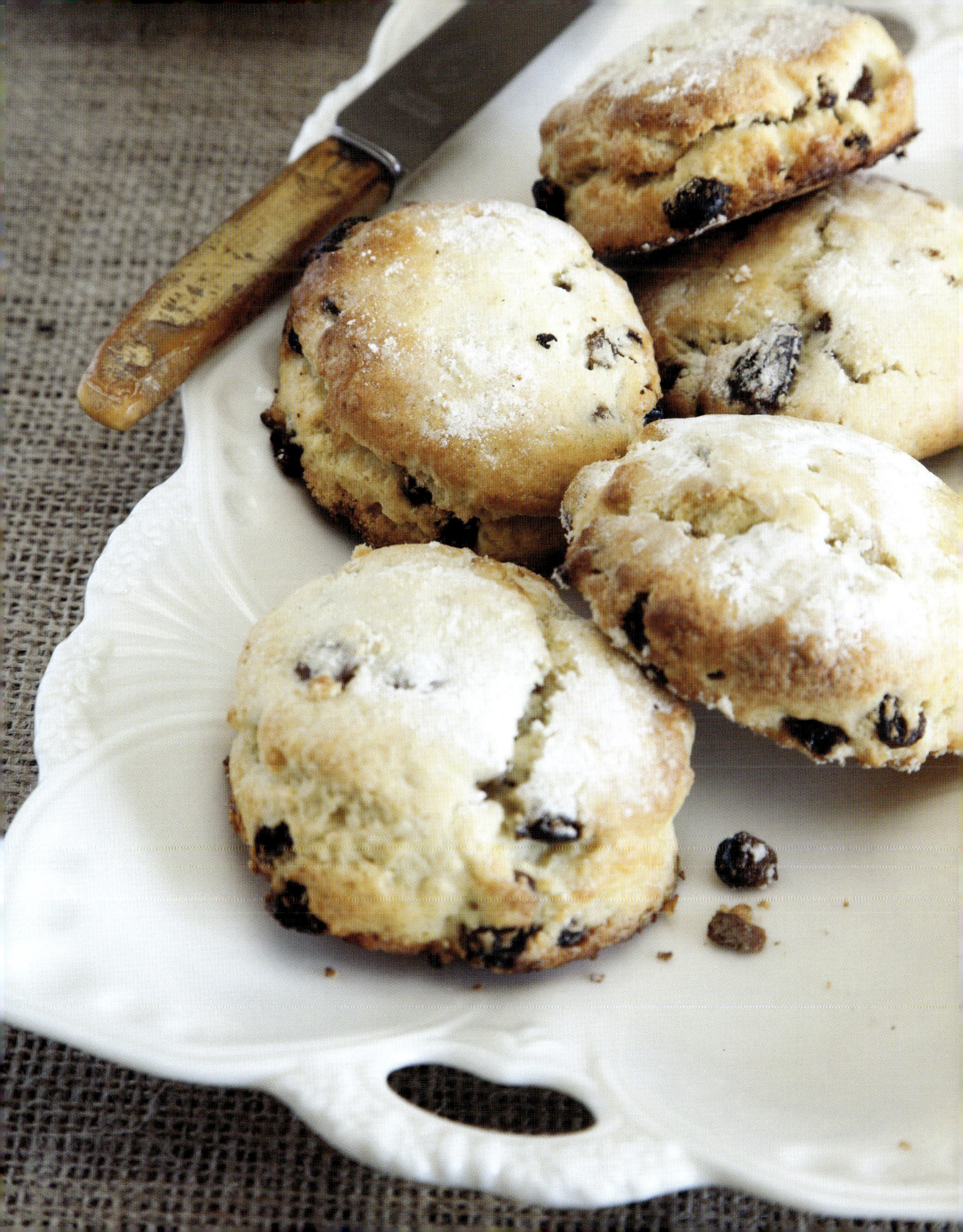

Maple Nut Scones

Gluten-Free/Dairy-Free Option

Makes 10 scones

Before we learned we needed to be gluten free, we used to treat ourselves occasionally to Maple Pecan Scones at Starbucks. Once we knew we couldn't eat them, we would look at them longingly when we were there to pick up a coffee. Now, I am happy to say, we make our own scones at home and enjoy them with our own freshly brewed coffee.

Scones

- 1½ cups Elizabeth's Gluten-Free Flour Blend (see Index) plus 1 tablespoon baking powder or 1½ cups The Pure Pantry Organic All Purpose Baking Mix and 2 teaspoons baking powder
- ½ teaspoon sea salt
- 1 cup gluten-free oats
- 3 tablespoons maple sugar, coconut sugar or brown sugar
- ¼ cup butter or butter alternative (see Index)
- 2 tablespoons maple syrup
- 1 egg or egg replacer (see Index)
- ½ cup So-Delicious brand Coconut Milk Creamer or half and half
- ½ teaspoon maple extract
- ½ cup chopped pecans

Glaze

- 1½ cups powdered sugar
- 1 teaspoon maple extract
- 1 tablespoon milk of choice (regular, rice, almond or coconut)

1. Preheat oven to 400° F. Grease a baking sheet with cooking spray. In a food processor or blender, finely grind oats. Or, alternatively, you may use gluten-free oat flour.

2. In large bowl, combine flour, baking powder, salt, oat flour, and sugar.

3. Cut butter, or butter alternate, into small pieces with a knife. Blend butter into dry ingredients with your fingers until it resembles coarse meal. Add maple syrup, beaten egg, cream and maple extract, stirring just until dry ingredients are moistened. Stir in pecans. Dough will be sticky.

4. Lightly dust a work surface and hands with gluten-free baking mix or rice flour. Turn dough out onto work surface. Knead lightly and pat dough into an 8-inch circle and place on parchment paper on a baking sheet. Score top of circle with knife, creating 10 wedges but not cutting all the way through dough. Or, using a large spoon drop dough ¼ cup at a time, 3 inches apart, onto greased baking sheet.

5. Bake for 25 minutes or until scones are golden brown. Cool completely. If you created the 8-inch circle, cut into 10 scones.

6. Prepare glaze by sifting powdered sugar into a medium bowl. Add maple extract and milk and blend with mixer. Spread glaze over scones and let set.

Apricot Amaranth Muffins

Gluten-Free/Dairy-Free

Makes 8 - 12 muffins

My Apricot Amaranth Muffins provide a powerhouse of nutrition in each muffin! Amaranth is an excellent gluten-free grain as it is high in fiber, protein, magnesium, calcium and iron. This recipe combines two great sources of iron: amaranth and apricots. One quarter cup of amaranth provides 60 percent of the recommended daily allowance for iron!

- 1 cup Elizabeth's Gluten-Free Flour Blend plus 1 teaspoon baking soda and 1 teaspoon baking powder or 1 cup plus 2 teaspoons The Pure Pantry Gluten-Free Organic All Purpose Baking Mix
- ½ cup amaranth flour
- 1 teaspoon cinnamon
- ½ cup puffed millet cereal, available at natural food stores
- ¼ cup coconut oil
- ¼ cup agave nectar, preferably Nature's Agave, Amber variety
- ¼ cup brown sugar or coconut sugar
- 2 eggs or egg replacer
- ½ cup milk of choice (regular, rice, almond or coconut)
- 1 cup chopped apricots, soaked in water for 15 minutes then drained (you can substitute cranberries or other dried fruit if you prefer)
- 1 teaspoon cinnamon and 1 teaspoon raw sugar, combined,
- ½ cup chopped walnuts, optional

1. Preheat oven to 350°F. Grease muffin tin with cooking spray. Mix flour blend, amaranth flour, cinnamon and cereal in a medium mixing bowl.

2. In a large bowl, combine coconut oil, agave nectar, eggs and milk with electric mixer. With mixer on low, add in dry ingredients.

3. Drain apricots and discard water. Stir in apricots and walnuts, if desired.

4. Pour batter into muffin tin. Combine cinnamon and raw sugar and sprinkle on top of muffins. Bake for 20 minutes. Cool on wire rack.

Banana Bread or Muffins

Gluten-Free/Dairy-Free

Makes 1 loaf or 14 muffins

- ½ cup butter at room temperature (or coconut oil or non-hydrogenated shortening)

- 2 eggs or egg replacer (see Index)

- 3-4 ripe bananas, mashed

- ¾ cup organic brown sugar

- 2 tablespoons agave nectar, preferably Nature's Agave, Amber variety

- 1 teaspoon vanilla

- 2 cups Elizabeth's Gluten-Free Flour Blend plus 1 teaspoon baking powder, or 2 cups The Pure Pantry Organic All Purpose Baking Mix*

- ½ cup milk of choice (regular, rice, almond or coconut milk)

1. Preheat oven to 350°F. Grease 9 x 5-inch loaf pan or muffin tin with cooking spray.

2. In large bowl, beat butter or coconut oil with electric mixer. Stir in brown sugar, agave nectar and vanilla. Add eggs, or egg replacer, and beat until well blended. Add mashed bananas and blend. Beat until well combined. Add baking mix half a cup at a time, stirring slowly after each addition. If using Elizabeth's Blend, stir in baking powder. Add milk and stir until well combined.

3. Place in greased loaf pan or muffin tin. Bake for 45 minutes or until toothpick inserted into the center comes out clean.

* *Alternative: Banana Flax Bread*
Substitute 2 cups of baking mix, with 1⅔ cups baking mix and ⅓ cup ground flax meal.

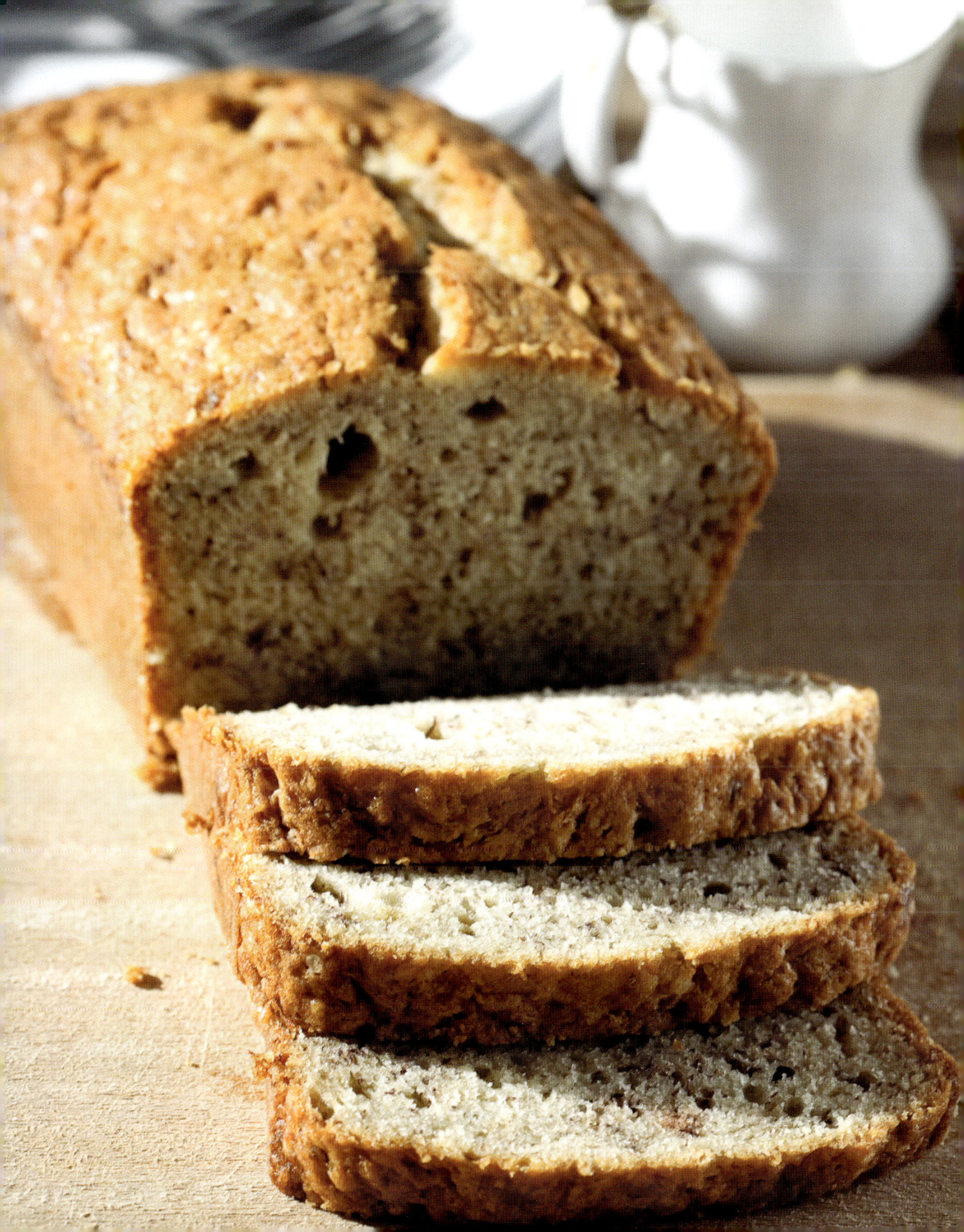

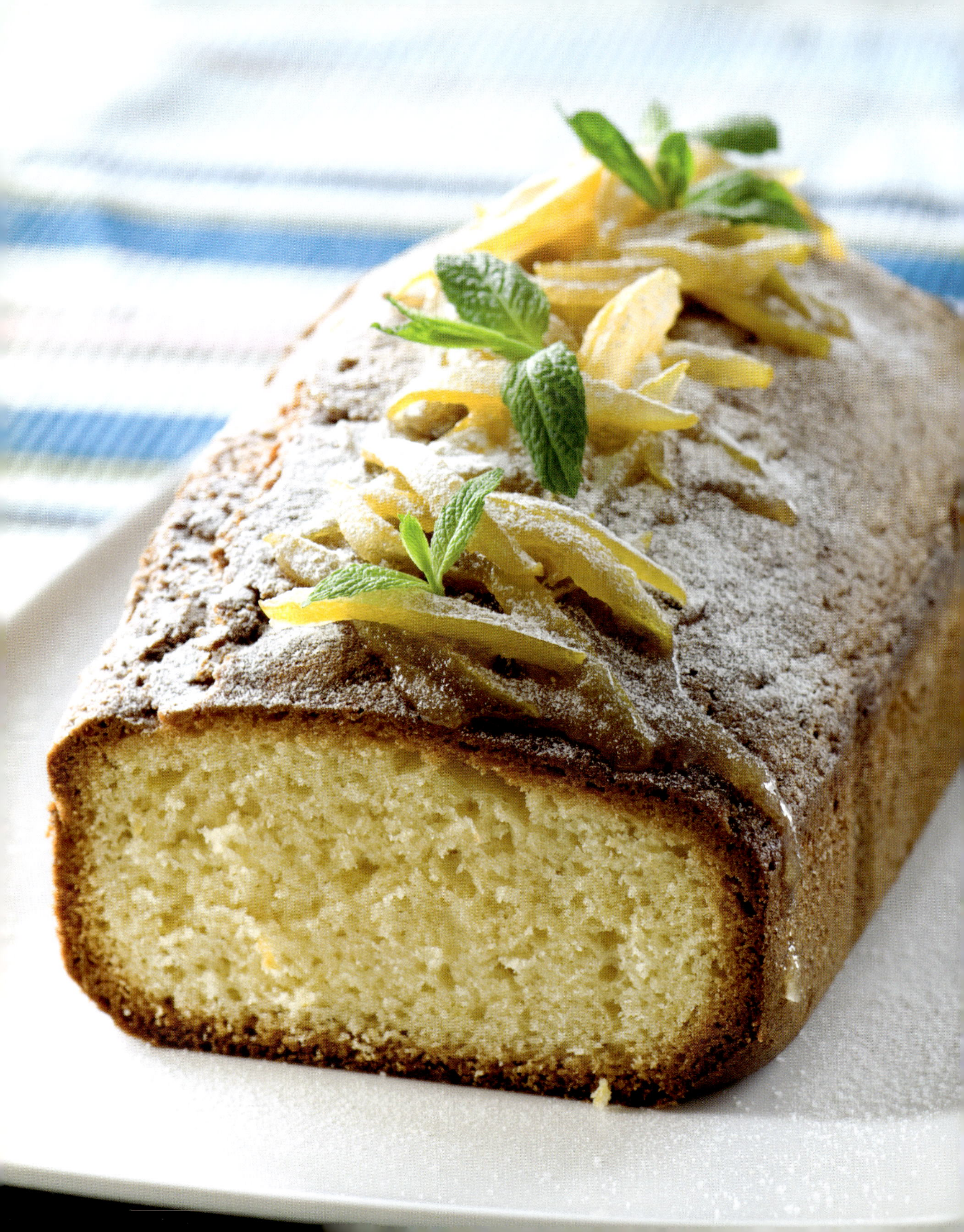

Lemon Tea Bread

Gluten-Free/Dairy-Free Options

Makes 2 large loaves or 4 small loaves

This recipe originally came from my best childhood friend, Denise. We used to bake together when we were kids. We had so much fun in the kitchen and this was one of our favorite things to make, and eat! I have the original recipe card that I had written out in 4th grade. It is splattered with stuff from over the years. I am so glad that this recipe easily converted to a gluten-free version!

¾ cup butter or coconut oil

1½ cups granulated sugar

4 eggs, slightly beaten

2 lemons, grated and juiced

1 cup milk or coconut milk

3 cups Elizabeth's Gluten-Free Flour Blend (see Index) plus 2 teaspoons baking powder and 2 teaspoons baking soda, or 3 cups The Pure Pantry Gluten-Free Organic All Purpose Baking Mix

¾ cup walnuts, optional

½ cup sugar for topping

1. Preheat oven to 350°F. Grease two large bread pans or four small pans with cooking spray. Cream butter or coconut oil with sugar until fluffy; add eggs and blend well. Grate lemon peel, yellow part only, with fine grater. Blend in grated lemon peel and milk with egg mixture.

2. Add baking mix (and baking powder and baking soda if using Elizabeth's Flour Blend). Stir until well combined. Add walnuts, if desired. Pour into two large greased bread pans or four small pans. Bake for 45 minutes.

3. In a small bowl, while bread is baking, combine ½ cup sugar with juice of two lemons. Stir until sugar dissolves. Spoon approximately 2 tablespoons of glaze over top of each loaf. Return to oven for 10 more minutes. Check doneness by inserting a toothpick to see if it comes out clean.

Pumpkin Streusel Bread

Gluten-Free/Dairy-Free

Makes 1 loaf or 14 muffins

Bread

2 cups Elizabeth's Gluten-Free Flour Blend (see Index) plus 1 teaspoon baking powder or 2 cups The Pure Pantry Organic All Purpose Gluten-Free Baking Mix

1 teaspoon cinnamon

¼ teaspoon cloves

¼ teaspoon ginger

¼ teaspoon nutmeg

3 eggs or egg replacer (see Index)

1⅓ cups canned pumpkin

1 cup organic dark brown sugar

2 tablespoons agave nectar, preferably Nature's Agave, Amber variety

½ cup safflower oil

1 teaspoon vanilla

¼ cup water

¾ cup chopped pecans (optional)

Crumb Topping (optional)

¾ cup Elizabeth's Gluten-Free Flour Blend (see Index) or ¾ cup The Pure Pantry Organic All Purpose Baking Mix

½ cup golden brown sugar, packed

1 teaspoon ground cinnamon

½ cup butter or butter alternative (see Index)

1. Preheat oven to 350°F. Grease 9 x 5-inch loaf pan or muffin tin with cooking spray. In a medium bowl, combine baking mix, baking powder (if using Elizabeth's Blend), cinnamon, cloves, ginger and nutmeg. Set aside.

2. Put eggs, or egg replacer, into large bowl of electric mixer. Beat until blended. Add pumpkin, sugar, agave nectar, oil, vanilla and water. Beat until well combined. Set aside. Fold the dry ingredients into the egg mixture, stirring until smooth. Stir in pecans, if desired. Set aside.

3. To make crumb topping, place baking mix, brown sugar and cinnamon in a bowl. Blend shortening or margarine with dry ingredients using fingertips until well mixed.

4. Pour batter into greased pan or muffin tin. Top loaf with crumb mixture or muffins with about ¼ cup crumb mixture each.

5. Bake 45 minutes or until a toothpick inserted comes out clean. Cool 10 minutes then turn out onto cooling rack until completely cool.

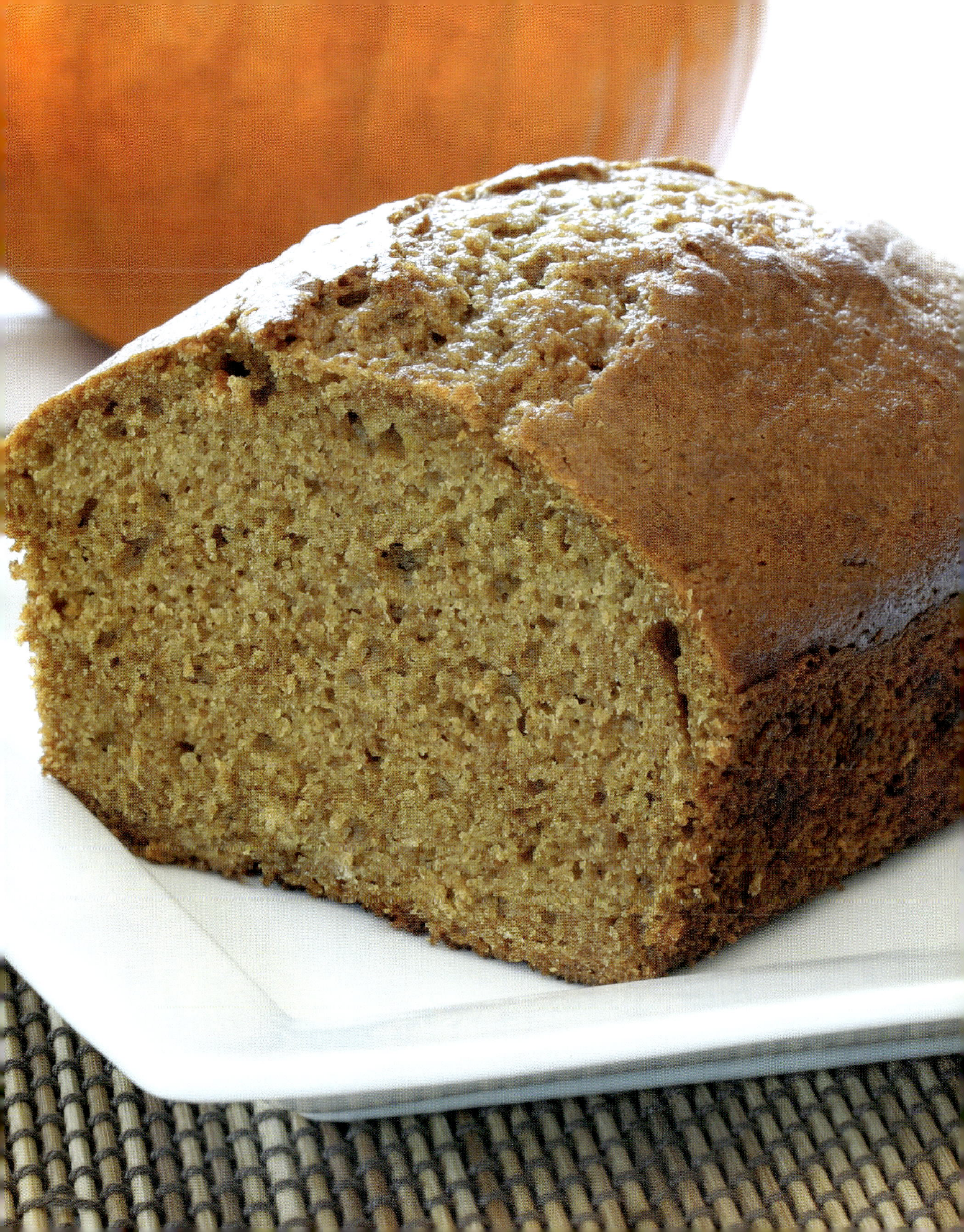

58　fresh from elizabeth's kitchen

Cornbread or Cornbread Muffins

Gluten-Free/Dairy-Free

Makes one 8-inch square pan or 12 muffins

This hearty, delicious gluten-free cornbread is easy to prepare. Try it with your favorite soup or salad, make stuffing with it, or enjoy as a nutritious addition to any meal.

- 1 cup Elizabeth's Gluten-Free Flour Blend plus 1 teaspoon baking powder and 1 teaspoon baking soda or 1 cup The Pure Pantry Gluten-Free Organic All Purpose Baking Mix or Gluten-Free Organic Buckwheat Flax Pancake and Baking Mix
- 1 cup organic yellow cornmeal
- ½ teaspoon sea salt
- 1 cup milk of choice (regular, rice, almond or coconut)
- ¼ cup agave nectar, preferably Nature's Agave, Amber variety
- ⅓ cup melted butter or butter substitute (see Index)
- 1 large egg, slightly beaten, or egg replacer (see Index)

1. Preheat oven to 400°F. Grease an 8-inch square baking pan, or muffin tin, with cooking spray.

2. Combine baking mix, cornmeal, and salt in a medium bowl. Combine milk, agave nectar, melted butter and egg in a small bowl; mix well. Add milk mixture to flour mixture; stir just until blended.

3. For bread, pour into prepared pan and bake for 20-22 minutes. For muffins, spoon batter two-thirds full into greased muffin tin, fill and bake 15-18 minutes. This recipe may be doubled and baked as above in a 9 x 13-inch baking pan.

Peach Cobbler Muffins

Gluten-Free/Dairy-Free Option

Makes 12 muffins

1½ cups Elizabeth's Gluten-Free Flour Blend (see Index) plus 1 teaspoon baking soda and 1 teaspoon baking powder or 1½ cups The Pure Pantry Gluten-Free Organic All Purpose Baking Mix

¾ cup brown sugar

¼ cup millet flour or almond flour

1 teaspoon cinnamon

½ teaspoon allspice

½ teaspoon nutmeg

2 eggs

5 fresh peaches, peeled and diced, or 1- 29 ounce can peaches, drained well and diced

1 teaspoon vanilla

¾ cup vegetable oil

¼ cup agave nectar, preferably Nature's Agave, Amber variety

½ cup milk of choice (rice, almond, coconut or regular milk)

2 tablespoons raw sugar, for topping

1. Preheat oven to 400°F. Grease muffin tin with cooking spray.

2. In large bowl, mix baking mix, (add baking soda and baking powder if using Elizabeth's Flour Blend), brown sugar, millet flour, cinnamon, allspice and nutmeg. Set aside.

3. In a separate bowl, whisk eggs. Add chopped peaches, vanilla, oil, agave nectar and milk. Pour egg mixture all at once into flour mixture. Stir by hand just until flour is moistened.

4. Spoon batter into greased muffin tin. Sprinkle top of muffins with ¼ teaspoon raw sugar. Bake 20 minutes or until a wooden toothpick comes out clean.

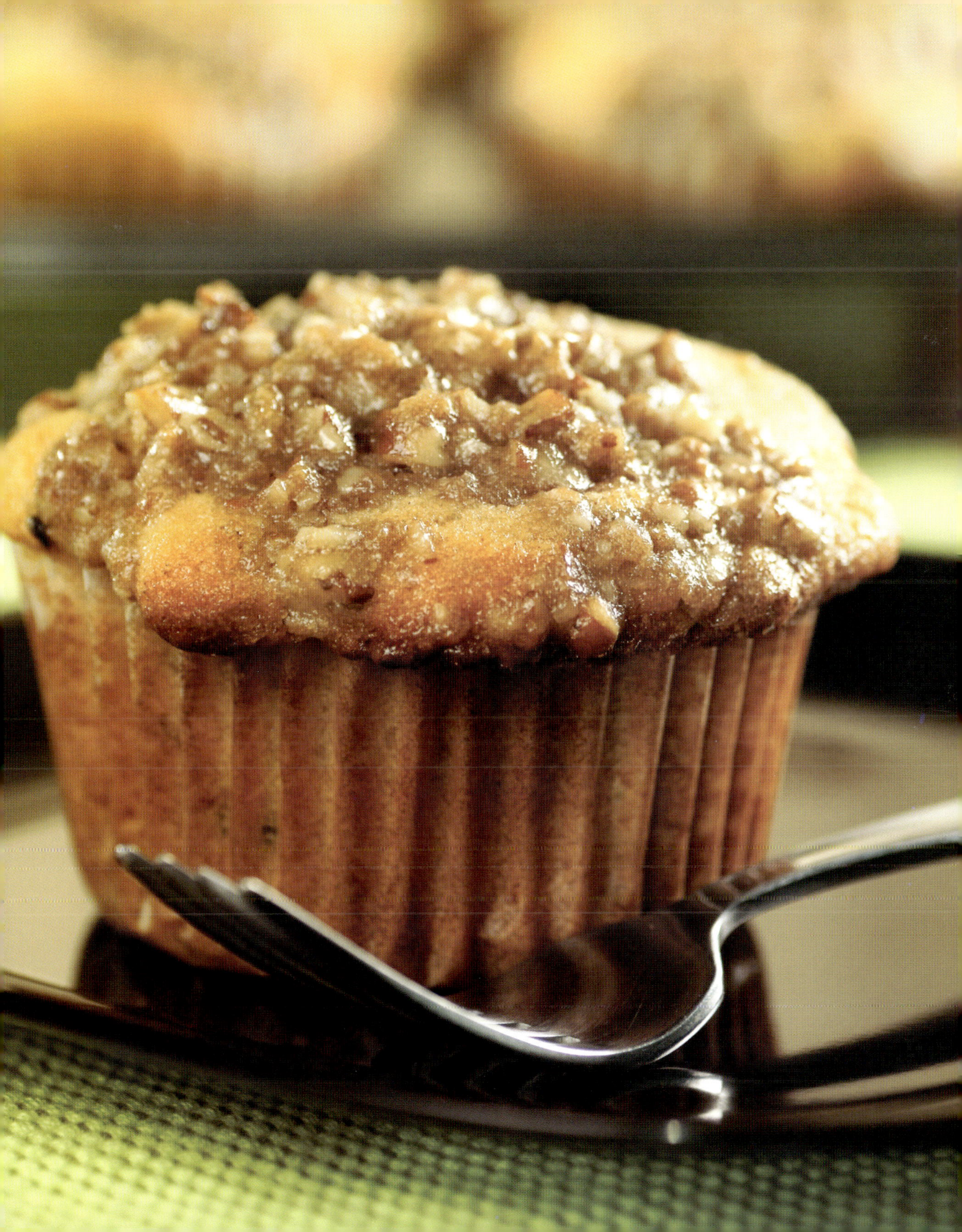

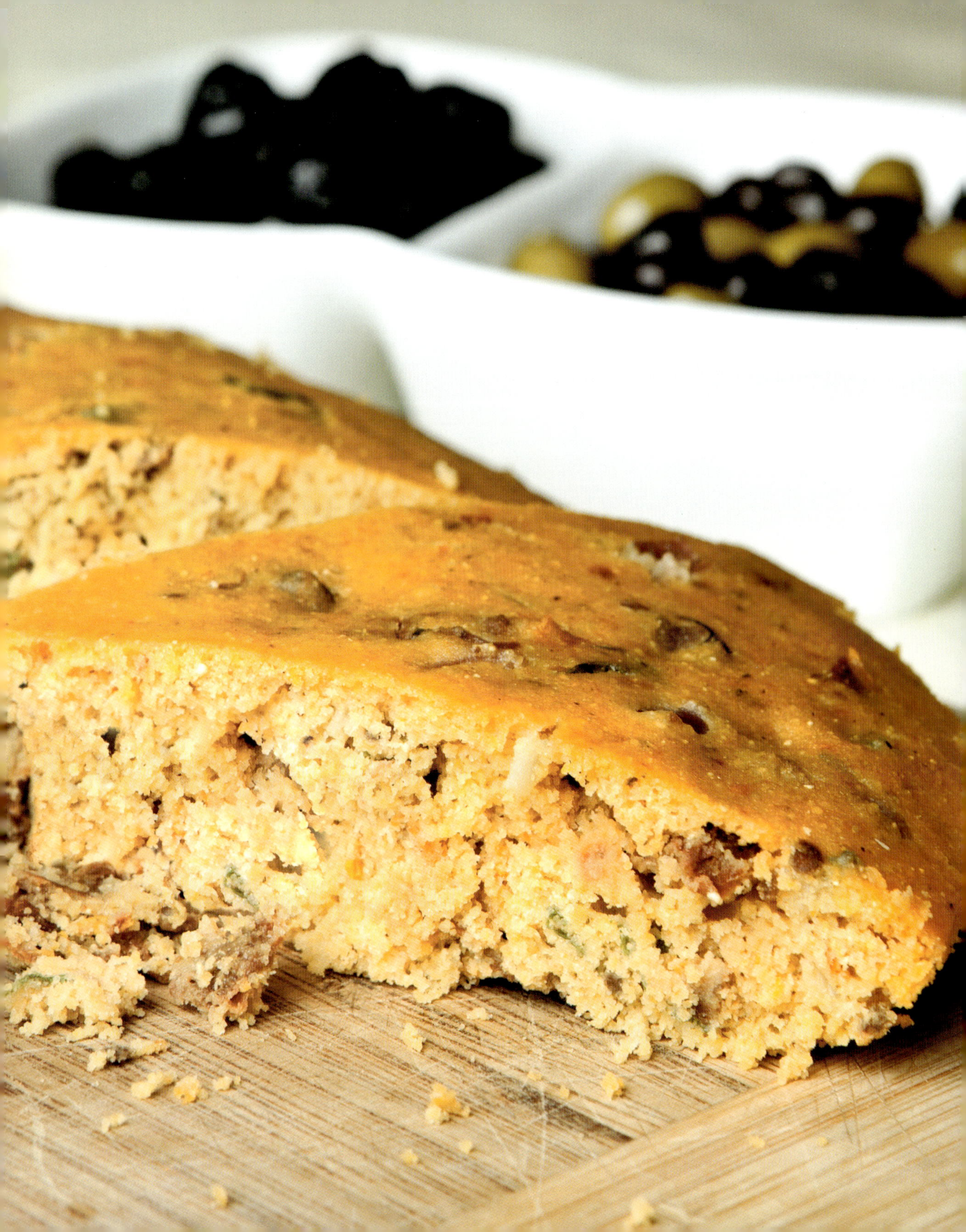

Savory Polenta Bread

Gluten-Free/Dairy-Free

Serves 8

1½ cups organic cornmeal or organic polenta cornmeal

½ cup Elizabeth's Gluten-Free Flour Blend plus 1 teaspoon baking soda, or ½ cup plus 1 teaspoon The Pure Pantry Organic All Purpose Baking Mix

½ teaspoon sea salt

2 tablespoons olive oil, divided

1¾ cups milk of choice (rice, almond, coconut or regular milk)

2 eggs, lightly beaten

½ cup pancetta or prosciutto, chopped

1- 8 ounce jar oil-packed sundried tomatoes, drained and chopped

2 tablespoons shallots, finely chopped

1 tablespoon fresh basil, chopped

1 tablespoon fresh rosemary, chopped

1. Preheat oven to 350°F. Grease 10-inch cast-iron or oven-proof skillet or 9-inch round baking pan with 1 tablespoon olive oil. Set aside.

2. In a medium bowl combine cornmeal, baking mix, (plus baking soda if using Elizabeth's Blend) and salt. Set aside.

3. In a large bowl, combine milk, eggs and 1 tablespoon olive oil, whisking together to blend. Stir in tomatoes, pancetta or prosciutto, shallots, basil, and rosemary.

4. Add cornmeal mixture to wet ingredients and stir until just combined but do not over stir. Pour into skillet or pan, and bake for 25 minutes.

Cheddar Drop Biscuits

Gluten-Free/Dairy-Free Option

Makes 12 biscuits or 12 muffins

These are fabulous served with Cranberry-Cherry Chutney (see Index). They also are wonderful for sandwiches. To make these dairy free, use Daiya Cheddar Cheese — an amazing cheese alternative that melts and tastes yummy!

- **2 cups Elizabeth's Gluten-Free Flour Blend plus 2 teaspoons baking powder or 2 cups The Pure Pantry Organic All Purpose Baking Mix**
- **½ teaspoon sea salt**
- **¼ cup cold butter or butter alternative (see Index)**
- **½ cup buttermilk (or rice milk with 2 teaspoons cider vinegar)**
- **2 beaten eggs or egg replacer (see Index)**
- **1 cup grated cheddar cheese or shredded Daiya cheese alternative**
- **½ teaspoon onion powder**
- **½ teaspoon finely chopped chives (optional)**

1. Preheat oven to 350°F. Grease baking sheet or muffin tin with cooking spray. In large mixing bowl, combine baking mix, (plus baking powder if using Elizabeth's Blend) and salt.

2. Cut butter into small pieces with a knife. Using your fingers, mix the butter into the flour so that there are no lumps of butter. Add the buttermilk (or rice milk and vinegar) and beaten eggs (or egg replacer) to the flour and combine with a fork. Add the cheese (or cheese alternative), onion powder and chives, if desired. Do not over stir.

3. To make 12 biscuits, use a large spoon to drop the dough, at least 3 inches apart, onto greased baking sheet. To make 12 muffins, spoon dough into greased muffin tin. Bake for 15 minutes.

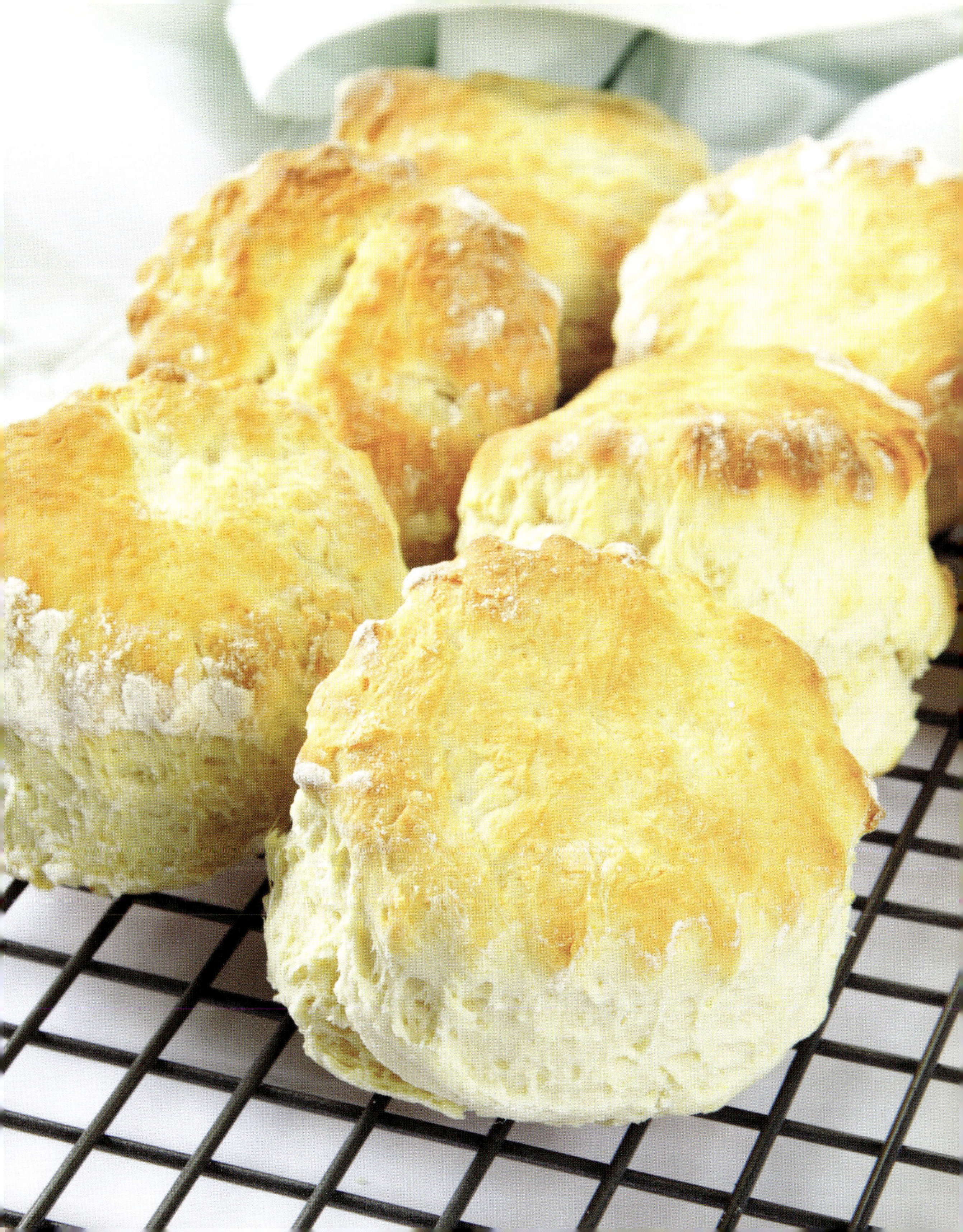

Chapter Three

Soups & Salads

Soups

David's Carrot Ginger Soup with Polenta Croutons

Lentil and Root Vegetable Soup

Gigi's French Onion Soup with Gruyere and Parmesan Cheeses

White Bean and Oregano Chili

Basic Chicken or Turkey Stock

Salads

Caesar Salad with Polenta Croutons

Greek Salad with Omega-Oregano Dressing

Ensalada Verano

Pear, Persimmon and Fennel Salad with Pear-Champagne Vinaigrette

Heirloom Tomato Mozzarella Stack with Edamame Pesto Hummus

Quinoa Tabouli

Rice and Lentils with Cranberries and Oranges

Curried Quinoa Mango Salad

Polenta Croutons

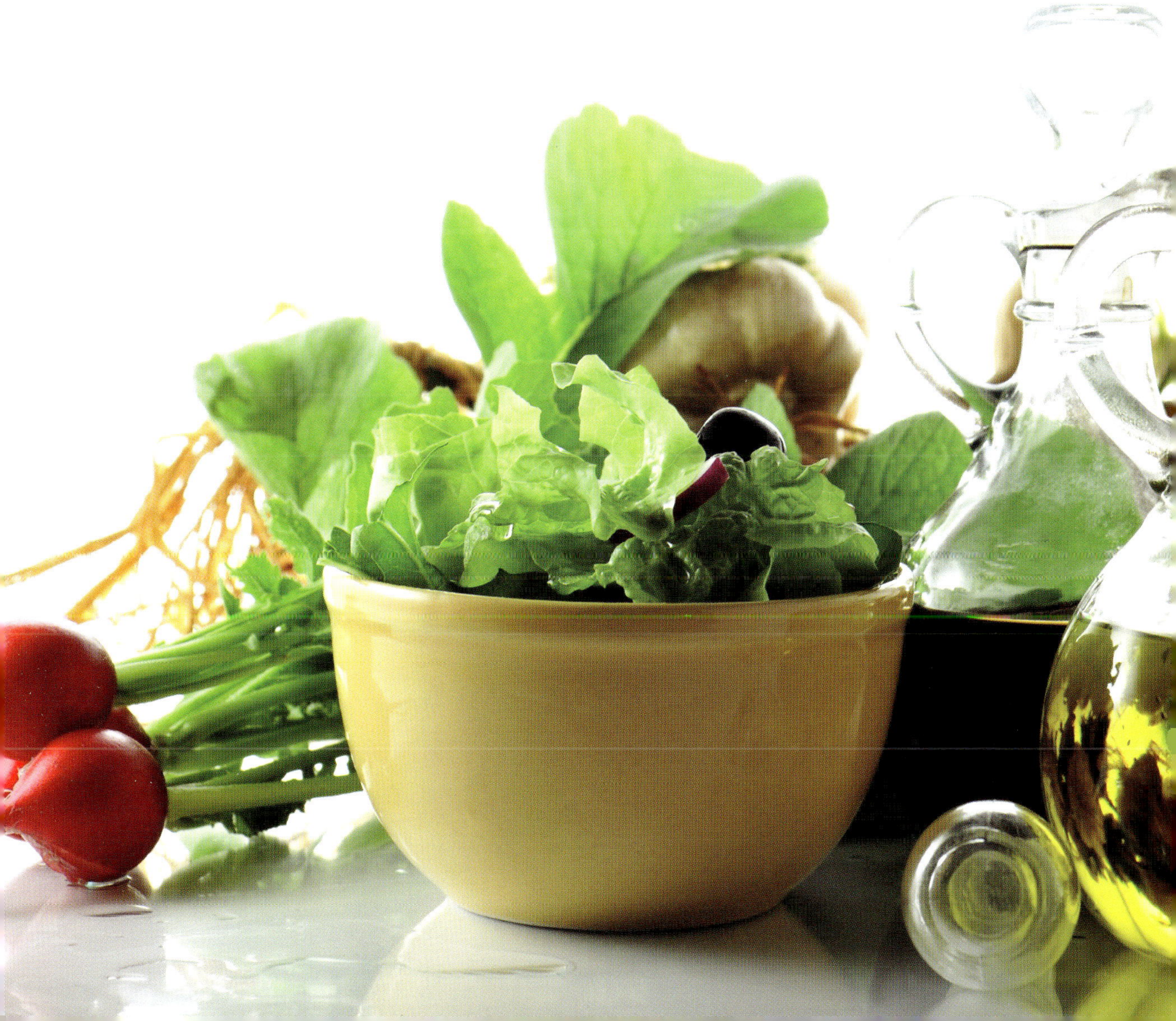

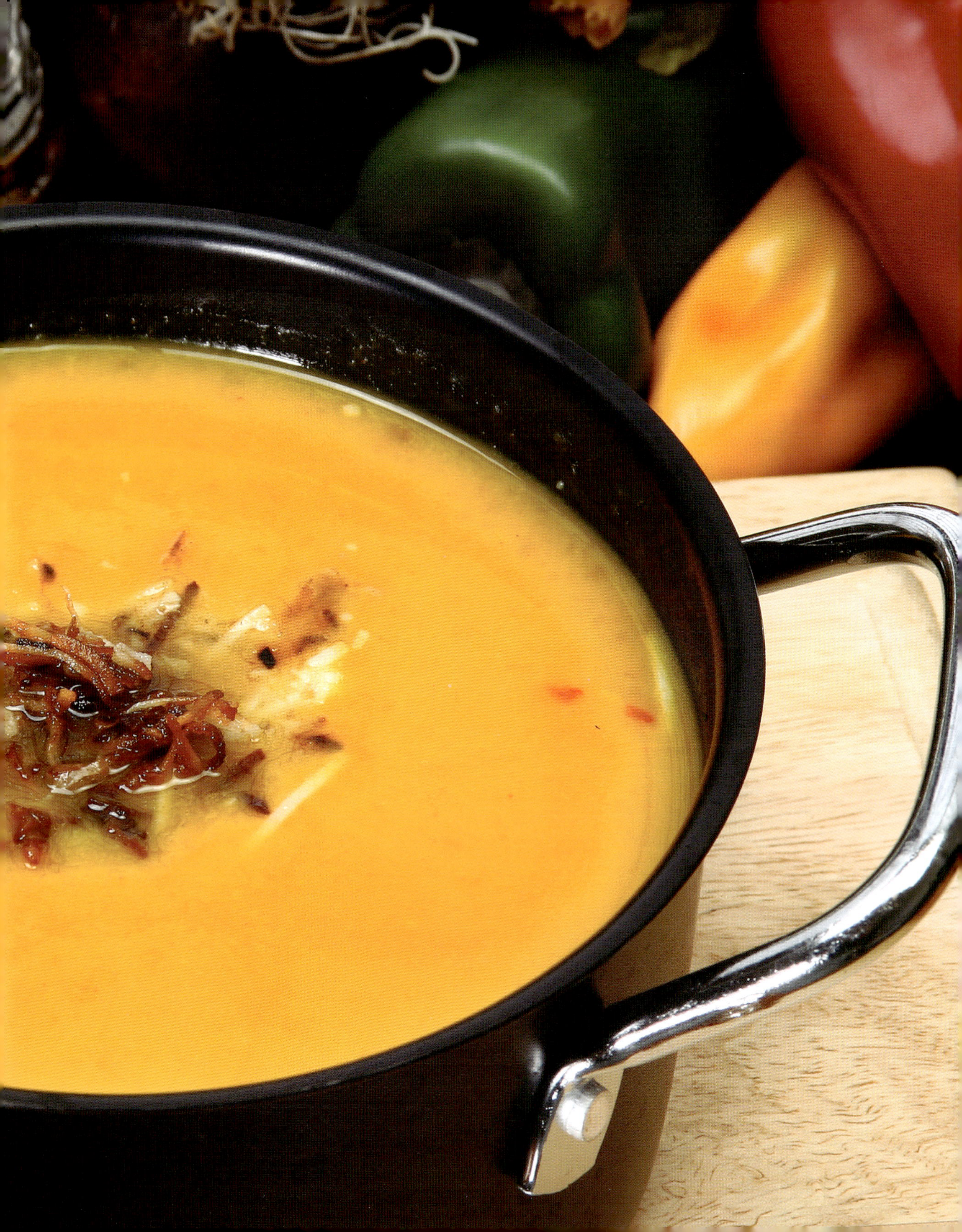

David's Carrot Ginger Soup
with Polenta Croutons

Gluten-Free/Dairy-Free with Vegetarian Options

Serves 8

1 yellow onion, chopped

2 tablespoons coconut oil

7 large carrots, peeled and cut into ¼-inch slices

1 tablespoon fresh ginger, minced

4 cups Basic Chicken or Turkey Stock (see Index), store-bought gluten-free chicken or vegetable stock

1 cup coconut milk, preferably So-Delicious brand, plain variety

½ cup freshly squeezed orange juice from 2 oranges

1 tablespoon grated orange zest

1 teaspoon sea salt

1 teaspoon freshly ground pepper

Polenta Croutons (see Index)

1. Sauté the onion in coconut oil in a large, heavy bottomed stockpot until translucent. Add the sliced carrots and ginger. Sauté over low heat for 4-5 minutes or until carrots are tender. Stir in 3 cups chicken stock. Bring to boil, reduce heat and simmer, covered, for 20 minutes.

2. Warm the coconut milk in a saucepan. Add warm coconut milk, remaining 1 cup stock, orange juice and orange zest to the carrots. Stir to combine and simmer on low for 2 minutes.

3. Puree the soup in batches in a blender. Return pureed soup to stockpot over low heat. Stir in salt and pepper. Ladle soup into heated soup bowls. Top with a few Polenta Croutons and a dollop of sour cream, if desired.

Lentil and Root Vegetable Soup

Gluten-Free/Dairy-Free with Vegetarian Option

Serves 8

- 3 tablespoons olive oil
- 2 medium yellow onions, chopped
- 3 parsnips, peeled and chopped
- 3 large carrots, peeled and chopped
- 1 small baking potato, peeled and chopped
- 4 ribs celery, chopped
- 1- 35 ounce can or box Italian plum tomatoes, with juice
- 6 cups Basic Chicken or Turkey Stock (see Index), or store-bought gluten-free chicken or vegetable stock
- ¾ cup dried French lentils, rinsed, preferably Gold Mine Natural Food Co. brand
- ½ cup dry white wine
- 3 cloves garlic, finely minced
- 1 teaspoon fresh thyme leaves or ½ teaspoon dried
- 1 teaspoon sea salt

1. Place olive oil in a large soup pot over medium heat. Add onions and sauté until soft. Add parsnips, carrots and potato and continue sauteing for 20 minutes. Add more olive oil if needed. Add celery, canned tomatoes with juice, and preferred stock. Bring to boil and add lentils.

2. Reduce heat and simmer, uncovered, for 20 minutes, stirring occasionally.

3. Stir in white wine, garlic, thyme and salt and simmer an additional 20-30 minutes. Taste lentils to ensure they are cooked. If still not done, continue cooking over low heat an additional 5-10 minutes until lentils are soft.

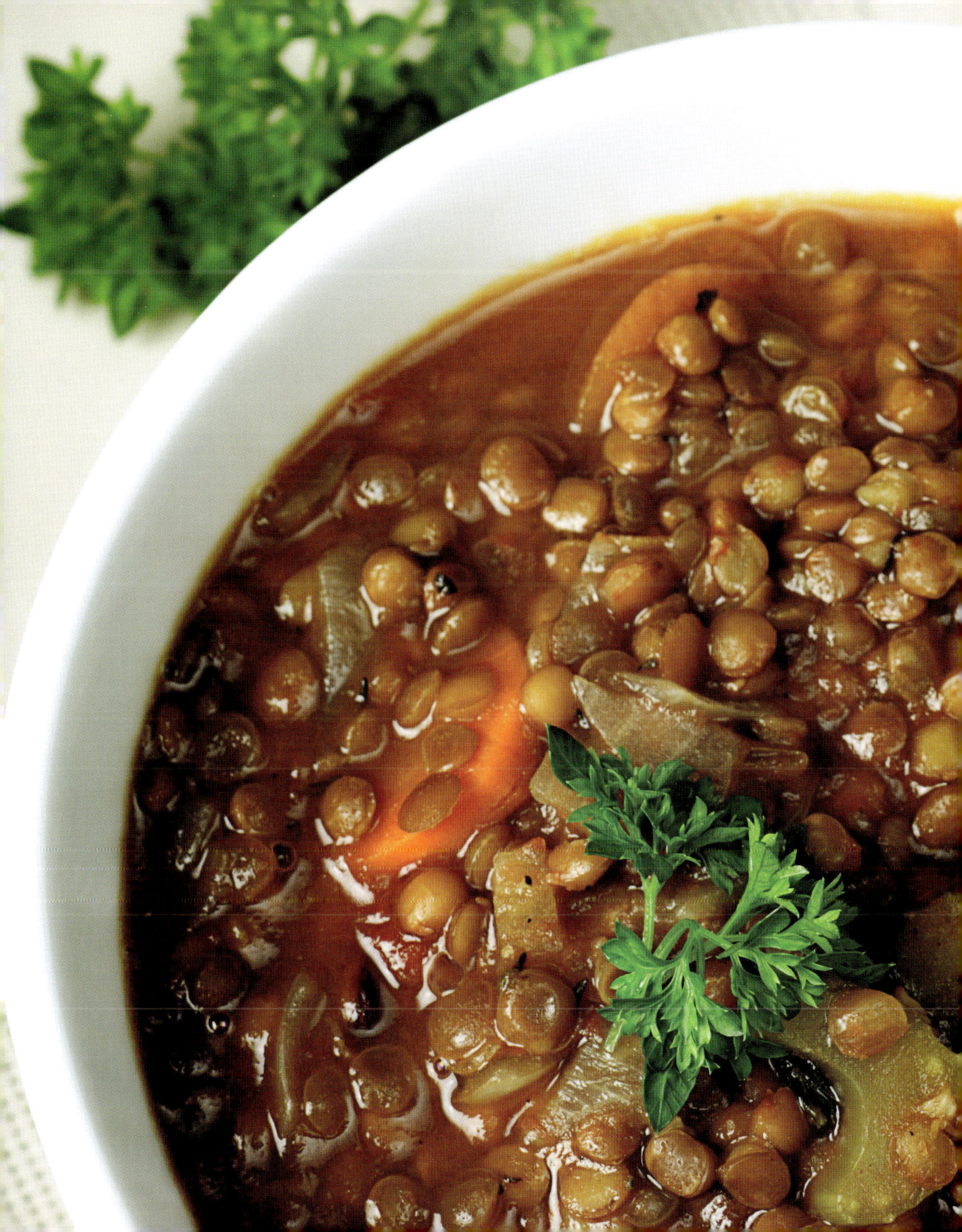

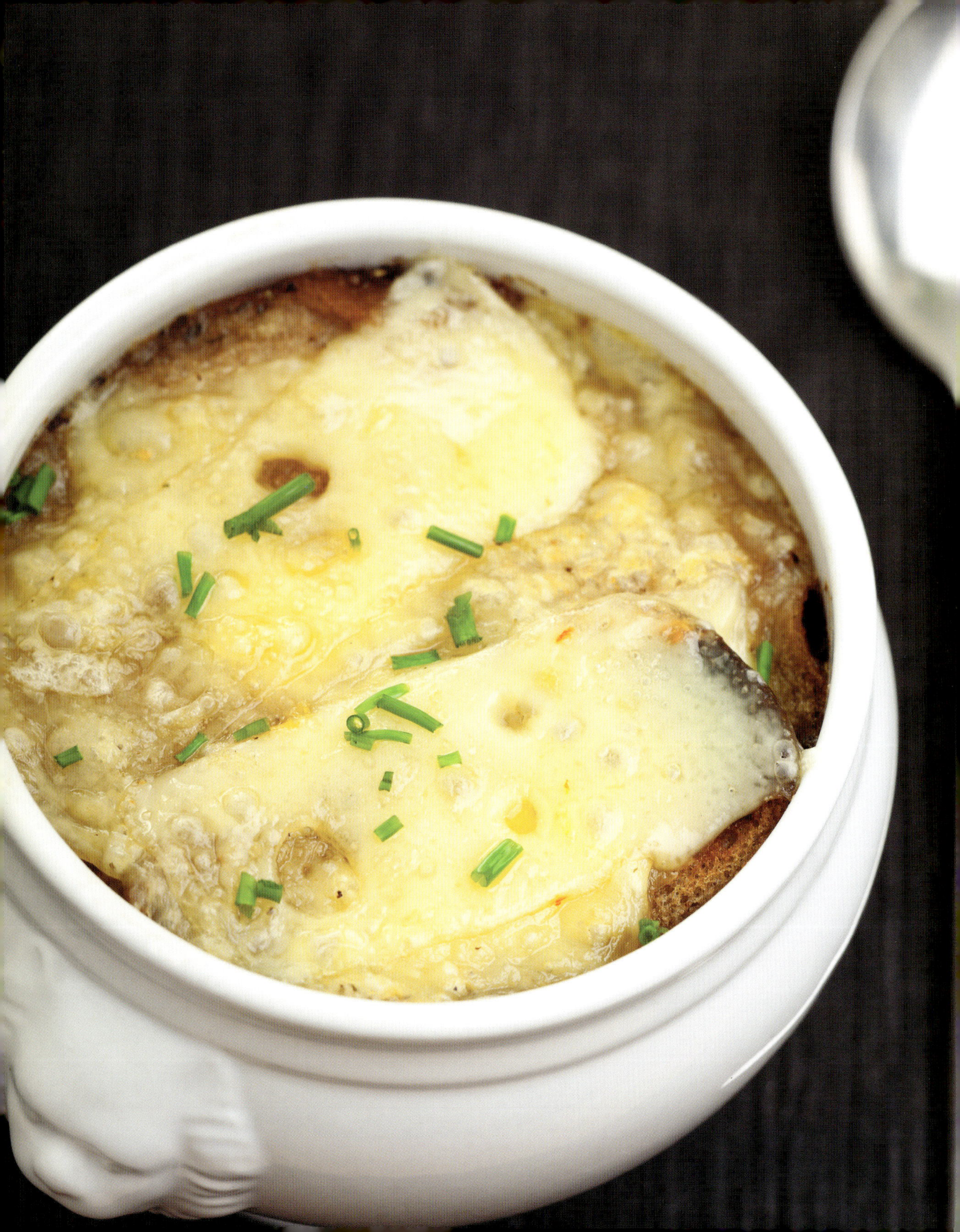

Gigi's French Onion Soup

Gluten-Free/Dairy-Free Options

Serves 8

What could be a better way of using that last morsel of turkey after a delicious turkey dinner? Even after all your favorite turkey sandwich makings are gone, if you have saved the turkey carcass and bones, you still have the primary ingredient for the best French onion soup ever! In our family, this soup is a tradition — usually the Sunday after Thanksgiving, Gigi begins making her amazing French Onion Soup. I am not sure which I like better, the Thanksgiving meal or the soup!

6 cups Basic Turkey Stock (see Index)

4 cups Basic Chicken Stock (see Index), or store-bought gluten-free chicken stock

½ cup white wine

¼ cup butter or Earth Balance Buttery Spread

4 teaspoons raw sugar

6 large onions, sliced in thin rings

2 tablespoons Elizabeth's Gluten-Free Flour Blend, or The Pure Pantry Gluten-Free Organic All Purpose Baking Mix

1 tablespoon gluten-free chicken bouillon

Sea salt and pepper to taste

1 cup turkey meat, shredded

6 slices gluten-free bread, toasted

1 cup each grated Gruyere and Parmesan cheese (or 2 cups Daiya Mozzarella cheese alternative)

1. Heat chicken stock, turkey stock and wine in a large soup pot over low heat.

2. While stock is heating, in a large heavy sauté pan melt 2 tablespoons butter. Add 1 teaspoon sugar and stir until golden brown. Add about a quarter of the onions and sauté while slowly adding 2-3 teaspoons gluten-free flour blend or baking mix. Once onions are caramelized, add onions to soup broth and repeat the same process with the remaining butter, onions and flour. Repeat the sauteing process until all onions have been cooked. Caramelizing the onions will enhance the rich flavor and color of the soup. Add chicken bouillon, sea salt and pepper to taste to the soup and continue cooking over low heat for an additional 15 minutes. Add shredded turkey meat and simmer 15 more minutes.

3. Ladle soup into individual oven-proof bowls. Place toasted bread covered with cheeses on top and brown under broiler until the cheese is melted and bubbly, about 1 minute. Serve piping-hot soup bowls on top of plates

White Bean Oregano Chili

Gluten-Free/Dairy-Free with Vegetarian Option

Serves 8

This is a great dish for a family or neighborhood potluck gathering. Set out chili with all the condiments and let people serve themselves. With some advanced planning, this is an easy and delicious meal!

- 1 pound dried white beans preferably Organic White Northern from Gold Mine Natural Food Co.
- 1 piece kombu, optional (a sea vegetable root available in natural food stores)
- 5 cups Basic Chicken or Turkey Stock (see Index), or store-bought gluten-free chicken or vegetable stock
- 3 cloves garlic, minced
- 1 yellow onion, chopped
- 1 tablespoon ground white pepper
- 1 teaspoon sea salt
- 1 tablespoon fresh oregano leaves, or 2 teaspoons dried leaves
- 1 tablespoon cumin
- 1 teaspoon mild hot sauce
- 1- 26 ounce can or box diced stewed tomatoes in juice
- 1 7-oz can chopped green chiles
- 5 cups chopped cooked chicken (for vegetarian option, substitute 5 cups roasted vegetables such as carrots, celery, zucchini and eggplant.)

1. Place beans in large pot and soak in cold water. Add a 2- to 3-inch piece of kombu (optional) to remove gas from beans. Let soak overnight or at least 5 hours. Drain beans in colander and remove kombu.

2. In a large soup pot or crockpot, combine beans, preferred stock, garlic, onion, pepper, salt, oregano, cumin and hot sauce. Simmer, covered, for 2 ½ - 3 hours or until beans are tender.

3. Stir in tomatoes, green chiles and chicken. For vegetarian option, substitute vegetables for chicken. Cover and simmer an additional hour. Serve chili with condiments.

Condiments:
Shredded mild cheddar cheese or Daiya Cheddar alternative

Sour cream or sour cream alternative such as Tofutti Sour Supreme

Avocado slices

Gluten-free tortilla chips, crumbled

Basic Chicken or Turkey Stock

Gluten-Free/Dairy-Free

Makes about 8 cups of stock

I like to freeze some stock in one- and two-cup containers and in ice cube trays for easy use with other recipes, such as risottos, sauces and soups. Two ice cubes of stock is approximately ¼ cup.

1 stewing hen (4 lbs), preferably organic, such as Rosie's, or entire leftover roasted chicken and bones or entire leftover roasted turkey carcass and bones with some meat still on bones

3 quarts water

2 teaspoons sea salt

1 large yellow onion, peeled and cut into quarters

4-5 celery ribs with leaves, cut into large pieces

4-5 carrots, peeled, cut into large pieces

1 bay leaf

Salt and pepper to taste

1. If using whole stewing hen, rinse it under cold water, then place in large stockpot. If using already roasted chicken or turkey, place in pot. Add water, salt, onion, sliced celery, carrots and bay leaf. Simmer stock for 2-3 hours, skimming foam from surface.

2. Cool for 30 minutes and strain broth through fine sieve. If using whole stewing hen, reserve meat for another use. Season with salt and pepper. Refrigerate stock until cold and skim any fat off top.

3. Pour stock into airtight containers and refrigerate or freeze.

Caesar Salad with Polenta Croutons

Gluten-Free/Dairy-Free Options

Serves 6

Dressing

2 teaspoons gluten-free miso paste (mellow white)

1 tablespoon Dijon or grainy Dijon organic mustard

1 teaspoon anchovy paste (optional)

1 lemon, juiced

1 garlic clove, crushed (optional)

1 teaspoon gluten-free tamari sauce, preferably San-J reduced sodium variety

1 teaspoon agave nectar, preferably Nature's Agave, Raw variety

2 tablespoons mayonnaise or Veganaise, grapeseed oil variety

½ cup olive oil

¼ cup raw apple cider vinegar, preferably Bragg's

Salad

1 head organic romaine lettuce, washed and torn into bite-size pieces

1 avocado, cut into chucks

Fresh Parmesan cheese, (optional)

1 recipe Polenta Croutons

1. Combine all dressing ingredients in blender. Process on medium speed until blended.

2. Toss dressing with romaine lettuce in large salad bowl. Top with avocado chucks. Sprinkle with fresh Parmesan cheese if desired and serve with Polenta Croutons.

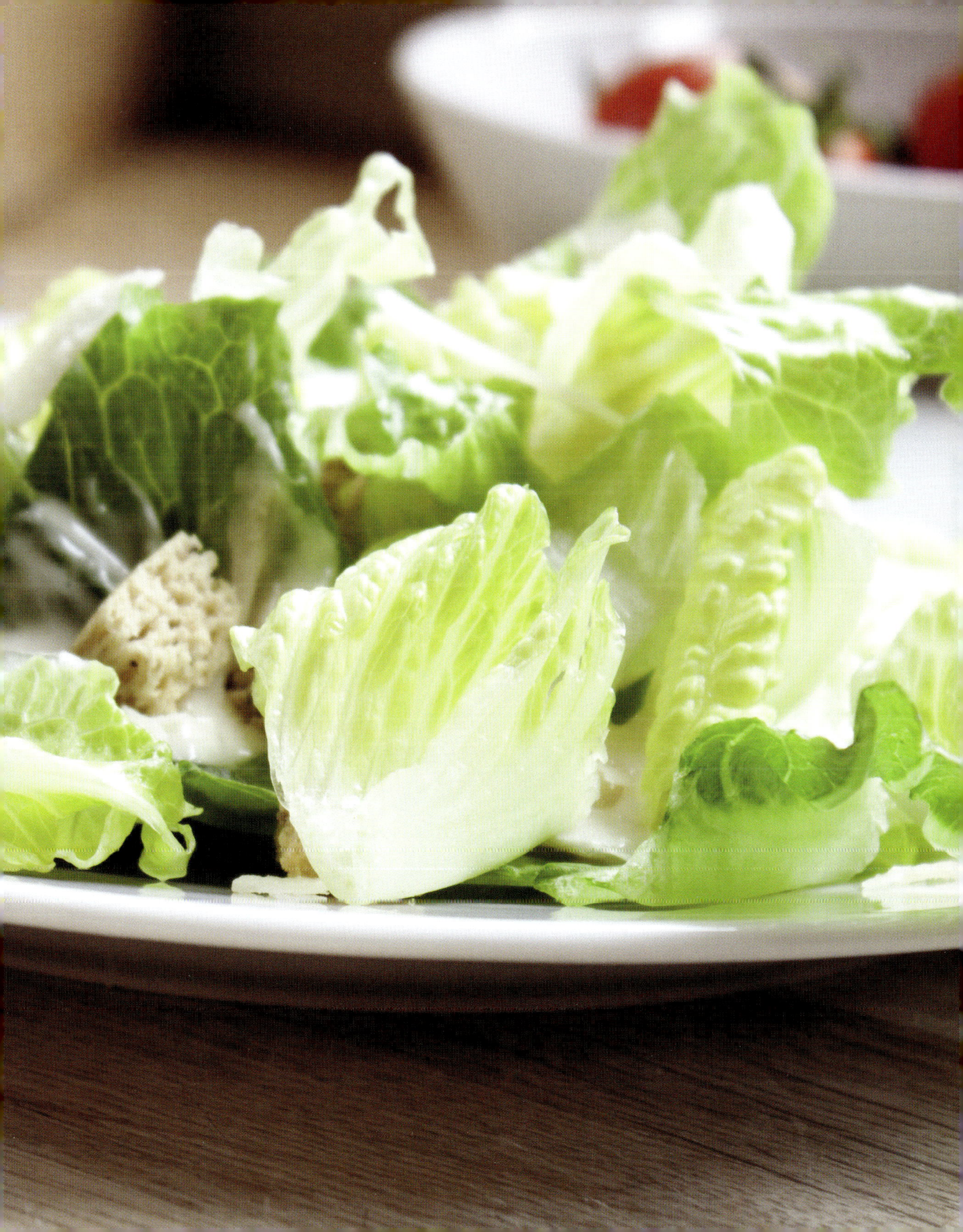

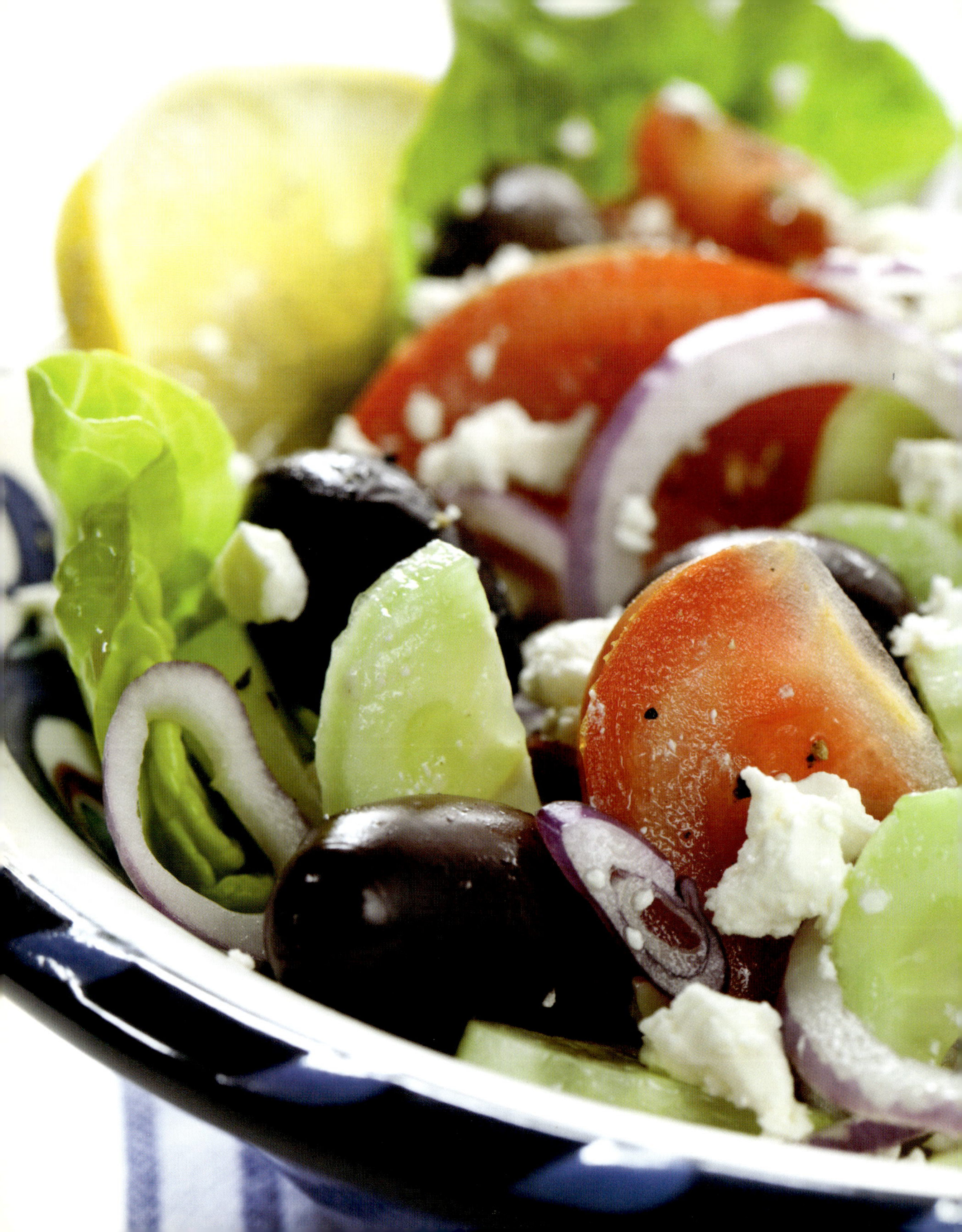

Greek Salad
with Omega-Oregano Dressing
Gluten-Free/Dairy-Free Options

Serves 6
Salad dressing makes 1½ cups

Salad
- 1 package baby romaine lettuce or 1 large head romaine, washed and torn into pieces
- 1 large ripe heirloom tomato or 1 pint Baby heirloom or Sweet 100 tomatoes
- 1 large cucumber, peeled and cut into 1/8-inch slices
- ½ red onion, sliced
- ½ cup Greek olives, pits removed
- ½ cup Greek feta cheese, cubed (optional)

Omega-Oregano Dressing
- ¾ cup extra virgin olive oil
- ¼ cup flax seed oil
- 2 tablespoons borage oil (optional, available at health food stores)
- ½ cup cider vinegar, preferably Bragg's brand
- 1 tablespoon lemon juice
- 2 cloves garlic, crushed
- 1 tablespoon organic Dijon mustard
- 1 teaspoon raw organic agave nectar, preferably Nature's Agave, Raw variety
- 1 teaspoon pepper
- ½ teaspoon sea salt
- 1 tablespoon oregano, finely chopped
- 2 tablespoons fresh herbs: basil, parsley or chives or a combination, finely chopped

1. Place romaine lettuce, tomatoes, cucumbers, onion and olives in a large salad bowl.
2. Place all dressing ingredients in a blender and process until smooth.
3. Toss the salad with about half the dressing and place remainder in a cruet and refrigerate. Sprinkle salad with feta cheese if desired.

Ensalada Verano (Summer Salad) with Balsamic Salad Dressing
Gluten-Free/Dairy-Free Options

Serves 6
Salad dressing makes 1½ cups

Avocado, hearts of palm, jicama and mango make a beautiful presentation in this salad.

- 5 cups baby lettuce, washed and patted dry (approximately 1½ bags)
- 2 ripe avocados, cut into ¼-inch slices
- 1 can hearts of palm, drained and cut into ¼-inch pieces
- 1 medium jicama, peeled and julienned
- 2 red bell peppers, cored, seeded and julienned
- 1 ripe mango, peeled and cut into ¼-inch slices
- ⅛ cup toasted macadamia nuts, chopped
- ½ cup crumbled feta cheese (optional)

Balsamic Salad Dressing:
- 1 cup extra virgin olive oil
- ½ cup good quality balsamic vinegar
- 1 tablespoon Dijon mustard
- 1 teaspoon agave nectar, preferably Nature's Agave, Amber variety, or honey
- 1 teaspoon fresh finely chopped herbs (such as basil, oregano, thyme, savory or chives) or ½ teaspoon dried herb blend, such as Herbs de Provence
- 1 teaspoon sea salt
- ½ teaspoon freshly ground pepper (for Ensalata Verano use dried chipotle powder in place of pepper)

1. Place washed baby lettuces on large oval platter. Arrange avocado slices around the edge of platter on top of lettuces. Arrange hearts of palm, jicama, red peppers and mango on top of lettuces. Sprinkle toasted macadamia nuts and crumbled feta on top of vegetables.

2. For Balsamic Salad Dressing, place all ingredients in a blender and process until smooth. Or, place in a mason jar with lid on and shake until combined. Drizzle desired portion over salad and refrigerate remainder.

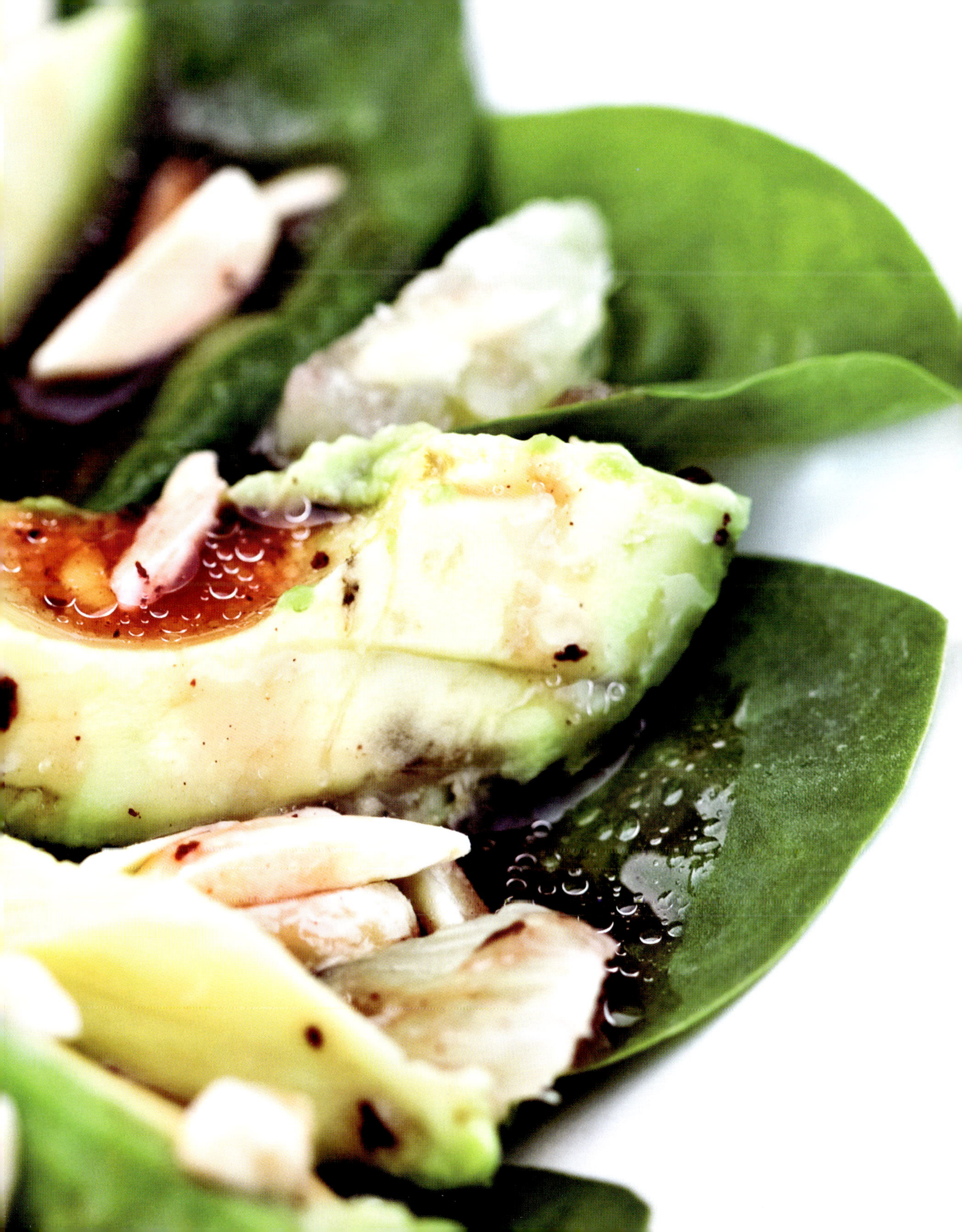

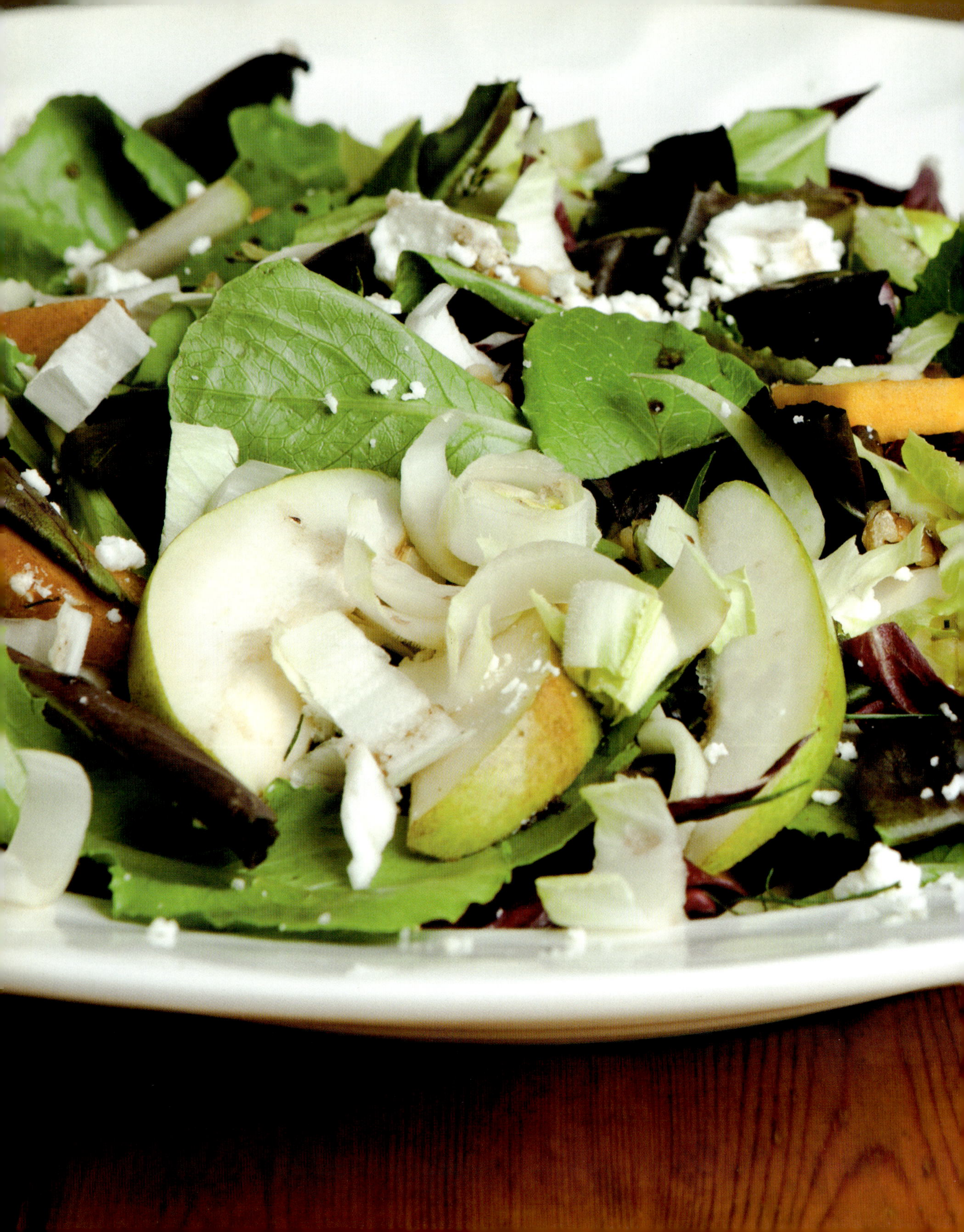

Pear, Persimmon & Fennel Salad
with Pear-Champagne Vinaigrette

Gluten-Free/Dairy-Free Options

Serves 8

Salad

- 8 cups mixed baby salad greens
- 4 Belgian endive: 2 chopped, 2 whole (remove stem but keep leaves whole)
- 1 medium fennel bulb, thinly sliced
- 4 Fuyu persimmons, peeled and cut into ½-inch wedges
- 4 D'Anjou or Asian pears, peeled and cut into ½-inch wedges
- 1 cup walnuts, chopped and toasted
- ½ cup goat feta cheese, crumbled (optional)

Pear-Champagne Vinaigrette

- 1 small ripe D'Anjou or Bartlett pear, peeled, cored and cut into quarters
- ½ cup extra virgin olive oil
- ¼ cup champagne vinegar or white wine vinegar
- 2 teaspoons minced shallots
- 1 teaspoon Dijon mustard
- ½ teaspoon sea salt

1. Divide mixed greens, chopped endive and fennel among chilled salad plates. Place whole endive leaves in spoke pattern, 3 per plate. Arrange persimmon and pear wedges around plate. Top with toasted walnuts.

2. To make vinaigrette, process the pear in a blender until pureed. Strain through fine sieve into a bowl. Whisk in the olive oil, vinegar, shallots, mustard and salt. Chill for 20-30 minutes in refrigerator. Drizzle salad dressing over salads and sprinkle with feta cheese, if desired.

Heirloom Tomato Mozzarella Stack with Edamame Pesto Hummus

Gluten-Free/Dairy-Free Option

Serves 8

Salad

4 Heirloom tomatoes, preferably of varying colors (orange, red, yellow), sliced into 16 $1/8$-inch slices

3- 8 ounce packages fresh Buffalo Mozzarella cheese, drained and sliced into 12 $1/8$-inch slices

1 batch Edamame Pesto Hummus

Fresh basil, for garnish

Salad Dressing

3 tablespoons extra virgin olive oil

1 tablespoon balsamic vinegar

1. Alternate tomato and mozzarella slices on individual salad plates, using 4 tomato slices and 3 mozzarella slices per plate.

2. Make Edamame Pesto Hummus recipe. Place a heaping tablespoon of Edamame Pesto Hummus next to the tomato-mozzarella stack.

3. Whisk together olive oil and balsamic vinegar. Drizzle over tomato-mozzarella stack. Garnish with fresh basil leaves.

Edamame Pesto Hummus

Gluten-Free/Dairy-Free

Makes 2 ½ cups

2 cups shelled organic edamame beans or lima beans

1 cup loosely packed fresh spinach leaves, rinsed and patted dry

¾ cup loosely packed fresh basil leaves

3 large cloves garlic, crushed

¼ cup olive oil, or more

1 teaspoon sea salt

1. Combine edamame or lima beans, spinach, basil and garlic in the bowl of a food processor fitted with chopping blade. With the food processing running, slowly drizzle the olive oil through the top and continue processing until smooth. Add salt and pulse several times to combine.

2. Serve as an appetizer with raw vegetables or gluten-free crackers.

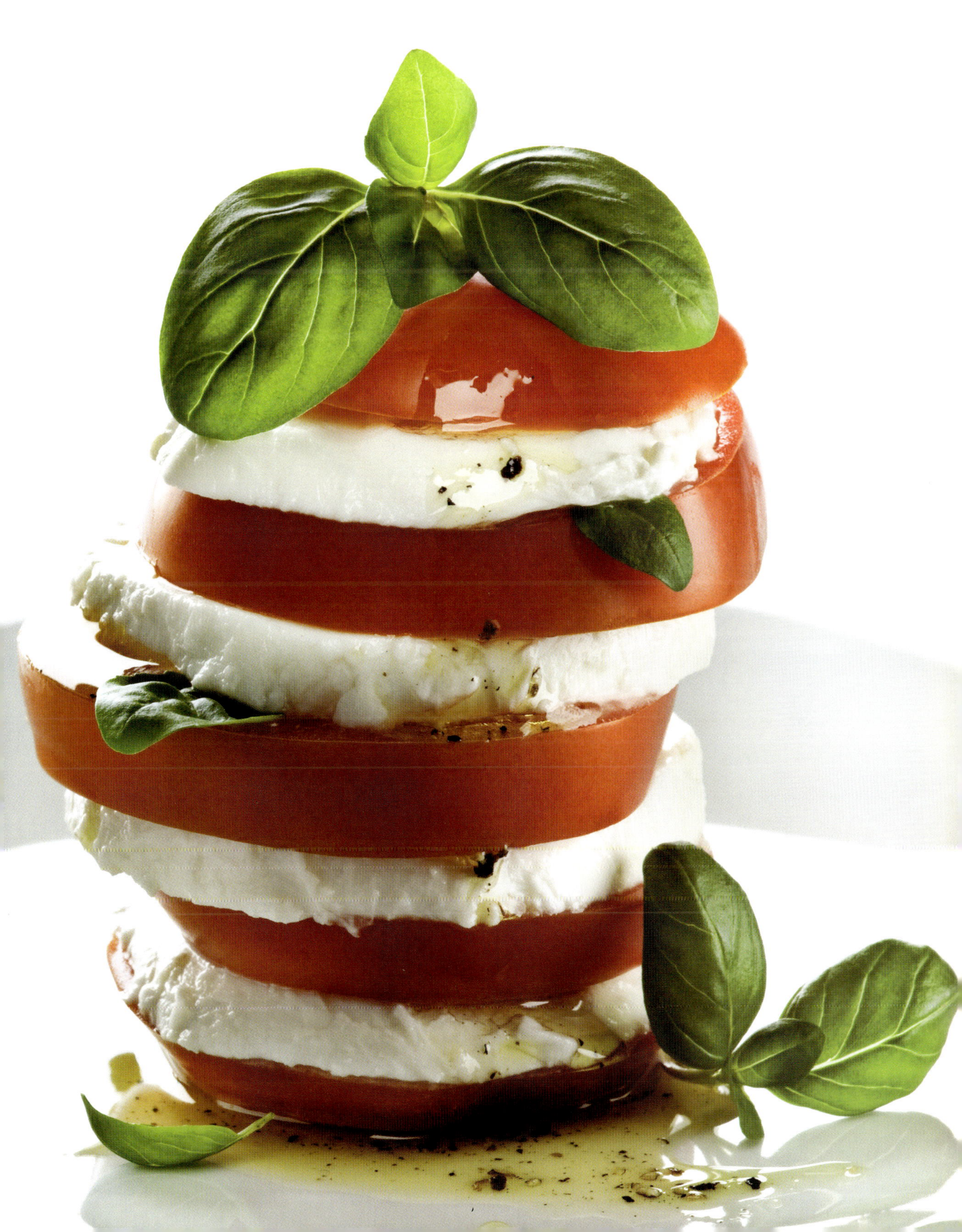

Quinoa Tabouli

Gluten-Free/Dairy-Free/Vegetarian

Serves 4

Try this Quinoa "Tabouli" with Grilled Salmon and Healthy Greek Salad with Omega-Oregano Dressing for a quick and nutritious supper

- 3 cups water
- 1 ½ quinoa
- ½ cup fresh lemon juice
- ¾ cup extra virgin olive oil
- 1 teaspoon pepper
- 2 teaspoons sea salt, or to taste
- 1 cucumber, peeled and chopped
- 2 small tomatoes, chopped
- 1 bunch green onions
- ½ cup fresh mint, chopped
- 2 cups fresh parsley, chopped
- 1 clove garlic, minced

1. Place water and quinoa in medium saucepan and bring to boil. Reduce to simmer and cover. Cook for 15 minutes or until the water is absorbed. Set aside to cool.

2. In a large mixing bowl, whisk together lemon juice, olive oil, pepper and salt. Add in cooled quinoa and toss until well incorporated. Mix in cucumber, tomato, onions, mint, parsley, and garlic.

Rice and Lentils with Cranberries and Oranges

Gluten-Free/Dairy-Free Option

Serves 6

1½ cups water

1 cup long-grain brown rice or brown basmati rice

½ teaspoon sea salt

½ cup French green lentils, preferably Gold Mine Natural Food Co. brand

¼ cup finely chopped shallots

2 tablespoons cider vinegar

1 tablespoon fresh lemon juice

1 orange

¼ cup orange juice

⅓ cup dried cranberries or currants

¼ cup olive oil

⅓ cup chopped fresh flat-leaf parsley

1. Bring water, rice, and salt to a boil in a 1½-quart heavy saucepan, uncovered and undisturbed, until steam holes appear and surface looks dry, about 8 minutes. Reduce heat to very low and cook, covered and undisturbed, 15 minutes more.

2. While rice cooks, cover lentils in 2 inches of water in a medium saucepan and simmer for 20 minutes or until just tender, then drain.

3. Stir together shallots, vinegar, and lemon juice and let stand. Finely grate zest from orange and cut away remaining peel and pith. Cut sections free from membranes and then cut sections into 1/2-inch pieces.

4. Toss warm rice with lentils, shallot mixture, orange, zest, juice, cranberries or currants, oil, and parsley and season with salt and pepper. Serve warm or at room temperature.

Curried Quinoa Mango Salad

Gluten-Free/Dairy-Free with Vegan Option

Serves 4

1½ cups Basic Chicken or Turkey Stock (see Index), or store-bought gluten-free chicken or vegetable stock

¾ cup quinoa

1 teaspoon finely chopped garlic

½ teaspoon sea salt

¼ teaspoon freshly ground pepper

1½ teaspoons curry powder

1 mango, peeled, seeded and diced, or 4 chopped apricots

3 green onions, chopped

¼ cup olive oil

½ cup slivered almonds, lightly toasted

1. Place stock, quinoa, garlic, salt and pepper in a saucepan and bring to boil over high heat. Reduce heat to a simmer, cover and cook until all water is absorbed, about 10-15 minutes.

2. Place cooked quinoa in a medium serving bowl and stir in curry powder, mango or apricots, and green onions. Toss in olive oil. Sprinkle with toasted almonds and serve hot or cool.

Polenta Croutons

Gluten-Free/Dairy-Free

Makes about 4 cups of croutons

- **2 ¾ cups canned low-salt chicken broth or vegetable stock**
- **1 cup yellow cornmeal**
- **3 tablespoons Elizabeth's Gluten-Free Flour Blend or The Pure Pantry All Purpose Organic Baking Mix**
- **¼ teaspoon rosemary**
- **¼ teaspoon thyme**
- **¼ teaspoon garlic powder**
- **2 tablespoons olive oil**
- **1 teaspoon sea salt**
- **½ teaspoon pepper**

1. Butter or oil a 9 x 12-inch-diameter glass baking dish.

2. Bring broth to boil in heavy medium saucepan. Gradually whisk in corn meal. Reduce heat to medium and whisk constantly until mixture thickens, about 6 minutes. Add rosemary, thyme, garlic powder and olive oil. Season with salt and pepper. Pour polenta into prepared dish. Spread evenly using buttered knife. Cool until polenta is firm, at least 1 hour.

3. Preheat oven to 350°F. Line baking sheet with foil and coat with olive oil. Cut polenta into bite size squares. Transfer squares, bottom side up, to prepared sheet, fitting closely together. Brush or spray with olive oil. Bake for 45 minutes.

4. Remove from oven and carefully turn over croutons to other side. Bake an additional 15 minutes or until golden brown. Let cool before tossing with salad.

soups & salads

Chapter Four

Family Dinners

Meat and Poultry Entrees
Apricot-Agave Glazed Meatloaf
Parsley, Sage, Rosemary & Thyme Crumb-Crusted Rack of Lamb
Chicken Grilled with Pomegranate-Chipotle BBQ Sauce
Mojito Chicken on Cilantro Rice
Rosemary-Scented Pork Tenderloin with Cranberry-Cherry Chutney

Fish Entrees
Almond-Encrusted Tilapia with Apricot-Orange Teriyaki Dipping Sauce
Grilled Salmon or Halibut with Dilly-Lemony "Tartar" Sauce
Grilled Salmon on Edamame Basil Pesto with Zucchini "Pasta"

Rice, Pasta and Grains - Entrees & Sides
Asian Veggies in Tamari-Sesame-Ginger Stir-Fry Sauce
Asparagus and Leek Risotto
Butternut Squash and Pumpkin Risotto
Cilantro Rice
Easy Fried Rice
Spaghetti with Turkey Meatballs
Quinoa with Roasted Eggplant Caponata

Vegetables - Sides
French Green Beans with Sundried Tomatoes and Pine Nuts
Sweet Potato Gratin with Pecan-Cinnamon Topping
Vegetable Sauté in Lemon-Thyme-Basil Sauce
Yukon Gold Potato-Goat Cheese Gratin
Zucchini Goat Cheese Gratin

family dinners 91

Apricot-Agave Glazed Meatloaf

Gluten-Free/Dairy-Free

Serves 4

Meatloaf

- 1 tablespoon olive oil
- 1 yellow onion, finely diced
- 4 garlic cloves, minced
- ½ cup dried apricots, diced
- 2 pounds organic ground beef or turkey, or a combination
- 2 links mild Italian sausage
- 1 large carrot, grated
- 1 large zucchini, grated
- ⅓ cup Pomegranate BBQ Sauce (see Index) or purchased gluten-free BBQ sauce, such as Annie's brand
- 1 tablespoon agave nectar, preferably Nature's Agave, Raw variety
- 2 eggs (for egg-free option, substitute 3 tablespoons olive oil)
- ¾ cup Elizabeth's Gluten-Free Flour Blend (see Index) or The Pure Pantry Gluten-Free All Purpose Baking Mix
- 1 teaspoon dried sage
- 1 teaspoon dried thyme
- 1 teaspoon curry powder
- 1 teaspoon sea salt
- 1 teaspoon pepper

Apricot-Agave Glaze

- 2 tablespoons brown sugar
- ⅓ cup agave nectar, preferably Nature's Agave, Raw variety
- ¼ cup apricot jam or fruit spread

1. Preheat oven to 350°F. In a medium skillet over medium heat, sauté onion and garlic in olive oil for 2-3 minutes. Add apricots and continue sautéing for an additional 2-3 minutes. Set aside to cool slightly.

2. In a large mixing bowl, place ground beef or turkey. Remove sausage meat from casings and add meat to mixing bowl. Add grated carrots and zucchini, BBQ sauce, agave nectar, eggs, baking mix and spices. Mix together until well combined but do not over mix. Spoon mixture into a large loaf pan. Smooth over top. Bake for 50 minutes.

3. While meatloaf is baking, prepare glaze. Combine all ingredients in a small bowl and whisk together.

4. Remove meatloaf from oven. Brush glaze over top of meatloaf and return to oven for 15 more minutes. Let cool for 5-10 minutes before slicing to serve.

Parsley, Sage, Rosemary & Thyme Crumb Crusted Rack of Lamb

Gluten-Free/Dairy-Free

Serves 6

Crust
¼ cup olive oil

3 large shallots, minced (about ¾ cup)

1 tablespoon finely chopped fresh rosemary

2 cloves garlic, crushed and finely chopped

1½ cups fresh gluten-free breadcrumbs (see below)

1 teaspoon sea salt

½ teaspoon freshly ground pepper

Gluten-free Breadcrumbs
6 slices gluten-free white bread, preferably Udi's brand white sandwich bread

¼ teaspoon sea salt

Lamb
1 tablespoon olive oil

2 well-trimmed racks of lamb (each 1¼ lb)

1 tablespoon Dijon mustard

1. For breadcrumbs, lightly toast bread for less than 1 minute in toaster or oven until just slightly crisp. Tear into pieces and place in food processor. Add ¼ teaspoon salt. Pulse on and off until breadcrumbs form.

2. For crust, place a large, heavy skillet over medium-high heat. Place olive oil, shallots, rosemary and garlic in skillet and sauté until shallots are soft, about 2 minutes. Add the breadcrumbs and sauté until golden brown, about 5 minutes. Add salt and pepper. Place crumb mixture in a small bowl and let cool.

3. Preheat oven to 400°F. In the same large skillet, add 1 tablespoon olive oil and turn heat on medium high. Working in batches, add the lamb racks to the skillet, rounded side down. Turn meat with tongs and sear tip of lamb chops. Sear until all sides are brown, cooking for about 4-5 minutes.

4. Transfer to a clean cutting board, seared side up. Spread Dijon mustard on seared side of each rack. Press the crumb topping into mustard, dividing crumb mixture evenly between the two racks of lamb. Place on rimmed baking sheet. Roast in the oven, until desired doneness, about 25 minutes for medium well. Let the lamb rest for 5-7 minutes before carving and serving.

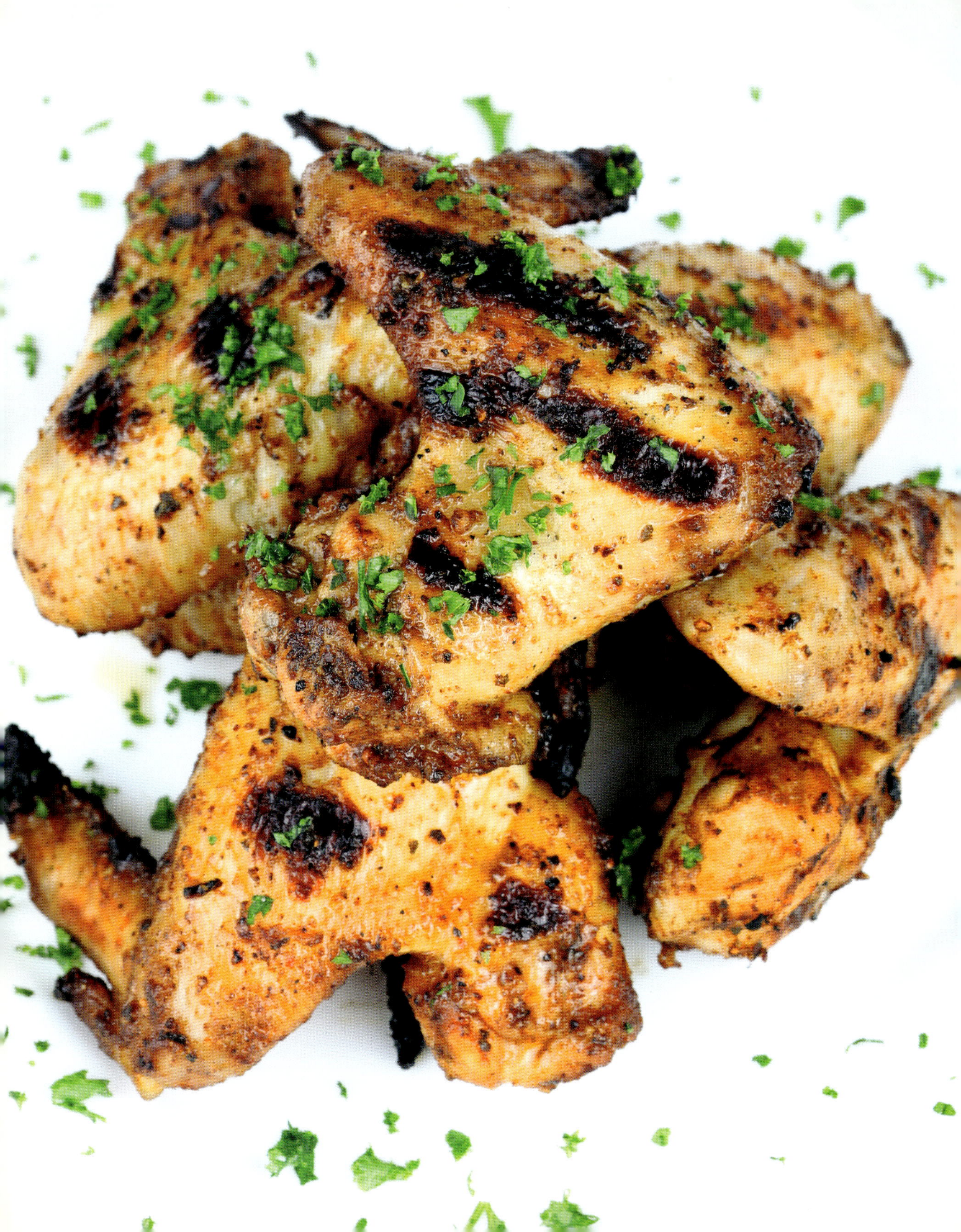

Chicken Grilled
with Pomegranate Chipotle BBQ Sauce

Gluten-Free/Dairy-Free

Serves 4

1 whole cut up chicken

1 teaspoon sea salt

½ teaspoon pepper

1 cup Pomegranate Chipotle BBQ Sauce, divided

1. Generously rub chicken pieces on all sides with salt and pepper.

2. Heat grill to medium heat (330°F) and grill chicken for 8 minutes per side. Brush with ½ cup BBQ sauce while on grill. Turn and brush other side of chicken pieces. Check for doneness with meat thermometer. Remove from grill and brush with reserved sauce. (For food safety, discard any sauce from the container used to brush chicken while on the grill.)

Pomegranate Chipotle BBQ Sauce

Gluten-Free/Dairy-Free

Makes 2 cups BBQ sauce

½ cup organic tomato paste

4 tablespoons organic balsamic vinegar

2 tablespoons organic blackstrap molasses

½ cup organic brown sugar

2 tablespoons organic gluten free tamari sauce, preferably San J brand

½ cup agave nectar, preferably Nature's Agave, Amber variety

½ cup pomegranate juice

½ teaspoon chipotle chile powder

1 tablespoon organic cornstarch or arrowroot

1. Mix all ingredients, except cornstarch or arrowroot, in a medium size bowl with whisk. Whisk in cornstarch or arrowroot.

2. Transfer to medium saucepan. Cook over medium heat while whisking for 2-3 minutes. Turn off heat and let cool.

3. Store in airtight container in refrigerator for up to two weeks.

family dinners

Mojito Chicken on Cilantro Rice

Gluten-Free/Dairy-Free

Serves 6

2 cloves garlic, minced

¼ cup yellow onion, minced

⅓ cup olive oil, divided

½ cup freshly squeezed orange juice

2 limes, juiced

½ cup dry white wine

1 teaspoon lime zest

2 tablespoons fresh cilantro, chopped

1 teaspoon sea salt

1 teaspoon ground cumin

3 skinless, boneless chicken breasts, cut in half or 6 chicken drumsticks

4 red bell peppers, halved, stems, seeds and white part removed

1 recipe Cilantro Rice (see Index)

Orange slices, for garnish

1. Place garlic and onion in large skillet with 2 tablespoons olive oil. Saute until soft, about 4 minutes. Add orange juice, lime juice, remaining olive oil and white wine. Simmer for 2 minutes over medium heat.

2. Remove from heat. Place in blender along with lime zest, cilantro, salt and cumin. Turn blender on and off three times to combine ingredients but not puree them. Reserve ⅓ cup marinade for use in Step 6.

3. Place chicken in large zipper-seal bag. Pour remaining marinade into bag and zip, making sure it is sealed. Move bag around to make sure marinade is soaking all the chicken pieces. Let sit in refrigerator for 15 minutes. Prepare Cilantro Rice (see Index) while chicken is marinading.

4. Heat oven or BBQ to 375°F. Remove chicken from marinade. Discard marinade. Roast chicken in oven for 20 minutes, turn pieces and roast an additional 5 minutes or until brown. Or, grill on BBQ, 10 minutes each side or until meat thermometer inserted in thickest part measures 165°F.

5. While chicken is cooking, grill red bell peppers on grill or roast in oven in ovenproof dish, cooking 3-5 minutes per side. Once skin of peppers begins to blacken, remove from oven or BBQ. Let cool slightly and cut into strips.

6. Place Cilantro Rice on large serving platter. Top with Mojito Chicken, red pepper strips and sprinkle with extra freshly chopped cilantro. Pour reserved marinade on top. For a nice presentation, garnish with orange slices.

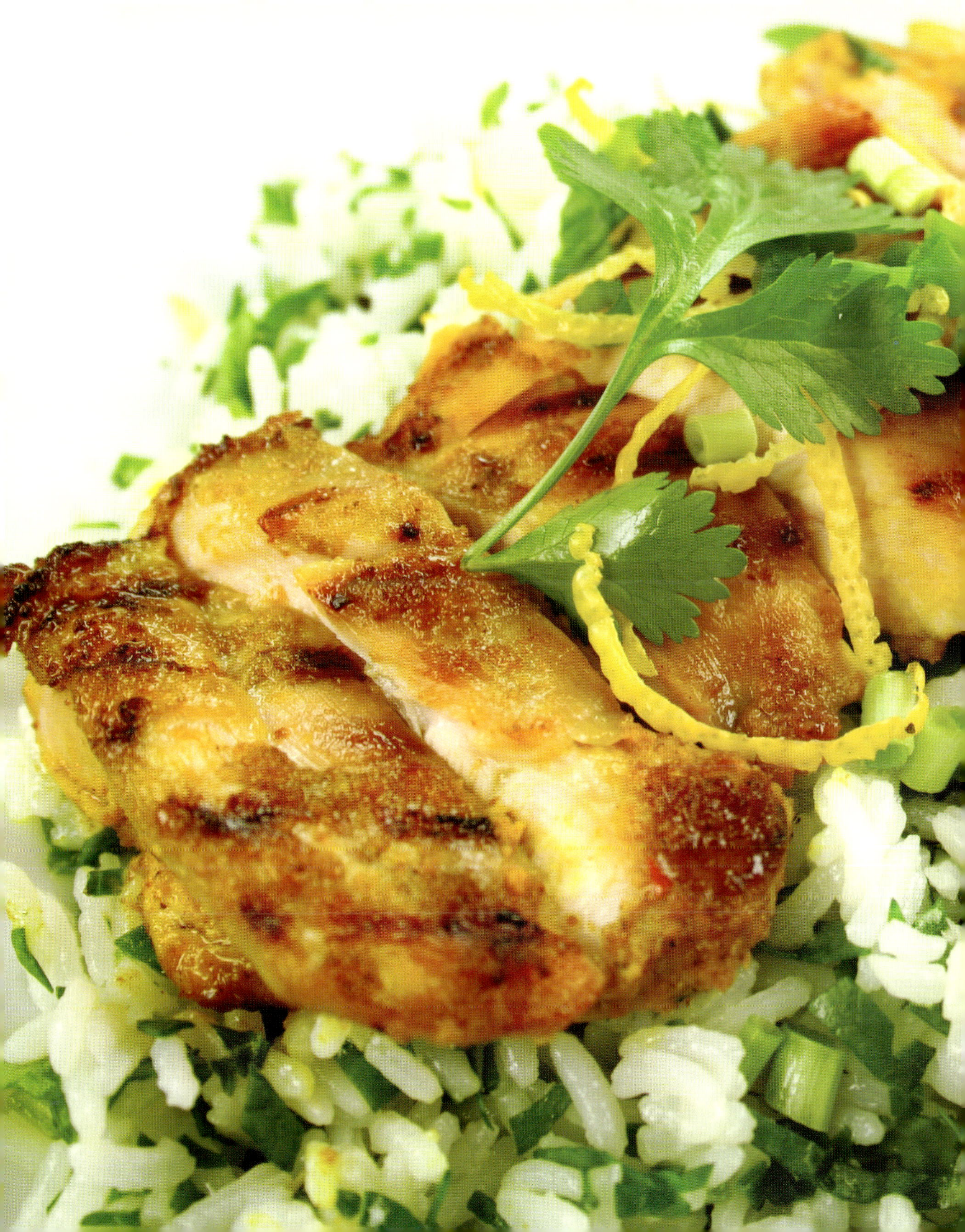

Rosemary-Scented Pork Tenderloin with Cranberry-Cherry Chutney

Gluten-Free/Dairy-Free

Serves 8

Pork Tenderloin
8 5-inch long sprigs fresh rosemary, or wooden skewers, soaked in water for 5 minutes

2 lean pork tenderloins, about 1 1/3 pound each

2 tablespoons finely chopped rosemary

1/4 cup Merlot wine

2 tablespoons olive oil

1 tablespoon gluten-free soy sauce, preferably San-J brand

Cranberry-Cherry Chutney
1 cup dried cherries (unsweetened)

1 cup dried cranberries (unsweetened)

2 shallots, finely chopped

1/2 cup dark brown sugar

1 cup Merlot wine

1 1/2 cups water

1/4 cup balsamic vinegar

1. Preheat oven to 375°F. Take rosemary sprigs and remove leaves except for one inch on the end to create rosemary skewers. Cut tenderloins into 3- to 4-inch pieces. Thread meat onto rosemary, or wooden skewers. Set aside.

2. Finely chop some of the rosemary leaves to equal 2 tablespoons.

3. In a small bowl, combine finely chopped rosemary, 1/4 cup Merlot wine, olive oil and soy sauce. Whisk together and pour over rosemary skewers. Turn skewers so all sides of meat are covered with marinade. Place meat in refrigerator for 1 hour or up to 4 hours.

4. Prepare Cranberry-Cherry Chutney while meat is marinating. Place all ingredients in medium saucepan on medium heat. Bring to simmer, stirring constantly. Lower heat and continue simmering until all liquid is absorbed, about 15-20 minutes.

5. Remove tenderloins from marinade and place on rack in roasting pan or in baking dish. Line up ends of skewers with rosemary leaves and cover ends with foil so they do not burn. Place in middle of oven for 6 minutes. Turn skewers over and bake an additional 6 minutes. Remove from oven and check with meat thermometer for doneness (180°F).

6. Brush skewers with plenty of chutney and tent with foil to keep warm. Serve with extra chutney on the side.

Almond-Encrusted Tilapia
with Apricot-Orange Teriyaki Dipping Sauce

Gluten-Free/Dairy-Free

Serves 8

This is a hit for kids who don't like fish since the Tilapia is mild and the almond crust along with the dipping sauce have such fantastic flavors.

1 lemon, juiced

1 tablespoon Dijon mustard

¼ cup olive oil

2 tablespoons white wine or cider vinegar

½ teaspoon sea salt

½ teaspoon ground pepper

¾ cup finely crushed gluten-free corn flake cereal

3 tablespoons Elizabeth's Gluten-Free Flour Blend (see Index) or The Pure Pantry Gluten-Free All Purpose Baking Mix

¾ cup almond meal

1 teaspoon turmeric

1 tablespoon fresh cilantro, finely chopped, or 1 teaspoon dried

1 tablespoon fresh Italian flat-leaf parsley, finely chopped or 1 teaspoon dried

6-8 tilapia fillets (or other mild white fish)

3 tablespoons sliced almonds

1. Preheat oven to 400°F. Grease baking sheet with coconut oil or olive oil. In a medium-size bowl, whisk together lemon juice, mustard, olive oil, white wine or vinegar, salt and pepper. Combine in another medium bowl the crushed corn flakes, baking mix, almond meal, turmeric, cilantro and parsley.

2. Dip tilapia in the lemon-mustard mixture, coating both sides of each fillet. Let excess drip back into the bowl. Dredge fillet in corn flake-almond mixture on both sides. Set fillets on greased baking sheet. Sprinkle any remaining crumbs over top of fillets.

3. Set oven rack in second from the top position. Bake fillets for 6 minutes. Carefully turn fillets over, sprinkle top of fillets with sliced almonds, bake an additional 4-6 minutes; depending on thickness of fillet, you may be able to bake for less time. Remove from oven and serve with Apricot-Orange Teriyaki Dipping Sauce.

Apricot-Orange Teriyaki Dipping Sauce

½ cup gluten-free teriyaki sauce, preferably San-J brand

½ cup apricot spread, preferably Crofter's Organic Fruit Spread

1 teaspoon minced fresh ginger or ½ teaspoon powdered ginger

1 teaspoon grated orange peel

1. Place teriyaki sauce, apricot spread, ginger and orange peel in a blender and blend for 20 seconds until combined.

Grilled Salmon or Halibut
with Dilly-Lemony "Tartar" Sauce
Gluten-Free/Dairy-Free Options

Serves 4

An easy weeknight entrée with a tangy twist!

- 4 center-cut wild salmon fillets or halibut fillets
- ¼ cup Vegenaise brand mayonnaise from Follow Your Heart
- ¼ cup plain Greek yogurt or Tofutti Sour Supreme
- 1 teaspoon fresh dill, finely chopped
- ½ teaspoon white pepper
- ½ teaspoon garlic salt
- 1 tablespoon fresh lemon juice
- 3 tablespoons cucumber, peeled, seeded and finely chopped, or fennel, finely chopped

1. Preheat grill to 375°F. Place 1 tablespoon Vegenaise in a small bowl. Brush salmon with Vegenaise. Grill salmon or halibut on one side for about 3 minutes, turn over to second side and grill an additional 3 minutes. Check for doneness.

2. Prepare "tartar" sauce by whisking together remaining Vegenaise, yogurt or substitute, dill, pepper, garlic salt and lemon juice. Add chopped cucumber or fennel.

3. Serve salmon or halibut on a plate with a heap of "tartar" sauce on top and lemon wedges on the side. Serve with Cilantro Rice (see Index).

family dinners 101

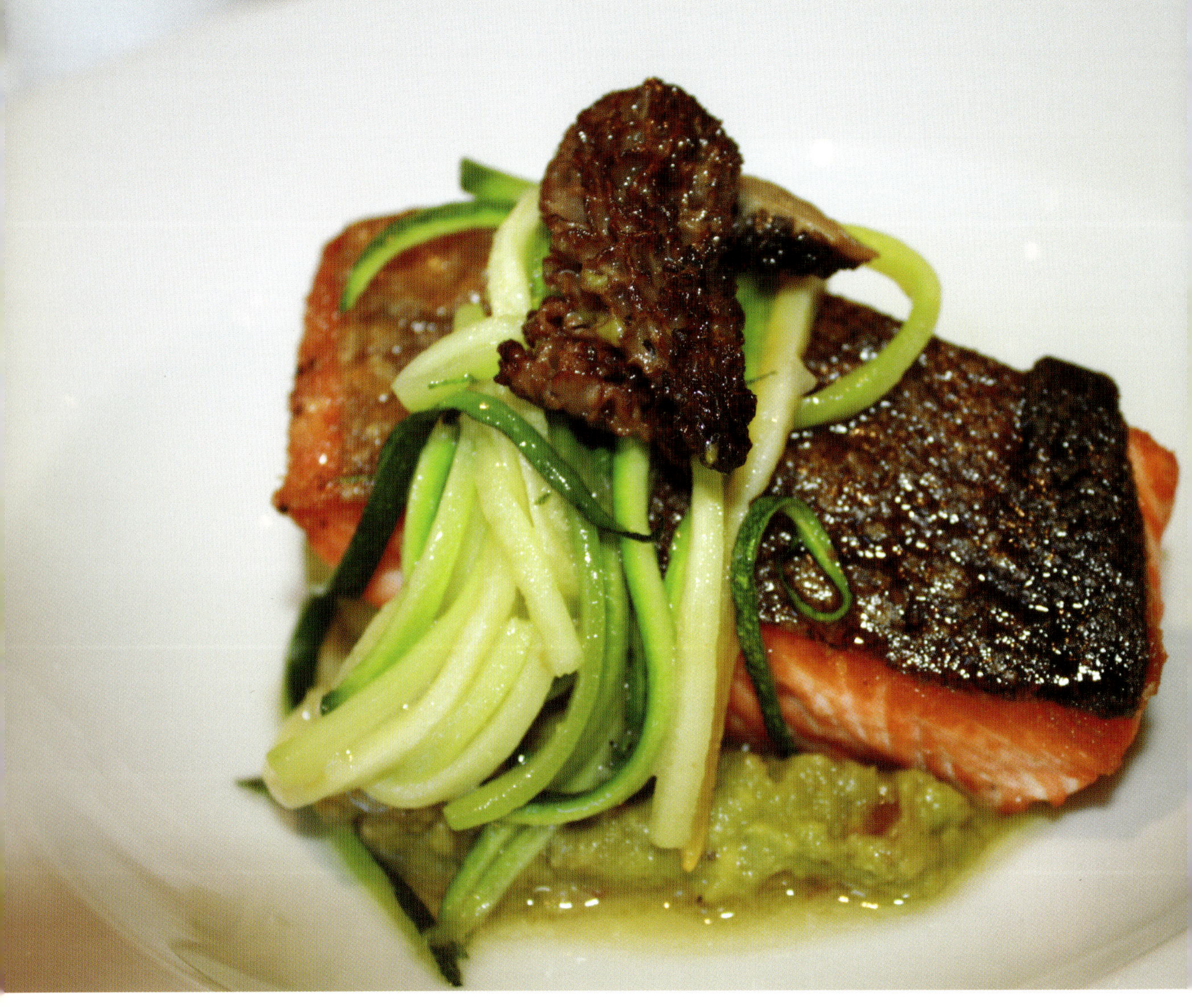

Grilled Salmon
on Edamame Pesto Hummus with Zucchini "Pasta"

Gluten-Free/Dairy-Free

Serves 4

This is an elegant entrée to serve at a dinner party or for a special occasion. You can prepare the Edamame Pesto Hummus up to four days in advance to help save time.

4 zucchini, washed and ends trimmed

4 tablespoons olive oil, divided

2 tablespoons white wine

2 cloves garlic, crushed and finely minced, divided

8 morel mushrooms, washed and ends of stems trimmed

1 tablespoon Dijon mustard

1 tablespoon maple syrup

1 teaspoon olive oil

1 teaspoon sea salt

4 center-cut wild salmon fillets with skin on

1 batch Edamame Pesto Hummus (see Index)

1. Prepare zucchini pasta by using a mandolin vegetable slicer with julienne blade or using a kitchen tool called a spiral slicer (available from Joyce Chen on Amazon.com). Toss zucchini strands with 1 tablespoon olive oil, white wine and 1 crushed and minced garlic clove.

2. Sauté morel mushrooms in 1 tablespoon olive oil and the remaining crushed garlic clove for 3-4 minutes until tender. Remove mushrooms from pan and cover.

3. Place zucchini pasta in the same pan and gently heat for 2-3 minutes just until warm. Do not overcook.

4. Whisk together Dijon, maple syrup, olive oil and salt in small bowl. Brush mixture over salmon fillets. Grill salmon fillets, flesh side down, for about 4 minutes or until salmon begins to slightly flake. Remove salmon and tent with foil to keep warm.

5. Place two heaping tablespoons of Edamame Pesto Hummus on center of plate. Place salmon fillet, flesh side down, on top. Place ¼ of the zucchini pasta on the side of the salmon and two morel mushrooms on top. Drizzle with a teaspoon extra virgin olive oil and a squeeze of fresh lemon and serve.

family dinners

Asian Veggies
in Tamari-Sesame-Ginger Stir-Fry Sauce
Gluten-Free/Dairy-Free

Serves 4

Tamari-Sesame-Ginger Stir-Fry Sauce

1 tablespoon sesame oil

3 tablespoon gluten-free tamari sauce, preferably San-J brand

1 tablespoon agave nectar, preferably Nature's Agave, Amber variety

2 tablespoons fresh ginger, finely chopped

1 clove garlic, finely chopped

¼ teaspoon Asian chili sauce (optional)

Veggies

1 teaspoon sesame oil

1 tablespoon coconut oil

4-6 cups chopped fresh vegetables: carrots, green beans, broccoli, Asian cabbage, kale, bean sprouts, celery, onion, etc.

2 tablespoons toasted sesame seeds

1. Whisk together 1 tablespoon sesame oil, tamari sauce and agave nectar. Add fresh ginger and garlic and stir. Add optional Asian chili sauce.

2. Place 1 teaspoon sesame oil and coconut oil in a hot wok. Stir-fry vegetables for 2 minutes in oil. Pour sauce over vegetables and stir-fry for an additional 3-4 minutes. Vegetables should be hot and slightly cooked at this point – do not overcook. Serve over jasmine rice or Easy Fried Rice (see Index) with toasted sesame seeds.

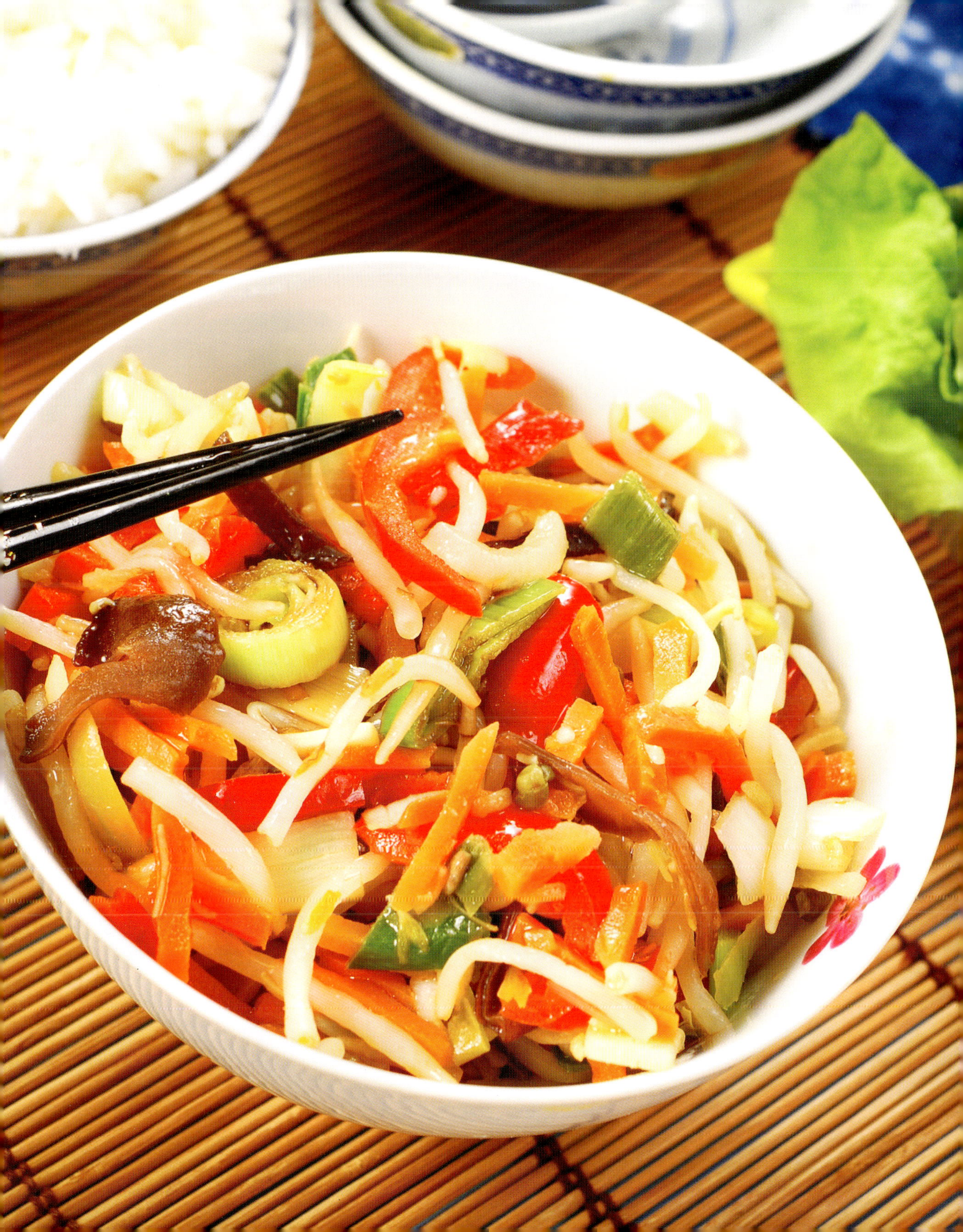

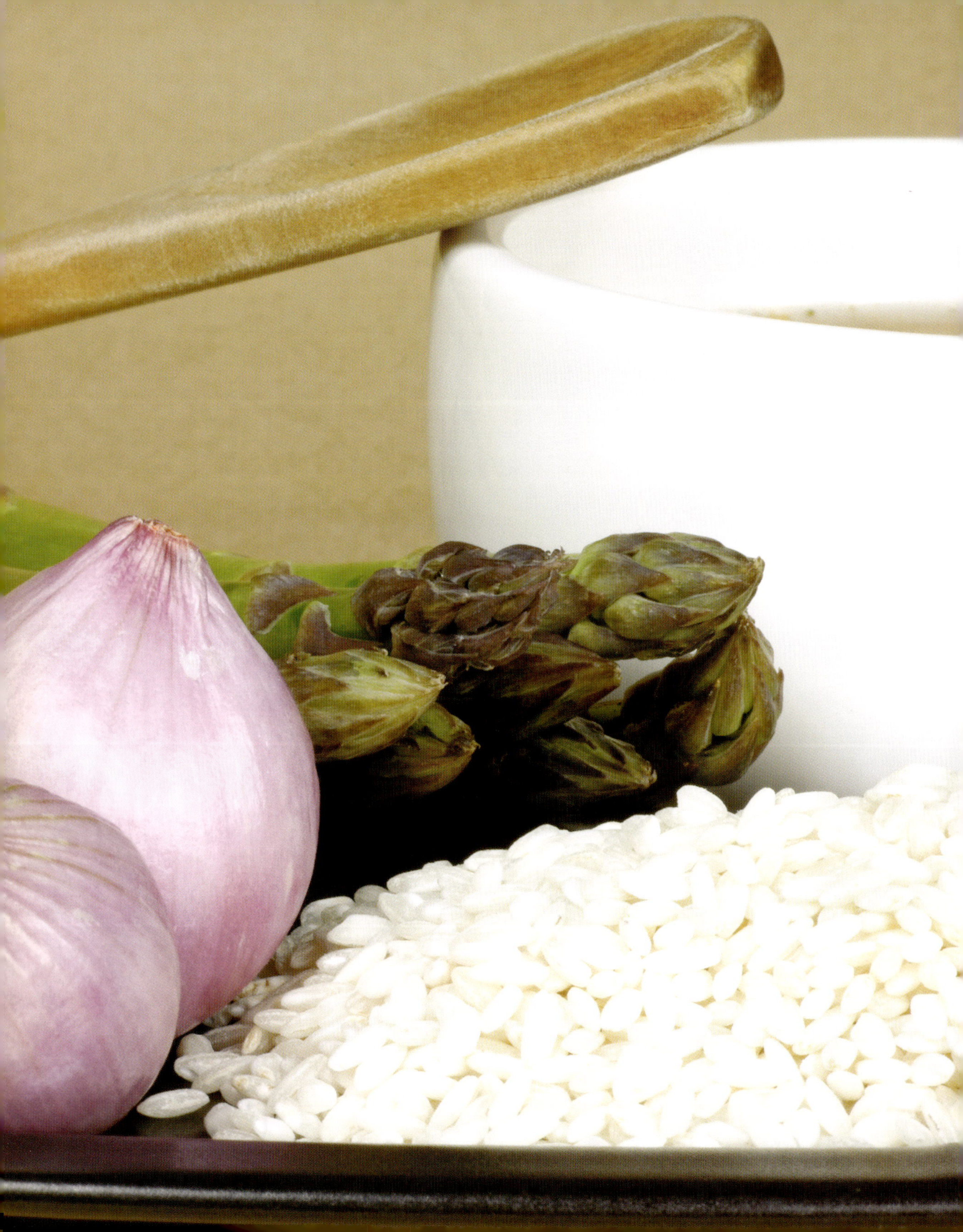

Asparagus and Leek Risotto

Gluten-Free with Dairy-Free & Vegetarian Options

Serves 6 as a side dish, 4 as a main dish

8-10 stalks asparagus

1 large leek

3 tablespoons olive oil, divided

1 teaspoon sea salt, divided

5½ cups Basic Chicken Stock (see Index) or store-bought gluten-free chicken stock

1 yellow onion, finely chopped

2 shallots, finely chopped

2 cloves garlic, minced

1¼ cups Arborio rice

½ cup dry white wine

¼ cup freshly chopped Italian flat-leaf parsley

2 tablespoons finely chopped basil

½ teaspoon white pepper

½ cup freshly grated Parmesan cheese, optional

1. Preheat oven to 350°F. Clean asparagus and trim ends. Cut green part off of leek. Cut white part of leek diagonally and rinse thoroughly under water to remove all dirt. Place asparagus and leek halves on baking sheet and toss with 1 tablespoon olive oil and ½ teaspoon salt. Roast in oven for 10 minutes. Let cool and cut into ½-inch pieces.

2. While vegetables are roasting, bring chicken or vegetable stock to simmer over medium heat. Cover and keep warm over low heat.

3. In a large, heavy saucepan, heat remaining 2 tablespoons olive oil and add chopped onion and shallots. Sauté until soft, about 6 minutes. Add garlic and sauté for 30 seconds until fragrant.

4. Add rice and stir over low heat until all rice grains have been coated with olive oil. Add one cup of the hot chicken stock and cook over low heat, folding in the stock gently so rice grains will not break. Simmer for about 6 minutes. Add another cup of hot stock and repeat process, cooking an additional 6 minutes. Continue adding stock, one cup at a time, and gently stirring it into the rice as it cooks over low heat, until all liquid is absorbed.

5. Add wine, roasted asparagus and leeks, folding ingredients gently, cooking for an additional 2-3 minutes until rice is hot and creamy. Gently fold in parsley, basil, remaining ½ teaspoon salt, pepper and optional Parmesan cheese. Serve and top with additional Parmesan, if desired.

Butternut Squash and Pumpkin Risotto

Gluten-Free

Serves 8

- 2 tablespoons olive oil, for greasing
- 4½ cups Basic Chicken or Turkey Stock (see Index), or store-bought gluten-free chicken or vegetable stock
- ½ cup dry white wine
- 2 cups Arborio rice
- 1½ cups butternut squash, diced (fresh or frozen)
- 1½ cups canned pumpkin
- 1 cup yellow onion, finely chopped
- 2 cloves garlic, minced
- 2 tablespoons fresh sage leaves, minced
- ½ cup grated Parmesan cheese

1. Preheat oven to 400°F. Grease Dutch oven or other ovenproof baking dish with lid, with olive oil. Combine broth, wine, rice, squash, pumpkin, onion, garlic and sage in Dutch oven.

2. Cover with lid and bake for 15 minutes. Remove from oven and stir gently.

3. Return to oven and bake an additional 15 minutes or until all liquid is absorbed. Remove from oven.

4. Stir in Parmesan cheese and top with freshly chopped sage leaves.

Cilantro Rice

Gluten-Free/Dairy-Free, Vegetarian

Serves 6

2 tablespoons butter or olive oil

¼ cup onion, finely chopped

2 cloves garlic, minced

1 cup basmati rice

2 cups vegetable stock

3 tablespoons cilantro, finely chopped

1. In a large saucepan, sauté onion and garlic in butter or olive oil for 3 minutes, until soft.
2. Add basmati rice and sauté until rice becomes slightly translucent.
3. Add vegetable stock and turn up heat to high. Bring to boil, cover, and reduce to low simmer.
4. Cook for 20 minutes. Remove lid and toss in chopped cilantro.

Easy Fried Rice

Gluten-Free/Dairy-Free, Vegetarian

Serves 4

2 tablespoons safflower oil

1 teaspoon sesame oil

3 cups cooked brown rice, purchased in frozen section

4 minced scallions

1 teaspoon freshly grated ginger

1 cup fresh or frozen peas

½ cup diced carrots

2 eggs

1½ tablespoons gluten-free soy sauce, preferably San-J brand

1. In a large skillet or wok, heat safflower oil and sesame oil over medium heat. Add cooked brown rice and sauté until hot.
2. Add scallions, ginger, peas and carrots. Cook for 1 minute over medium-high heat, stirring constantly with wooden spoon.
3. Reduce heat and make a hollow in center of rice. Break eggs in center and scramble with fork until semi-cooked, then stir into rice mixture.
4. Stir in soy sauce. Serve hot.

family dinners

Spaghetti with Turkey Meatballs

Gluten-Free/Dairy-Free

Serves 6

I like to hide lots of veggies in my tomato sauce so I always make it from scratch. If you'd like to save time, you can improvise by purchasing a quality gluten-free tomato sauce and adding extra veggies.

½ cup carrots, diced

½ cup zucchini, diced

½ cup broccoli rabe, chopped (trim end and peel tough part off stem of broccoli and you have the "rabe" part)

1 cup yellow onions, finely chopped

3 tablespoons olive oil

2 cloves garlic, minced

1- 35 ounce can or box diced plum tomatoes with juice

2 tablespoons tomato paste

¼ cup dry red wine

1 teaspoon dried oregano

1 bay leaf

1 batch Turkey Meatballs (see Index)

1 pound gluten-free spaghetti, preferably Tikinyada brand

1 tablespoon fresh basil

1 tablespoon fresh Italian flat-leaf parsley

Grated Parmesan cheese (optional)

1. In large Dutch oven, sauté carrots, zucchini, broccoli rabe, and onion in olive oil until soft, about 5 minutes.

2. Add garlic and sauté an additional minute. Add tomatoes, tomato paste, wine, dried oregano and bay leaf.

3. Cover and continue cooking over low heat for 20 minutes. Prepare meatballs (see Index) while sauce is simmering.

4. Add browned meatballs to sauce and cook for 25 minutes, turning meatballs occasionally.

5. Boil pasta according to package instructions. Rinse in colander. Serve spaghetti with sauce and meatballs. Top with fresh basil, parsley and grated Parmesan, if desired.

Turkey Meatballs

Gluten-Free/Dairy-Free

Serves 4 - 6

Rice and baking mix replace bread crumbs in this tasty recipe. Serve meatballs as an appetizer with Pomegranate Chipotle BBQ Sauce or for a main course in Spaghetti with Meatballs recipe.

1 medium yellow onion, finely chopped

2 cloves garlic, finely chopped

1 tablespoon olive oil

1 lb. lean ground turkey

½ cup cooked basmati rice

¼ cup Elizabeth's Gluten-free Baking Mix or The Pure Pantry Organic All Purpose Baking Mix

½ cup water

½ teaspoon sea salt

½ teaspoon pepper

½ teaspoon garlic powder

½ teaspoon oregano

1. Place medium sauté pan on medium heat. Add olive oil, finely chopped onion and garlic. Sauté for 3 minutes. Set aside and let cool.

2. In large bowl, combine the turkey meat, rice, baking mix, water, salt, pepper, garlic powder and oregano. Add onion-garlic mixture and mix well with hands.

3. Form golf ball size meat balls using your hands. In large skillet over medium heat, brown meatballs for 3-4 minutes in 1 tablespoon olive oil, cooking in batches. Turn meatballs on all sides to brown all over.

4. For Spaghetti and Meatballs see recipe (on previous page) for next steps.

Quinoa
with Roasted Eggplant Caponata

Gluten-Free/Dairy-Free

Serves 8

Caponata is a traditional Sicilian dish made with eggplant. This roasted caponata recipe is wonderful with quinoa or by itself served with gluten-free crackers or bread.

1/3 cup extra virgin olive oil

2 tablespoons lemon juice

1 tablespoon agave nectar, preferably Nature's Agave, Amber variety

1½ teaspoons sea salt

½ teaspoon freshly ground black pepper

1 small eggplant, diced

2 stalks celery, diced

2 plum tomatoes, diced

1 red bell pepper, diced

1 yellow bell pepper, diced

2 zucchini, diced

1 yellow onion, diced

2 garlic cloves, minced

2 cups quinoa

4 cups chicken stock or water

1 teaspoon oregano, finely chopped

1 teaspoon basil, finely chopped

½ cup Italian black olives, pits removed, sliced (optional)

2 tablespoons capers, rinsed

Garnish

¼ cup pine nuts, toasted

¾ pound feta, 1/2-inch diced, not crumbled, (optional)

15 fresh basil leaves, cut into julienne

1. Preheat the oven to 425°F. In a glass measuring cup, whisk together olive oil, lemon juice, agave nectar, salt and pepper. Toss vegetables and garlic with olive oil mixture on large baking sheet with rim. Roast for 40 minutes, until soft, turning once with a spatula.

2. While the vegetables are roasting, place 1 cup quinoa and 2 cups chicken stock or water in a 1½ quart saucepan and bring to boil. Reduce to simmer, cover and cook until all liquid is absorbed, about 10 minutes.

3. Place the roasted vegetables in a medium bowl, scraping all the liquid and seasonings from the roasting pan into the bowl. Toss in fresh herbs, olives, capers and cooked quinoa. Garnish with pine nuts, feta and basil. Serve warm or at room temperature.

Shortcut: For a quicker version of this recipe, use purchased Eggplant Caponata. Trader Joe's sells a 19 ounce jar – you will need two jars to replace the homemade version above.

French Green Beans
with Sundried Tomatoes and Pine Nuts

Gluten-Free/Dairy-Free

Serves 6

2½ pounds fresh French green beans (haricot vert)

1 tablespoon white wine vinegar or champagne vinegar

10 sundried tomatoes in oil, sliced (reserve 1 tablespoon of the sundried tomato oil)

2 tablespoons extra virgin olive oil

2 garlic cloves, minced

½ cup chopped fresh basil plus 2 tablespoons for garnish

½ teaspoon sea salt

½ teaspoon fresh ground pepper

½ cup pine nuts, toasted

1. Steam green beans until they are just tender but still crisp.

2. Place green beans in bowl and toss with sundried tomatoes, vinegar, sundried tomato oil (reserved from jar), olive oil, garlic, chopped basil, salt and pepper. Place on platter and top with toasted pine nuts and garnish with chopped basil.

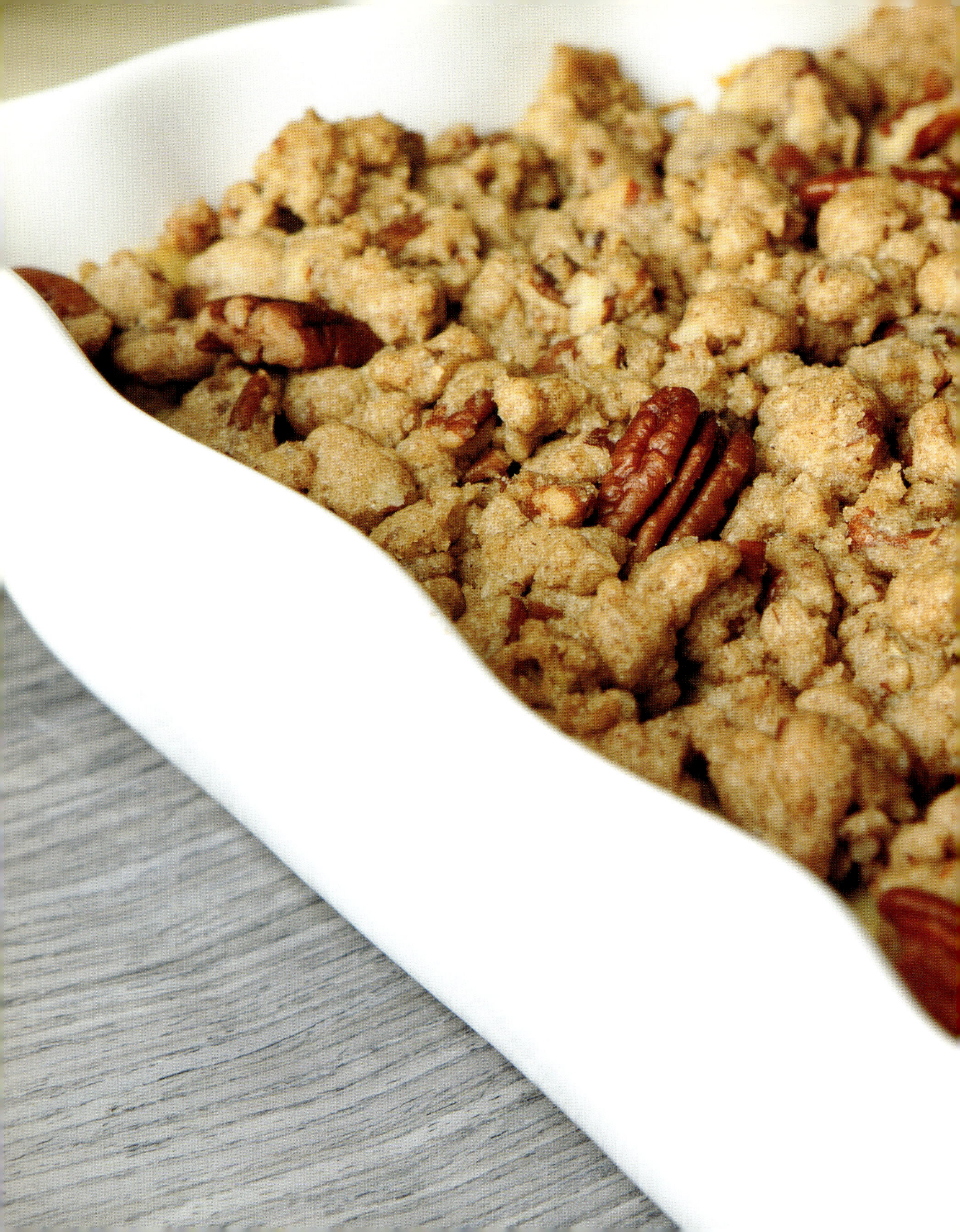

Sweet Potato Gratin
with Pecan-Cinnamon Topping

Gluten-Free/Dairy-Free with Egg-Free Option

Serves 6

Sweet Potato Gratin

3 pounds sweet potatoes

2 large eggs*

2 tablespoons coconut oil or margarine, melted

2 tablespoons agave nectar, preferably Nature's Agave, Amber variety

1½ teaspoons ground cinnamon

½ teaspoon ground nutmeg (preferably freshly ground)

Topping

½ cup Elizabeth's Gluten-Free Flour Blend (see Index) or The Pure Pantry Gluten-Free Organic All Purpose Baking Mix

¼ cup firmly packed golden brown sugar

½ teaspoon ground cinnamon

½ cup coconut oil or margarine

½ cup chopped pecans

1. Preheat oven to 350°F. Place sweet potatoes in baking pan and bake until all are tender, about 1 hour.

2. Butter 8 x 8-inch square glass baking dish. Scrape sweet potato pulp from skins into large bowl. Using electric mixer, mash sweet potatoes. Add eggs, melted coconut oil or margarine, agave nectar, cinnamon and nutmeg. Beat until smooth. Season to taste with salt and pepper. Spoon potatoes into prepared dish.

3. Combine baking mix, brown sugar and cinnamon in medium bowl. Add coconut oil or margarine and cut in until mixture resembles coarse crumbs. Mix in chopped pecans. Sprinkle topping over potatoes. Bake for 30 minutes. Serve warm.

* *To omit eggs, increase coconut oil or margarine to ½ cup and add ¼ cup more baking mix to potato mixture.*

Vegetable Sauté
in Lemon-Thyme-Basil Sauce

Gluten-Free/Dairy-Free/Vegetarian

Serves 4

Lemon-Thyme-Basil Sauce

1 lemon, juiced

2 tablespoons olive oil

1 tablespoon lemon zest

2 cloves garlic, minced

2 tablespoons basil, finely chopped

2 tablespoons Italian flat-leaf parsley, finely chopped

1 teaspoon sea salt

1 teaspoon Dijon mustard

1 tablespoon Vegenaise, Follow Your Heart brand

4 cups vegetables, chopped

1. Combine all sauce ingredients in a small bowl and mix together.

2. Sauté your choice of 4 cups of vegetables with sauce until vegetables are tender. Here are some great combinations:

   Zucchini and Yellow Squash

   Swiss Chard and Shiitake Mushrooms

   Tomato, Leek and Kale

   Cauliflower and Broccoli

Yukon Gold Potato-Goat Cheese Gratin

Gluten-Free/Dairy-Free Option

Serves 8

This hearty gluten-free (and dairy-free optional) version of potatoes au gratin is a sure hit with everyone. If you are dairy sensitive but can tolerate goat's milk, you can substitute goat cheeses and goat's milk in this recipe.

2 tablespoons olive oil

2 tablespoons Elizabeth's Gluten-Free Flour Blend (see Index) or The Pure Pantry Gluten-Free Organic All-Purpose Baking Mix

1 teaspoon chopped fresh thyme (or ½ teaspoon dried)

1 teaspoon chopped fresh rosemary

1 clove garlic, minced

2 cups milk of choice (rice, almond, coconut or regular milk)

1 cup grated Parmesan cheese or Daiya dairy-free cheese substitute

1½ teaspoons sea salt

¼ teaspoon freshly ground pepper

3 pounds Yukon gold potatoes, washed and cut into ⅛-inch slices

1. Preheat oven to 375°F. Grease a 9 x 13-inch baking pan with olive oil. Place olive oil in a small saucepan over medium heat. Sprinkle olive oil with baking mix and cook for two minutes, stirring constantly with a whisk as it thickens to a paste.

2. Stir in thyme, rosemary and garlic. Gradually add milk. Stir with a whisk over medium heat until slightly thick, about 3 minutes.

3. Stir in ½ cup Parmesan or Daiya cheese and continue cooking over low heat until cheese melts. Stir in salt and pepper. Remove from heat.

4. Arrange one quarter of the potatoes in the bottom of the pan. Pour about ¾ cup sauce over potatoes. Repeat layers twice. Sprinkle top with remaining cheese. Cover with foil and bake for 30 minutes. Uncover and bake an additional 30 minutes, or until potatoes are tender and top is golden brown. Remove from oven; let stand 10 minutes before serving.

family dinners

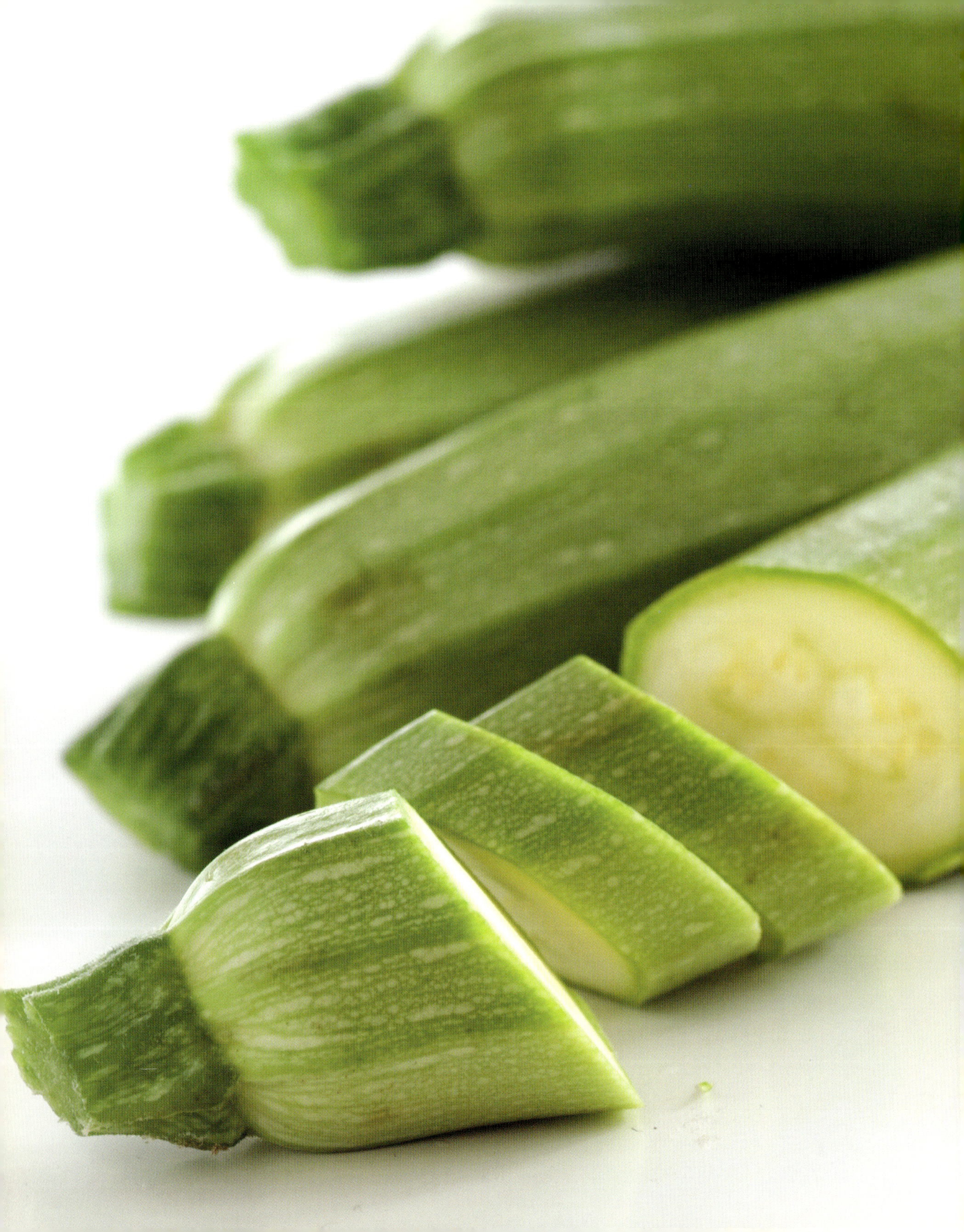

Zucchini Goat Cheese Gratin

Gluten-Free

Serves 8

6 large zucchini, cut into rounds

8 ounces grape tomatoes, halved

3 tablespoons olive oil

2 tablespoons Elizabeth's Gluten-Free Flour Blend (see Index) or The Pure Pantry Gluten-Free Organic All Purpose Baking Mix

1¾ cups low-fat milk or plain rice milk

3 ounces herbed goat cheese

3 ounces grated Parmesan cheese plus 2 ounces for topping

3 tablespoons Spinach-Pesto Sauce (see Index)

½ teaspoon sea salt

½ teaspoon fresh ground pepper

2 tablespoons chopped fresh basil

1. Preheat oven to 350°F. Grease oblong baking dish with olive oil. Layer sliced zucchini rounds in baking dish with halved grape tomatoes.

2. Place olive oil in a small saucepan over medium heat. Sprinkle olive oil with baking mix and cook for two minutes, stirring constantly with a whisk as it thickens to a paste.

3. Gradually add milk. Stir with a whisk over medium heat until slightly thick, about 3 minutes.

4. Add herbed goat cheese and Parmesan cheese. Add pesto sauce, salt and pepper. Pour sauce over zucchini and top with additional Parmesan cheese. Bake for 25 minutes. Top with freshly chopped basil before serving.

Divine Desserts

Pies
Banana Coconut Cream Pie

Chocolate Bourbon Pecan Pie

Pumpkin-Agave Pie

Key Lime Meringue Pie

Whole-Grain Graham Cracker Crust

Pie Crust

Cakes & Cupcakes
Carrot Cake with Heavenly Cream Cheese Frosting

Cranberry Ginger Pound Cake

Chocolate Chocolate-Chip Cupcakes

Flourless Chocolate Decadence

Sticky Toffee Pudding with Warm Caramel Sauce

Other Treats
Blueberry Cheesecake

Pumpkin Cheesecake

Brownie Sundaes

Chocolate Agave Sauce

Chocolate Agave Frosting

Chapter Five

Shown above: Sticky Toffee Pudding, Chocolate Bourbon Pecan Pie, and Chocolate Chip Cookies (made with The Pure Pantry cookie mix)

divine desserts 121

Banana Coconut Cream Pie

Gluten-Free/Dairy-Free Option

Serves 6 - 8

⅓ cup agave nectar, preferably Nature's Agave, Clear variety

1 cup coconut milk (either canned or So-Delicious brand)

6 large egg yolks, beaten (save whites for another use)

2 tablespoons coconut oil

⅛ teaspoon sea salt

3 tablespoons arrowroot

1 teaspoon vanilla

½ cup plus 2 tablespoons shredded coconut

1 banana

1 Whole-Grain Graham Cracker Crust, (see Index)

1 cup whipping cream (optional)

1 tablespoon agave nectar, preferably Nature's Agave, Clear variety (optional)

---

1. Preheat oven to 375°F. In a heavy-bottomed saucepan or double boiler, combine agave nectar, coconut milk, beaten egg yolks, coconut oil and salt. Whisk together over medium heat until bubbles begin to rise. Lower heat and continue whisking for about 1 minute.

2. Remove about ¼ cup of mixture to a small bowl. Whisk in arrowroot until well blended. Pour mixture back into saucepan and continue whisking over low heat until pastry cream begins to thicken, about 1-2 more minutes. Whisk in vanilla. Set aside.

3. Toast coconut in oven for 5 minutes until golden brown. Let cool. Reserve 2 tablespoons for top of pie. Stir remainder into pastry cream.

4. Peel and slice banana into small circles. Arrange banana slices on top of the graham cracker crust in pie plate. Pour cooled pastry cream over banana slices.

5. If using whipping cream, whip using mixer until soft peaks form. Blend in 1 tablespoon agave nectar. Spread whipping cream on top of pastry cream. Sprinkle with extra coconut. If not using whipping cream, sprinkle extra coconut directly on top of pastry cream. Chill in refrigerator for one hour before slicing.

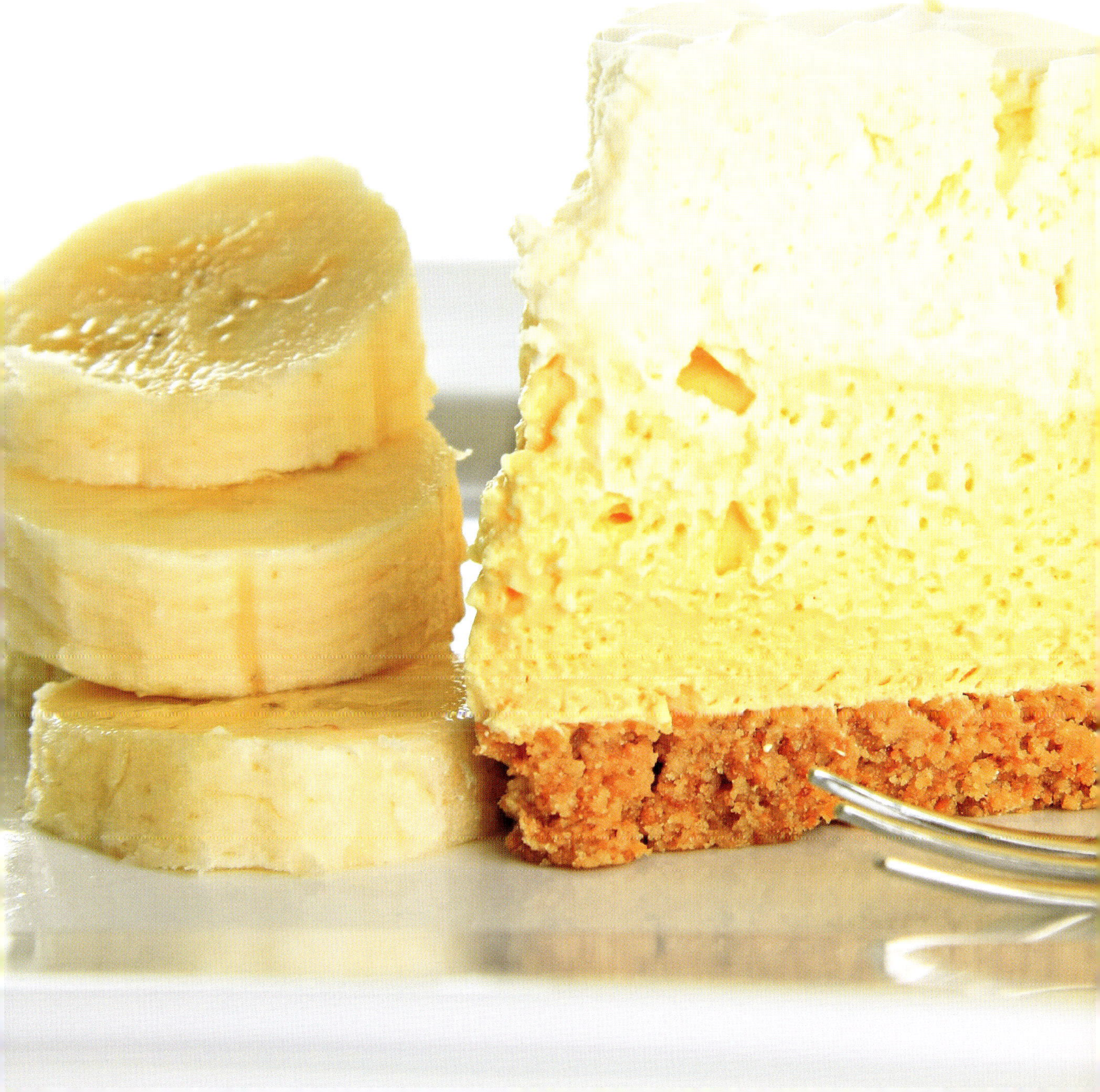

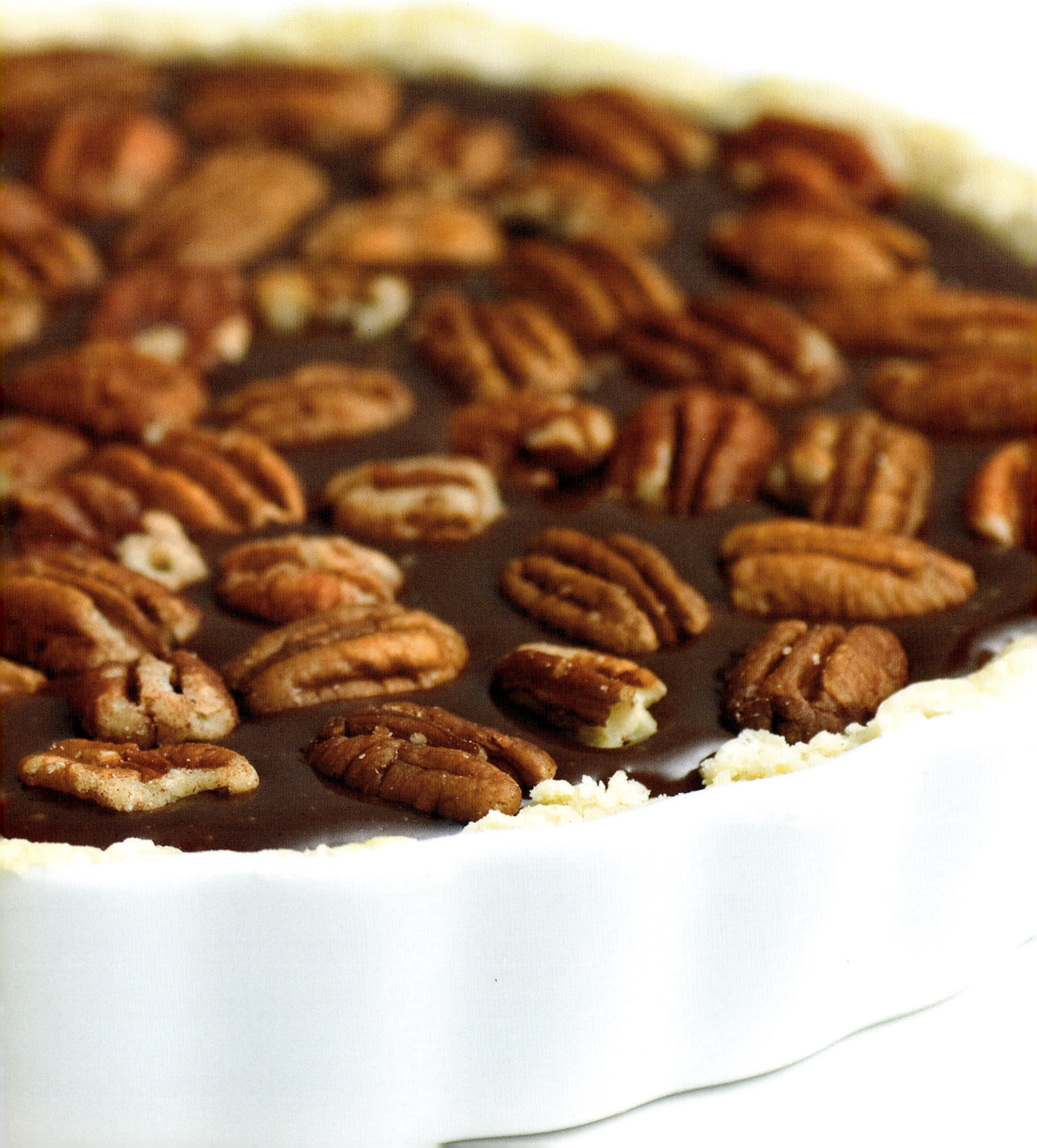

Chocolate Bourbon Pecan Pie

Gluten-Free/Dairy-Free

Serves 10

½ cup coconut oil

1 cup quality bittersweet chocolate

½ cup coconut milk

¾ cup light brown sugar

5 eggs

½ cup agave nectar, preferably Nature's Agave, Amber variety

2 tablespoons blackstrap molasses

1 teaspoon vanilla

¼ teaspoon sea salt

2 tablespoons Elizabeth's Gluten-Free Flour Blend (see Index) or The Pure Pantry Gluten-Free Organic All Purpose Baking Mix

1½ cups chopped pecans

1 gluten-free Pie Crust in 10-inch fluted tart pan, chilled

3 tablespoons bourbon

1 cup whipping cream sweetened with 1 teaspoon agave nectar, preferably Nature's Agave, Clear variety and laced with 1 teaspoon bourbon (optional)

1. Preheat oven to 400°F. Combine coconut oil and chocolate in saucepan over low heat and stir until melted. Add coconut milk and brown sugar and stir to combine. Let cool.

2. In mixer with paddle attachment, beat eggs with agave nectar, molasses, vanilla, salt and baking mix. Add cooled chocolate mixture and blend. Turn off mixer and fold in chopped pecans.

3. Pour mixture into chilled piecrust. Bake for 20 minutes. Reduce temperature to 350°F and bake an additional 20 minutes until set. Remove pie from oven. Let cool for 10 minutes. With a skewer poke small holes in the surface and brush with bourbon. Serve with whipped cream or vanilla ice cream, if desired.

Pumpkin-Agave Pie

Gluten-Free/Dairy-Free

Serves 8

2 cups organic canned pumpkin

1- 14 ounce can light coconut milk

2 eggs

¼ cup agave nectar, preferably Nature's Agave, Amber variety

⅓ cup organic brown sugar

⅓ cup maple sugar

3 tablespoons cornstarch

1½ teaspoons cinnamon

½ teaspoon ground ginger

½ teaspoon nutmeg

¼ teaspoon allspice

¼ teaspoon ground cloves

½ teaspoon sea salt

1 gluten-free Pie Crust (see Index)

1. Preheat oven to 400°F. In large mixing bowl, beat together pumpkin, coconut milk and eggs. Add agave nectar. In a small bowl whisk together both sugars, cornstarch, spices and salt. Add to wet ingredients and blend until well combined.

2. Pour into prepared crust and bake for 15 minutes; then reduce temperature to 350°F and bake for 40 minutes longer or until an inserted tester comes out clean.

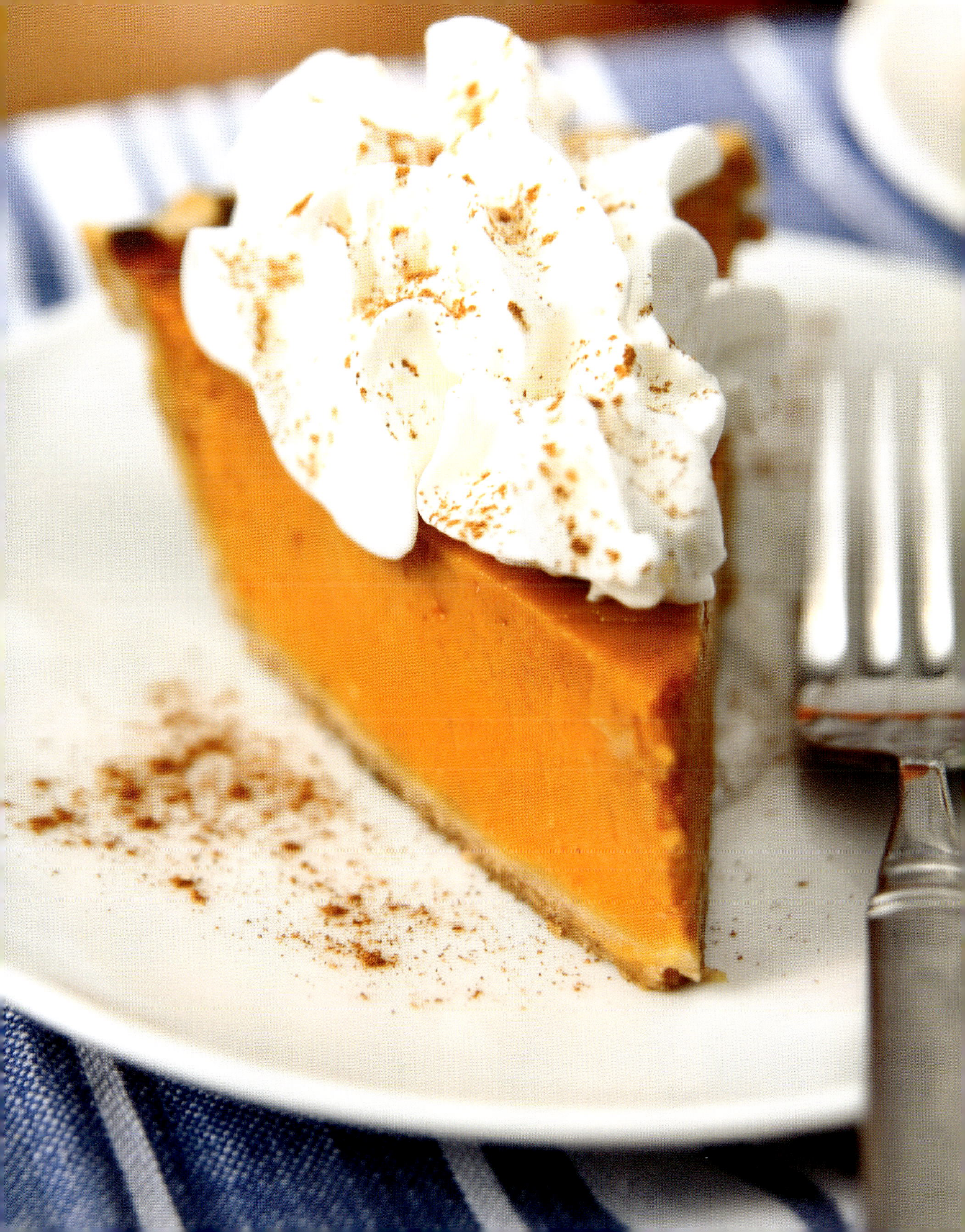

Key Lime Meringue Pie

Gluten-Free/Dairy-Free

Serves 8

A number of people have written to me asking for a gluten-free/dairy-free version of key lime pie. Since key lime pie uses whipped cream as a topping, I created this version that is a cross between a meringue pie and a cream pie.

1 gluten-free Whole-Grain Graham Cracker Crust (see Index)

Pastry Cream

1/3 cup agave nectar, preferably Nature's Agave, Amber variety

1 cup coconut milk (either canned or So-Delicious brand)

6 large egg yolks, beaten (save whites for another use)

2 tablespoons coconut oil

1/8 teaspoon sea salt

1/2 cup fresh lime juice

3 tablespoons arrowroot

1 teaspoon vanilla

1 tablespoon lime zest

Meringue

4 large egg whites

1/4 teaspoon cream of tartar

1/4 teaspoon salt

1/4 cup agave nectar, preferably Nature's Agave, Clear variety

1. Prepare Whole-Grain Graham Cracker Crust and set aside. Preheat oven to 350°F.

2. In a heavy-bottomed saucepan or double boiler, combine agave nectar, coconut milk, beaten egg yolks, coconut oil and salt. Whisk together over medium heat until bubbles begin to rise. Lower heat and continue whisking for about 1 minute.

3. In a small bowl, whisk together lime juice and arrowroot. Add vanilla and stir. Whisk lime mixture into egg mixture over low heat and cook an additional 1-2 minutes until it begins to thicken. Let cool for 10 minutes, then add lime zest. Pour into prepared crust.

4. Prepare meringue by beating egg whites, cream of tartar and salt in bowl with electric mixer until soft peaks form. Slowly add agave nectar and continue beating for 30 seconds. Place cloudlike spoonfuls of meringue along the rim of the pie. Bake for 10-12 minutes until meringue is set and golden brown. Remove from oven and let cool. Chill in refrigerator for 1 hour before serving.

Whole-Grain Graham Cracker Crust

Gluten-Free/Dairy-Free Option/ Vegetarian

Makes 1 crust for 9-inch pie plate

14-15 gluten-free Whole-Grain Graham Crackers (see Index) or store-bought gluten-free graham crackers

½ cup maple sugar or regular sugar

4 tablespoons coconut oil, melted

1. Place graham crackers in food processor fitted with metal blade and pulse until fine crumbs form. Add sugar and melted coconut oil. (Add optional coconut or chopped nuts and coconut oil.) Pulse 2-3 times until combined.

2. Press into pie plate or tart pan. Chill crust for 30 minutes. This step is important or filing will disintegrate the crust.

Other crust options:

Gingersnap Crust:
Use purchased gluten-free gingersnaps (Midel brand works well).
Pulse in food processor approximately 2 cups ginger snaps (1 package Midel) and follow directions above.

Coconut or Pecan Crust:
Add ¼ cup toasted, shredded coconut or ¼ cup toasted finely chopped pecans. Increase coconut oil by 1 teaspoon. Follow direction above.

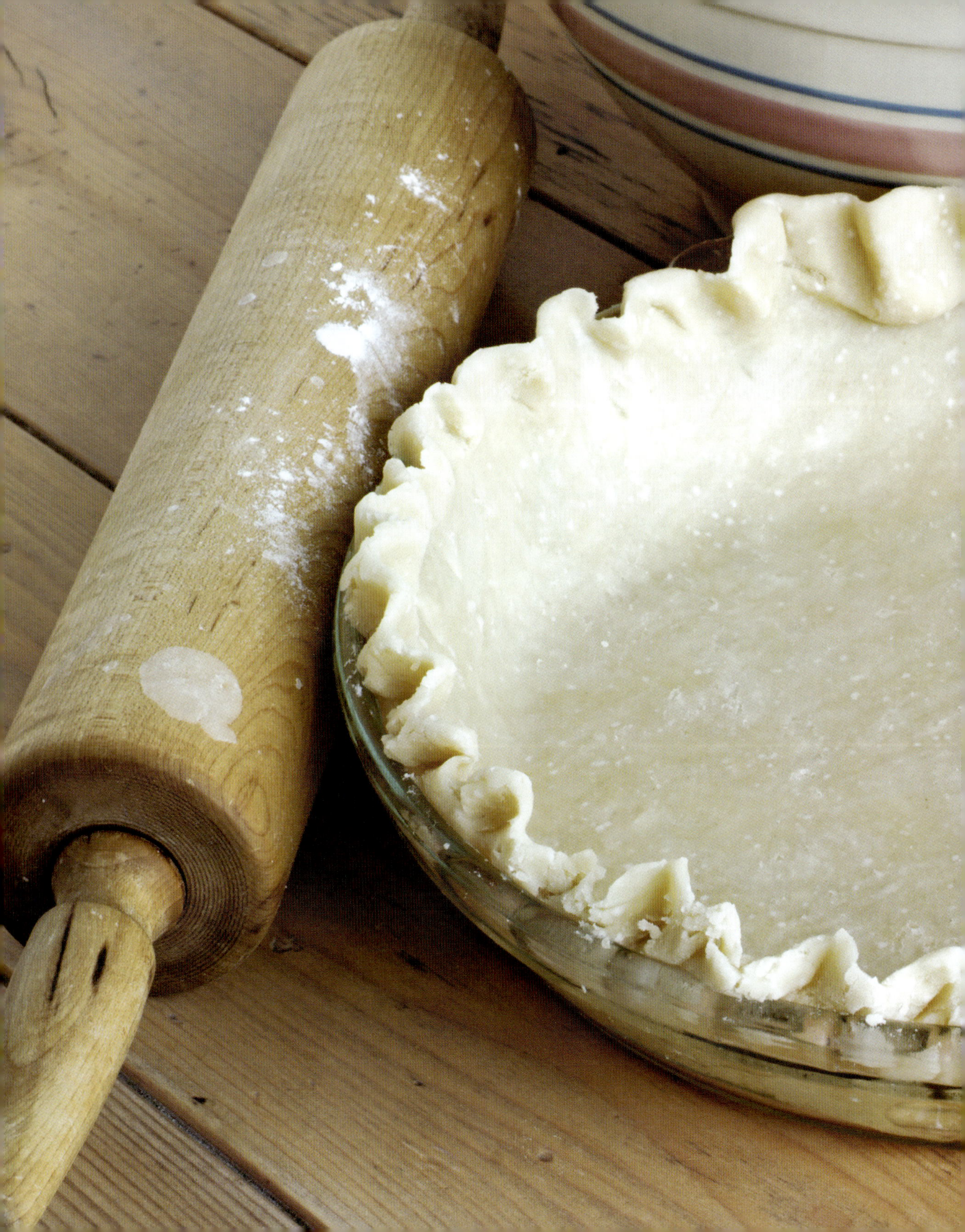

Pie Crust

Gluten-Free/Dairy-Free Option

Makes 1 pie crust for 10-inch pie plate

- ½ **cup (1 stick) chilled butter or coconut oil**
- ½ **cup non-hydrogenated shortening by Spectrum**
- ½ **cup rice flour**
- ½ **cup sweet rice flour**
- 1 **cup potato starch flour**
- ½ **cup cornstarch**
- 1 **teaspoon xanthan gum**
- 2 **tablespoons sugar**
- 1 **egg or equal equivalent egg replacer (see Index)**
- 2 **tablespoons cold water**
- 1 **teaspoon cider vinegar**

1. Cut butter or margarine into small pieces with a knife. Blend butter and shortening with dry ingredients using fingertips.

2. Add egg, cold water and cider vinegar and blend until well combined. If too sticky, add a small amount of rice flour. Roll dough into ball and flatten. Cover with waxed paper and chill for 30 minutes.

3. On floured surface, roll out and fit into pie plate. Trim and crimp edges. If pie recipe requires bake shelled, prick pie crust all over with fork and bake at 400°F for 10 minutes.

Carrot Cake or Cupcakes
with Heavenly Cream Cheese Frosting

Gluten-Free/Dairy-Free Option

Serves 8

- 3 large organic free-range eggs
- ½ cup light vegetable oil
- 1 cup organic light brown sugar, packed
- ⅓ cup plain yogurt, coconut yogurt or applesauce
- 2 teaspoons vanilla
- 1 tablespoon agave nectar, preferably Nature's Agave, Amber variety
- ½ teaspoon ground cinnamon
- 1 teaspoon pumpkin pie spice
- 2 cups Elizabeth's Gluten-Free Flour Blend (see Index), and 1 teaspoon baking powder, or 2 cups of The Pure Pantry Gluten-Free Organic All Purpose Baking Mix
- 1½ cups finely grated carrots
- ½ cup raisins
- ½ cup toasted chopped walnuts or pecans

1. Preheat the oven to 350°F. Grease two 9-inch round cake pans or 12-cup muffin tin with cooking spray.

2. In a mixing bowl, beat the eggs; add the oil and beat; add the brown sugar and beat until smooth. Beat in the yogurt or applesauce, vanilla, agave nectar, cinnamon and spice. Add in the baking mix, and baking powder if using Elizabeth's Blend, and beat until combined. Add the carrots, raisins and nuts; stir until combined.

3. Spread the batter evenly in the cake pan or muffin tin and place pan in center of oven. Bake until the cake is firm and a wooden toothpick inserted into the center emerges clean, about 35 minutes for cake and 20 minutes for cupcakes. When cool, frost with Heavenly Cream Cheese Frosting.

Heavenly Cream Cheese Frosting

Gluten-Free

Makes enough frosting for 12 cupcakes or one two layer 9-inch round cake

- ½ cup unsalted butter, at room temperature
- 8 ounces cream cheese, at room temperature
- 2 cups confectioner's sugar
- ½ cup agave nectar, preferably Nature's Agave, Amber variety
- 1 teaspoon vanilla

1. In large mixing bowl fitted with paddle attachment, cream butter in mixing bowl. Add cream cheese and beat until combined. Slowly sift in sugar and beat until fluffy. Add agave nectar and vanilla and continue beating. If frosting is too thin, add up to 2 tablespoons confectioner's sugar. For a two-layer cake, double the recipe.

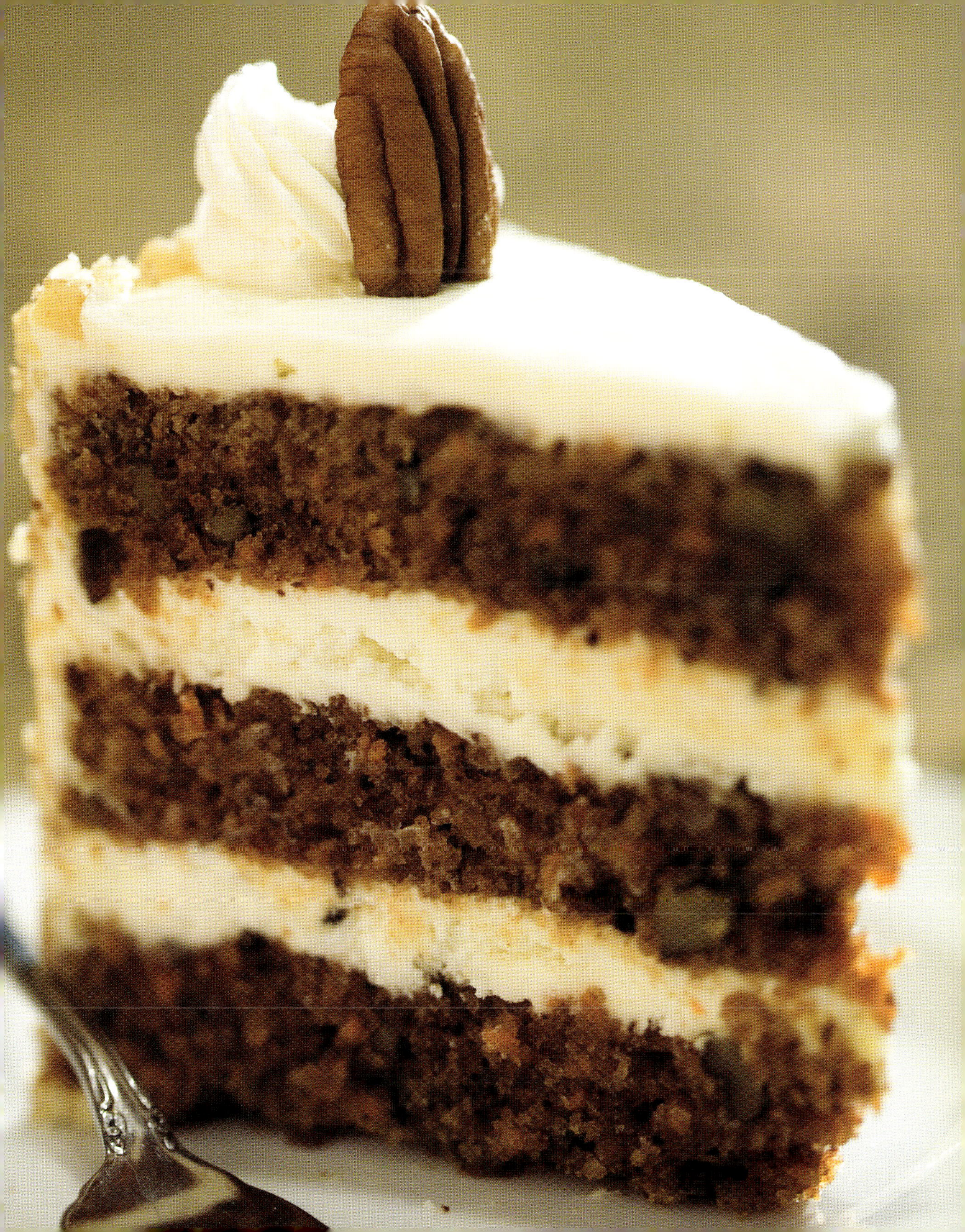

Cranberry Ginger Pound Cake

Gluten-Free/Dairy-Free Option

Serves 10

Cake
1 cup unsalted butter or Earth Balance, Buttery Spread

1 cup brown sugar

½ cup agave nectar, preferably Nature's Agave, Amber variety

4 eggs

2½ cups Elizabeth's Gluten-Free Flour Blend (see Index), and 1 teaspoon baking powder, or 2½ cups of The Pure Pantry Gluten-Free Organic All Purpose Baking Mix

⅓ cup buttermilk

2 tablespoons ground ginger

2½ cups dried cranberries

Glaze
½ cup water

½ cup lemon juice

½ cup sugar

½ cup fresh cranberries

2 teaspoons grated lemon peel

1. Preheat oven to 350°F. Grease one bundt pan or three small loaf pans with cooking spray. In a large mixing bowl fitted with paddle attachment, mix butter, sugar and agave nectar together until fluffy. Add one egg at a time, blending after each addition. Add half the baking mix, and baking powder if using Elizabeth's Blend, and beat until combined, then add buttermilk and blend. Add remaining baking mix and blend until well combined. Add ginger and cranberries.

2. Spoon into bundt pan or three small bread pans. Bake for 1 hour and 20 minutes. Let cool.

3. To make glaze: Bring water and lemon juice to boil in a medium sauce pan. Turn heat to medium, add sugar and stir until dissolved. Add fresh cranberries and continue stirring as cranberries pop. Cook over medium heat for 5-7 minutes or until cranberry mixture resembles cranberry sauce. Cool slightly and pour into a fine sieve over a small bowl. Push solids through sieve. Scrape bottom of sieve to get the glaze that is on the bottom. Add grated lemon peel to glaze.

4. Turn cooled cake out onto plate. Brush top and sides of cake with cranberry glaze.

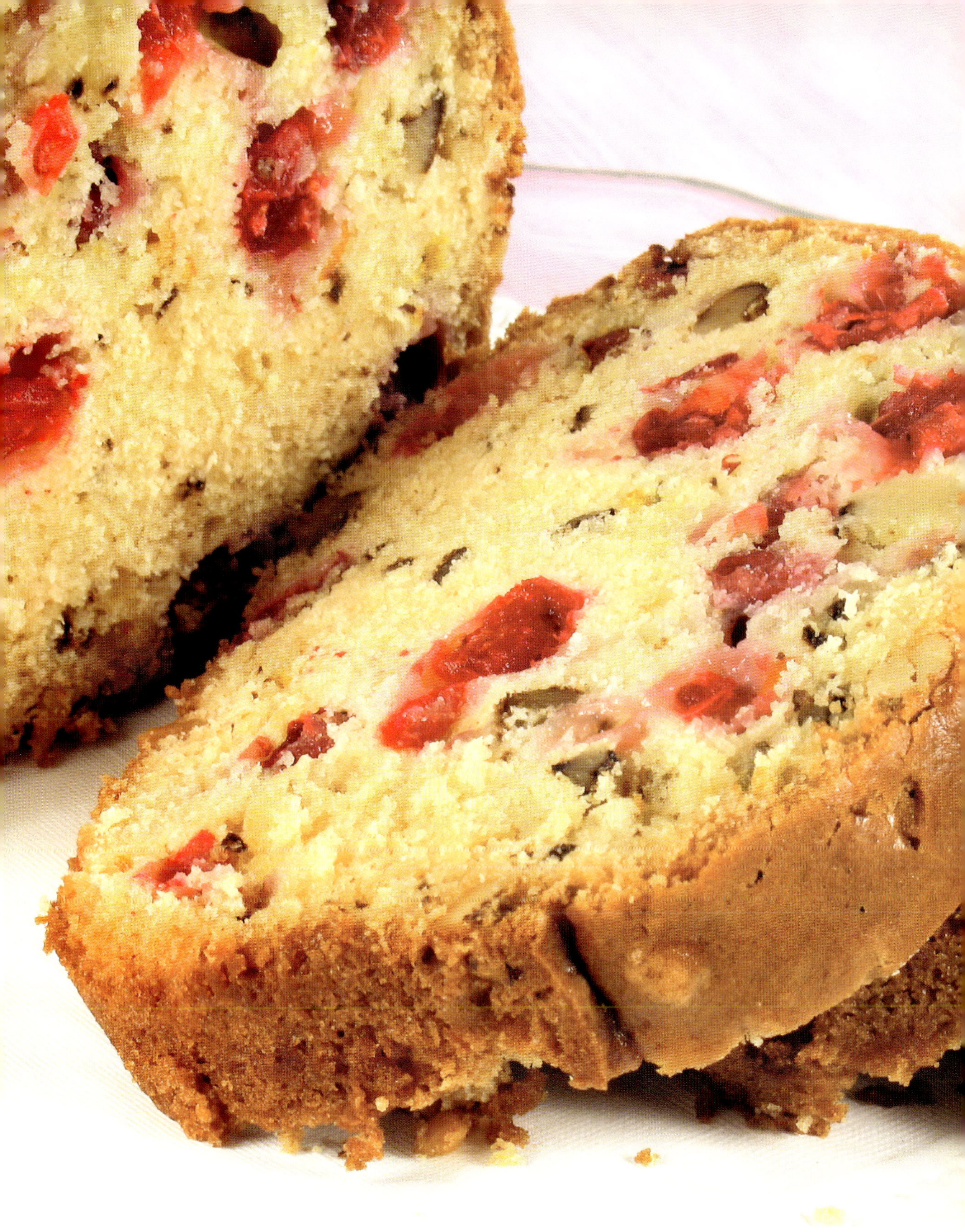

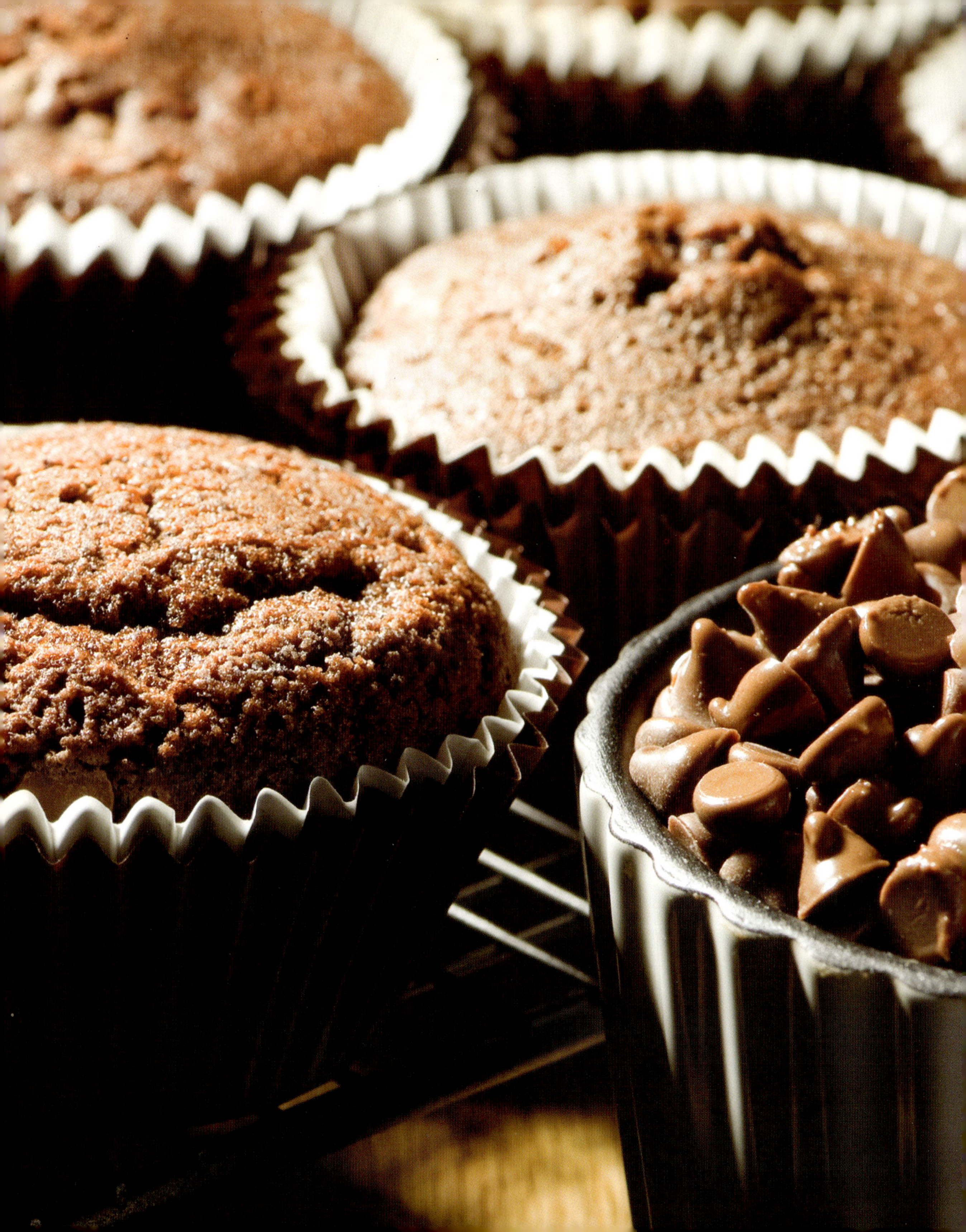

Chocolate Chocolate-Chip Cupcakes

Gluten-Free/Dairy-Free Option

Makes 12 cupcakes

½ **cup good quality bittersweet chocolate, melted**

½ **cup coconut oil or butter substitute such as Earth Balance, Buttery Spread**

½ **cup sugar**

2 large eggs

1 teaspoon vanilla

¼ **cup milk of choice (regular, rice milk or coconut milk)**

1 cup Elizabeth's Gluten-Free Flour Blend (see Index), and 1 teaspoon baking powder, or 1 cup of The Pure Pantry Gluten-Free Organic All Purpose Baking Mix

½ **teaspoon sea salt**

½ **cup semi-sweet dairy-free chocolate chips, such as Enjoy Life brand**

1. Preheat oven to 350°F. Grease muffin tin. Melt chocolate in double boiler over medium heat. Set aside to cool.

2. Using an electric mixer, cream coconut oil or butter with sugar and mix until fluffy. Add eggs and vanilla. Stir in milk.

3. With mixer on low setting, slowly add the baking mix, and baking powder if using Elizabeth's Blend, and beat until combined, baking powder and salt. Add melted chocolate and blend on low speed. Fold in chocolate chips. Scoop into muffin tin and bake for 25 minutes or until wooden toothpick comes out clean.

4. Frost with Chocolate Agave Frosting (see Index)

divine desserts

Flourless Chocolate Decadence

Gluten-Free

Serves 10

12 ounces semisweet chocolate, coarsely chopped

4 ounces unsweetened chocolate, chopped

1½ cup (3 sticks) unsalted butter, diced

½ cup freshly brewed espresso or 1 tablespoon instant espresso powder dissolved in ½ cup water

1 cup golden brown sugar, packed

4 large eggs, beaten

Fresh raspberries

1. Preheat oven to 350 °F. Grease 9-inch diameter springform cake pan with removable bottom or individual ramekins, with cooking spray.

2. Place both chocolates in a large bowl. Bring butter, espresso and sugar to boil in a medium saucepan, stirring to dissolve sugar. Add to chocolate; whisk until chocolate is melted and smooth. Cool slightly. Whisk in eggs.

3. Pour batter into prepared pan or ramekins. Place cake pan or ramekins in a roasting pan. If using cake pan, pour enough hot water into roasting pan to come halfway up the sides. If using ramekins, add just an inch of water. Bake until wooden toothpick inserted into center comes clean, about 1 hour. Remove pan or ramekins, from water. Chill for at least 2 hours, or overnight, in refrigerator.

4. Run a knife around the edge of cake to loosen it. Turn over to cake platter. Lift off cake pan and peel off parchment paper. For ramekins, just serve dessert in the ramekin. Dust with powdered sugar and serve with fresh raspberries.

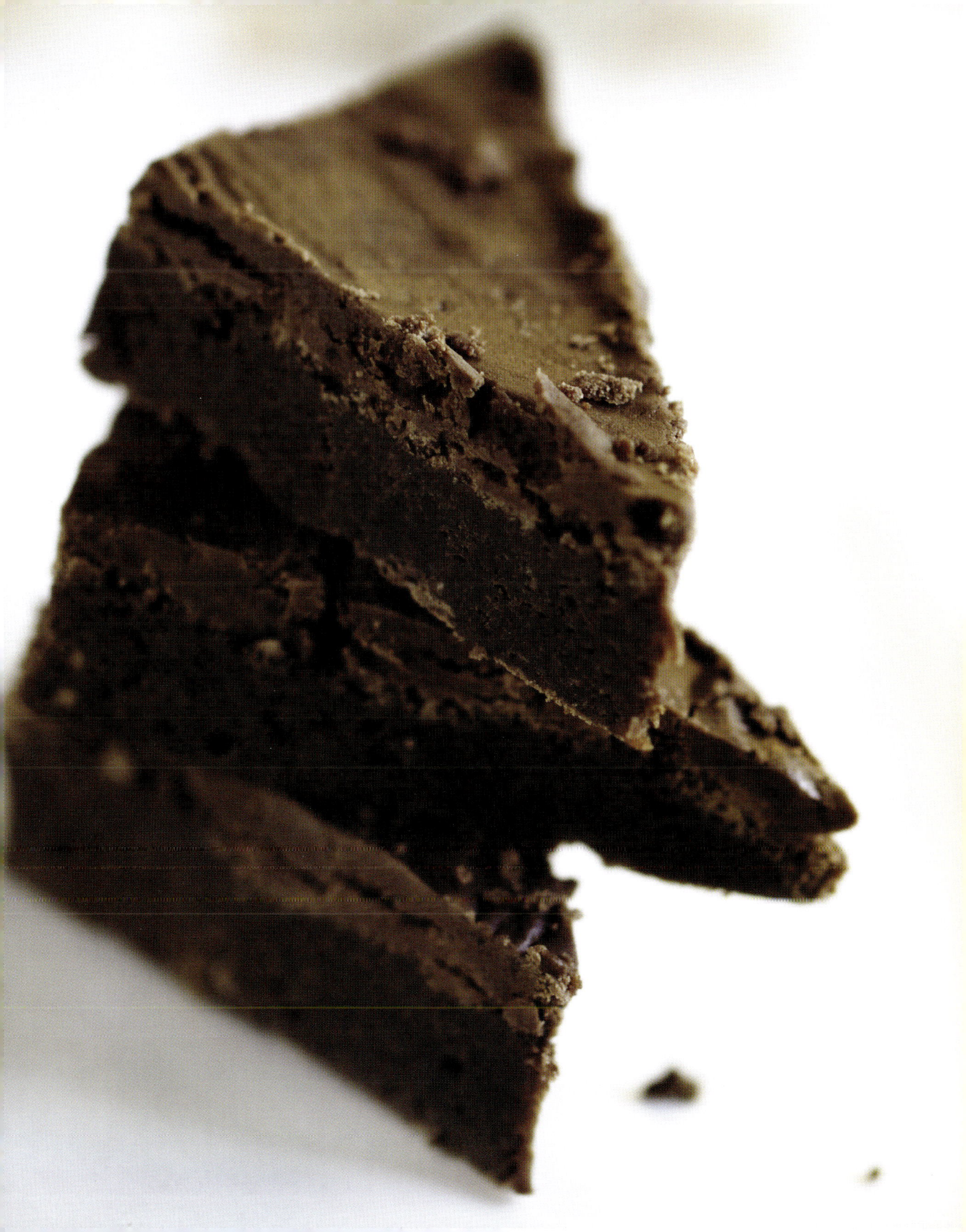

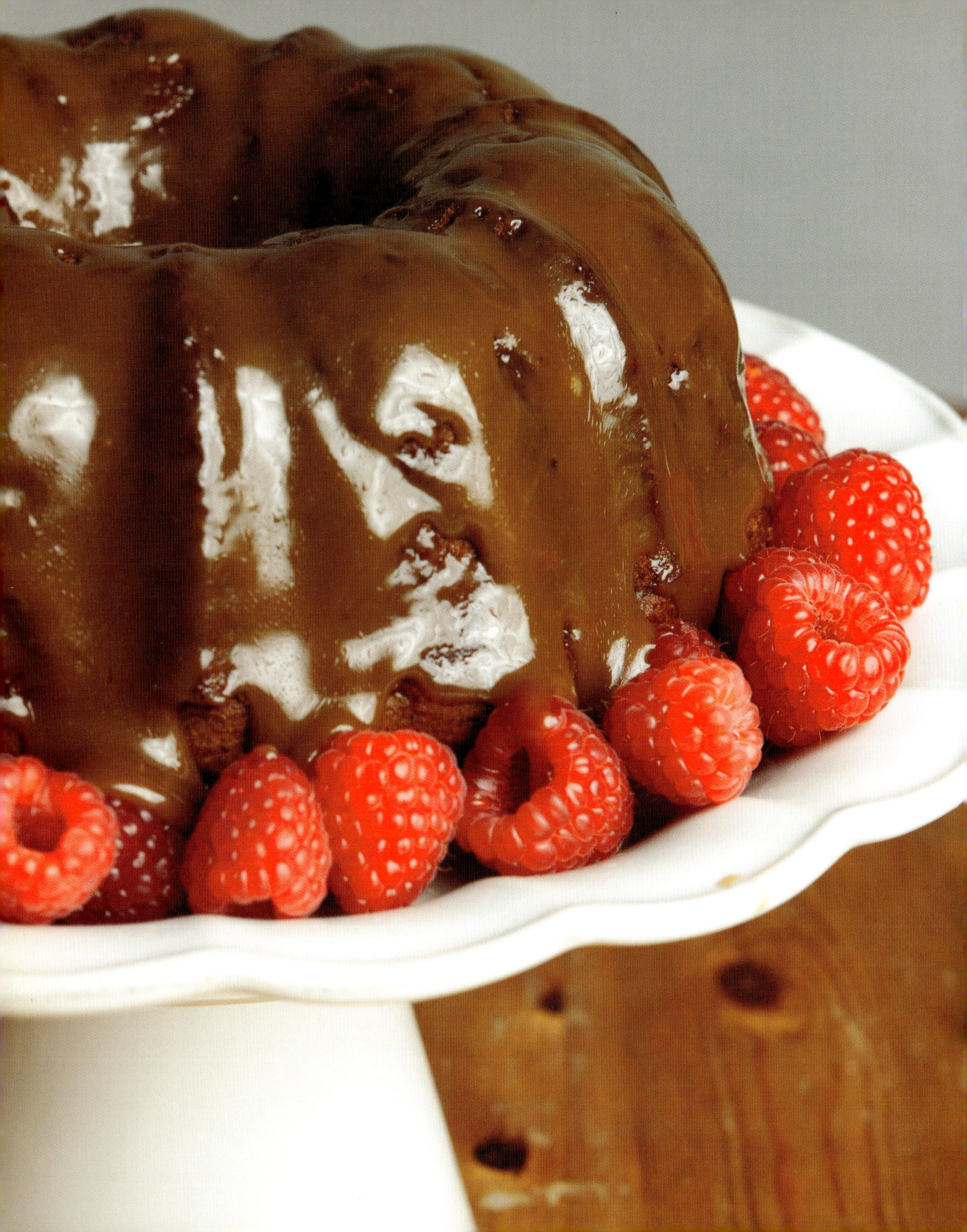

Sticky Toffee Pudding with Warm Caramel Sauce

Gluten-Free/Dairy-Free Option

Serves 8

My mom and stepdad toured England and Scotland for their honeymoon and one afternoon had the most delicious dessert called Sticky Toffee Pudding at a special tea shop. (In England all desserts are called puddings.) They asked me to recreate it when they returned and we've been making it gluten free ever since! It is a special treat we all love to devour.

Cake

- 1½ cups water
- 1¼ cups Medjool dates, pitted and chopped
- 2 teaspoons baking soda
- 1 cup (2 sticks) unsalted butter, room temperature
- ⅔ cup sugar
- 4 large eggs
- 2 teaspoons vanilla extract
- 2½ cups Elizabeth's Gluten-Free Flour Blend (see Index) plus 2 teaspoons baking powder, or 2½ cups plus 2 teaspoons The Pure Pantry Gluten-Free Organic All Purpose Baking Mix
- Fresh raspberries (optional)

Caramel Sauce

- 2 cups whipping cream
- 1 cup dark brown sugar
- ½ cup (1 stick) unsalted butter
- 1 teaspoon vanilla

1. Preheat oven to 350°F. Butter a 12-cup bundt pan. Combine water, dates and baking soda in heavy medium saucepan and bring to boil. Remove from heat and cool.

2. Using electric mixer, beat butter and sugar in large bowl until fluffy. Beat in eggs one at a time. Add vanilla and half the baking mix, and baking powder if using Elizabeth's Blend, and beat until combined. Add the date mixture. Blend in remaining baking mix. Pour into greased bundt pan.

3. Bake cake about 35 minutes or until tester comes out clean.

4. While cake is baking, prepare the caramel sauce. Bring cream, brown sugar and butter to boil in a medium saucepan, stirring constantly. Reduce heat and simmer sauce for about 5 minutes or until it thickens. Add vanilla and set aside.

5. Let cake cool for 1 hour, then run a knife around edges to loosen cake. Turn over onto a cake plate. Re-warm caramel sauce over low heat, stirring constantly. Brush sauce on cake with a pastry brush to evenly spread all over cake. Line rim of cake with fresh raspberries. Serve cake with whipped cream sweetened with agave nectar or with vanilla ice cream.

Blueberry Cheesecake

Gluten-Free/Dairy-Free Option

Serves 8 - 10

3- 8 ounce packages cream cheese or Tofutti brand cream cheese substitute

1/2 cup regular milk or coconut milk

2 eggs

½ cup maple sugar or coconut sugar

½ cup agave nectar, preferably Nature's Agave, Amber variety

1 teaspoon lemon zest

Topping
1 cup sour cream or Sour Supreme by Tofutti

¼ cup maple sugar or coconut sugar

1 tablespoon lemon juice

1 cup fresh blueberries

1 gluten-free Whole-Grain Graham Cracker Crust (see Index) or gluten-free Pie Crust, prebaked for 10 minutes at 350°F (see Index)

1. Preheat oven to 350° F. Using electric mixer with paddle attachment, beat the cream cheese until softened. Add milk and one egg at a time, blending well between additions. Add sugar, agave nectar and lemon zest. Beat until thoroughly blended. Pour the mixture into the prepared crust and bake for 50 minutes.

2. While cheesecake is baking, blend together sour cream, sugar and lemon juice. Remove cheesecake from oven and check for doneness, it should be firm.

3. Spread sour cream mixture over the top of cheesecake. Arrange blueberries on top of sour cream. Bake an additional 10 minutes.

4. Cool cheesecake on wire wrack and then chill in refrigerator for at least 2 hours before slicing.

divine desserts 143

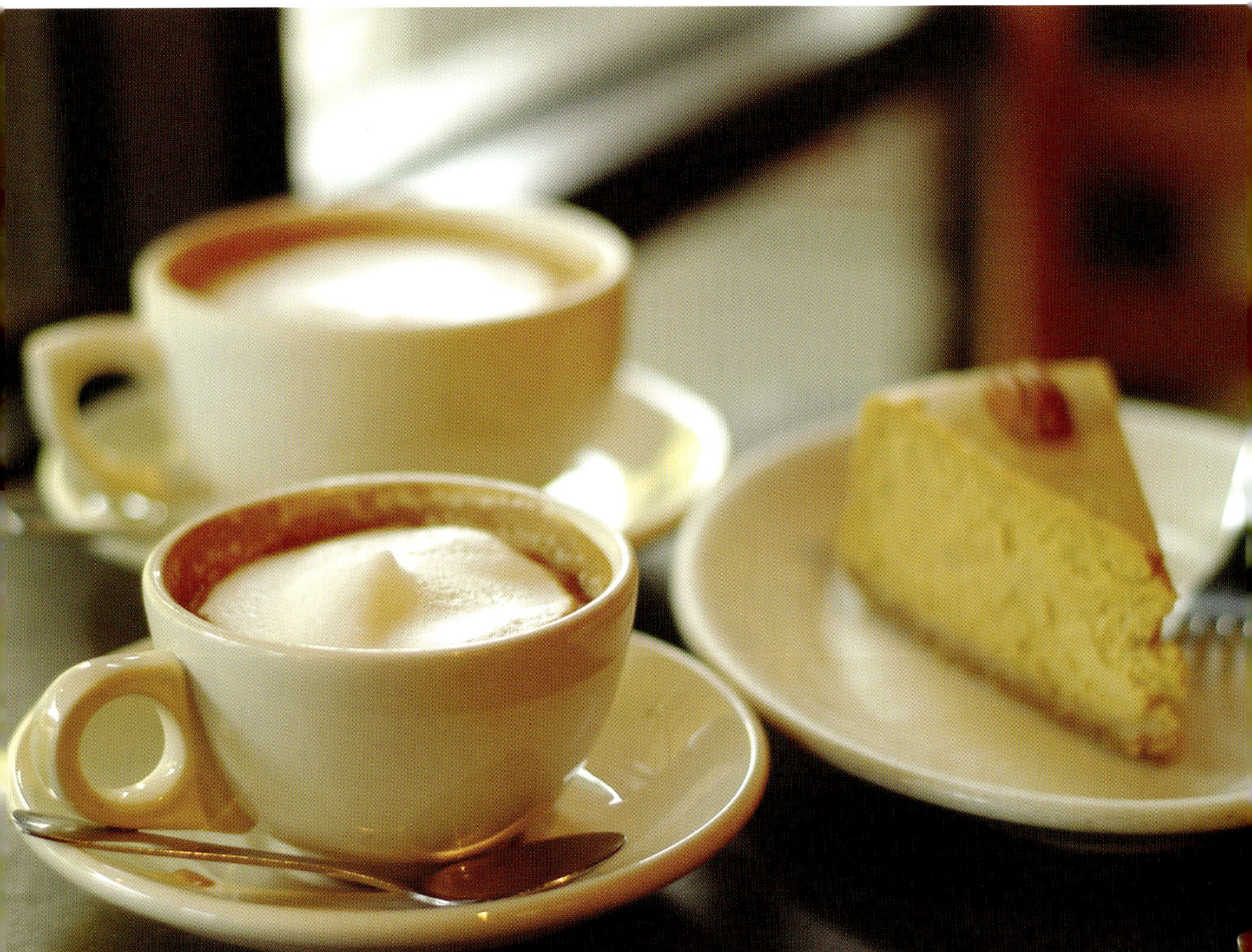

Pumpkin Cheesecake

Gluten-Free/Dairy-Free Option

Serves 8 - 10

1 gluten-free Whole-Grain Graham Cracker Crust or gluten-free Gingersnap Crust (see Index)

2- 8 ounce packages cream cheese or Tofutti brand cream cheese substitute

½ cup regular milk or coconut milk

2 eggs

1 cup canned pumpkin

½ cup maple sugar or coconut sugar

½ cup agave nectar, preferably Nature's Agave, Raw variety

1 teaspoon cinnamon

½ teaspoon nutmeg

½ teaspoon ginger

Topping

1 cup sour cream or Sour Supreme by Tofutti

½ cup brown sugar

1 teaspoon vanilla

1. Preheat oven to 350° F. Prebake crust for 10 minutes.

2. Using electric mixer with paddle attachment, beat the cream cheese until softened. Add milk and eggs one at a time, blending well between additions. Add pumpkin, sugar, agave nectar and spices. Beat until thoroughly blended. Pour the mixture into the prepared crust and bake for 50 minutes.

3. While cheesecake is baking, blend together sour cream, brown sugar and vanilla. Remove cheesecake from oven and check for doneness; it should be firm. Spread sour cream mixture over the top and bake an additional 10 minutes.

4. Cool cheesecake on wire rack and then chill in refrigerator for at least 2 hours before slicing.

Brownie Sundaes

Gluten-Free/Dairy-Free Option

Makes 6 sundaes

1 recipe baked Dark Chocolate Brownies (see Index) cut into 3 x 4-inch brownies

1 cup Chocolate Agave Syrup (see Index)

1 pint gluten-free/dairy-free vanilla coconut ice cream, preferably Coconut Bliss brand

½ cup chopped nuts, optional

1. Place 1 cup Chocolate Agave Sauce in saucepan on low heat, stirring constantly for one minute, to warm.

2. Using six large dessert plates, place a large brownie on each plate. Top with a large scoop of ice cream. Drizzle with warm Chocolate-Agave Sauce and sprinkle with optional nuts. Serve immediately.

divine desserts

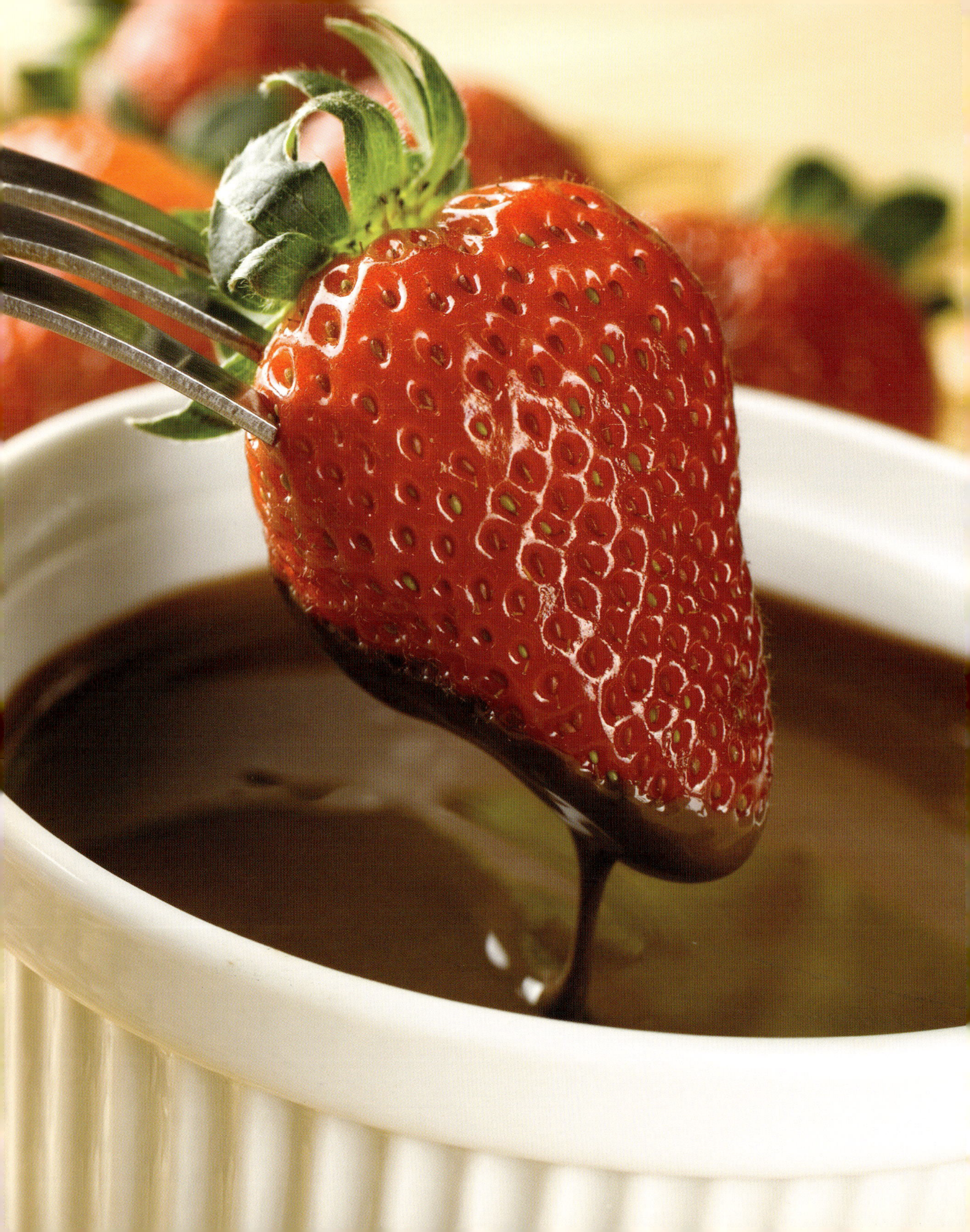

Chocolate-Agave Sauce

Gluten-Free/Dairy-Free

Makes 2¾ cups

This recipe is a fantastic dairy-free dessert sauce that is so versatile. Use it on crêpes, drizzled over cakes, with ice cream or as a base for Chocolate Agave Frosting (below)

2 cups semi-sweet chocolate chips

⅓ cup agave nectar, preferably Nature's Agave, Amber variety

½ cup canned coconut milk (not light)

1 teaspoon vanilla

1. In a double boiler, place chocolate chips over low heat. Stir until melted. Add agave nectar, coconut milk and vanilla and continue stirring until combined.

2. Cool chocolate sauce and place in an airtight glass container. Store in refrigerator. When ready to use, melt by placing glass container in a container of hot water (not on stovetop) for 5 minutes.

Chocolate-Agave Frosting

Gluten-Free/Dairy-Free

Frosts one large double layer cake or 24-28 cupcakes

1 batch Chocolate-Agave Sauce

4 cups sifted confectioner's sugar

1 teaspoon vanilla

1-2 tablespoons coconut milk or rice milk

1. Prepare the Chocolate-Agave Sauce and let cool.

2. Place sauce in mixing bowl. Add sifted confectioner's sugar, one cup at a time, blending after each addition. Add vanilla. Check consistency. If too thin, add a few more tablespoons of sugar. If too thick, add a few tablespoons of coconut milk or rice milk. Store in airtight container in refrigerator – but watch out for little sticky fingers – you may need to disguise the container!

divine desserts

The Allergy-free Cookie Jar

Chapter Five

Cookies & Bars

Allergy-Free Gingerbread Pals with Vanilla Icing

Chocolate Swirl Meringues

Chocolate-Dipped Molasses Ginger Cookies

Hazelnut Chocolate Chip Biscotti

White Chocolate Mac-Toffee Cookies

Whole-grain Graham Crackers

Coconut Lemon Curd Squares

Dark Chocolate Brownies

Almond Joy Bars

Mexican Wedding Cakes

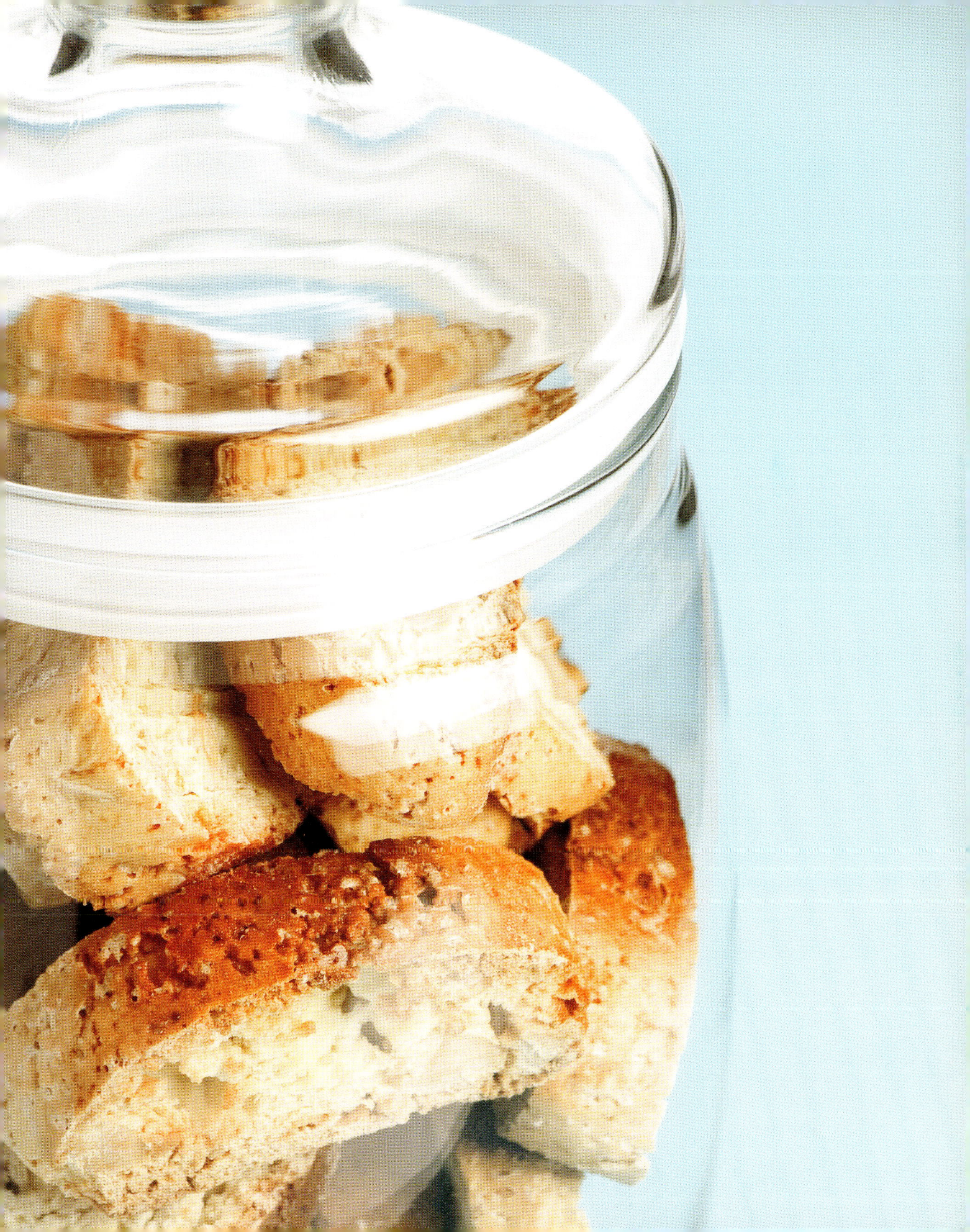

Allergy-Free Gingerbread Pals

Gluten-Free/Dairy-Free Option

Makes 14-16 large cut-out cookies

Have fun with your children decorating these allergy-free cookies free of gluten, dairy/casein and eggs! The blackstrap molasses provides 14 percent of the daily requirement for iron and gives these cookies a wonderful flavor! The vanilla icing is gluten free, dairy free and vegan. Happy baking!

- 2 cups Elizabeth's Gluten-Free Flour Blend (see Index) plus 1 teaspoon baking powder, or 2 cups plus 1 teaspoon The Pure Pantry Gluten-Free Organic All Purpose Baking Mix
- 1 teaspoon cinnamon
- ½ teaspoon ground ginger
- ¼ teaspoon ground cloves
- ¾ cup dark brown sugar, firmly packed
- 2 tablespoons blackstrap molasses
- ½ cup coconut oil (solidified and cold, not at melting point), Earth Balance Buttery Sticks or Spectrum shortening
- 1½ tablespoons coconut milk or rice milk
- Gluten-free chocolate chips or raisins

1. Preheat oven to 350°F. In a medium mixing bowl, combine baking mix, cinnamon, ginger, and cloves. Stir to mix.

2. In a large mixing bowl fitted with paddle attachment, combine brown sugar, molasses and coconut oil (or Earth Balance Buttery Sticks or Spectrum non-hydrogenated shortening) and beat until well blended. Add coconut or rice milk and beat until blended. With mixer on low speed, add half the baking mix, and baking powder if using Elizabeth's Blend, and beat until combined. Add remaining baking mix and, using your hands, knead dough until it is smooth and blended.

3. Divide dough in half and shape into two balls. Refrigerate dough for 30 minutes. In the meantime, make Vanilla Icing for Decorating Cookies.

4. Lightly flour a work surface and rolling pin with rice flour. Roll out chilled ball of dough into a rectangle about ¼-inch thick. Press gingerbread pal cookie cutter into dough to cut out shapes.

5. Transfer cookies to greased baking sheets. Repeat with second ball of dough. Gather scraps of dough into a ball, roll out and continue cutting out cookies until all dough is used. Bake cookies until golden brown, about 8-10 minutes. Cool on racks.

6. Frost cooled cookies with thin amount of icing. Place gluten-free chocolate chips or raisins for eyes, nose, mouth and buttons. Icing can be placed in a pastry bag to pipe designs on cookies.

Vanilla Icing for Decorating Cookies

Gluten Free/Dairy Free/Vegan

2 tablespoons cold water

1 tablespoon vanilla

1 tablespoon agave nectar, preferably Nature's Agave, Clear variety

1 tablespoon non-hydrogenated margarine, such as Earth Balance

1-16 ounce box confectioner's sugar

1. In a large mixing bowl fitted with paddle attachment, blend cold water, vanilla, agave nectar and margarine.

2. Sift into bowl one box confectioner's sugar. Blend on low speed until combined. If too dry, add 1 teaspoon cold water. If too wet, add 1 tablespoon more sugar. Beat until blended.

the cookie jar

Chocolate Swirl Meringues

Gluten-Free/Dairy-Free

Makes 24 meringues

Simple and elegant, these can be prepared and stored for up to a week in an airtight container.

4 ounces bittersweet chocolate, chopped

5 egg whites

¼ teaspoon cream of tartar

1 cup sugar

1. Preheat oven to 275°F. Line two baking sheets with parchment paper.

2. Melt chocolate in double boiler over medium heat. Set aside to let cool.

3. In a large mixing bowl fitted with whisk attachment, beat egg whites and cream of tartar until stiff peaks form. Add sugar and continue beating for one minute.

4. Drizzle melted chocolate over egg white mixture and fold in with a spatula to make chocolate swirls in the meringue.

5. Drop by tablespoons, 2 inches apart, onto lined baking sheets. Bake about 40 minutes. Let cookies cool completely before removing them from parchment.

Options:

Chocolate Peppermint Meringues: Add ¼ cup finely crushed peppermint candies before adding the chocolate.

Meringue Nests: This meringue mixture can be carefully placed in a pastry bag fitted with wide tip and piped into circles. Fill in the bottom of the circle with the mixture to create a small "nest." Bake for 50 minutes at same temperature. Cool completely before removing from parchment. Fill with sorbet and fresh fruit.

Chocolate-Dipped Molasses Ginger Cookies

Gluten-Free/Dairy-Free

Makes 12-14 cookies

These cookies call for both fresh and powdered ginger, so they have a very distinct ginger flavor. If you don't have fresh ginger, you can double the powdered ginger.

½ cup coconut oil or palm-fruit shortening, such as Spectrum brand

½ cup dark brown sugar

¼ cup white sugar

1 tablespoon vanilla

1 egg or egg replacer (see Index)

3 tablespoons molasses

1½ cups Elizabeth's Gluten-Free Flour Blend (see Index) plus 1 teaspoon baking powder, or 1½ cups plus 1 teaspoon The Pure Pantry Gluten-Free Organic All Purpose Baking Mix, or 1½ cups The Pure Pantry Gluten-Free Organic Buckwheat-flax Pancake and Baking Mix

2 teaspoons powdered ginger

2 teaspoons freshly grated ginger

½ cup good quality bittersweet chocolate

1. Preheat oven to 350°F. Cream shortening with both sugars. Add vanilla and mix until well blended. Add egg or egg replacer. Add molasses and blend well. Fold in baking mix, and baking powder if using Elizabeth's Blend, and beat until combined. Add powdered ginger.

2. Peel away the outer peel of a 1-inch piece of ginger and grate the flesh part with a ginger grater or the fine holes of a regular grater. Add fresh ginger to cookie mix and blend well.

3. Place tablespoon-size balls of dough on a greased baking sheet and bake for 10 minutes or until golden brown.

4. Melt chocolate in a double boiler over medium heat. Place waxed paper on baking sheet. Dip one side of cooled cookies into chocolate and let excess chocolate drip off. Lay on waxed paper to dry.

Hazelnut Chocolate Chip Biscotti

Gluten-Free/Dairy-Free

Makes 12-14 biscotti

These biscotti are heavenly with a nice cup of java, or hot chocolate for the kids.

- 2 tablespoons butter or coconut oil
- ½ cup brown sugar
- ⅓ cup white sugar
- 1 egg plus 2 egg whites, or equivalent egg replacer (see Index)
- 1 cup Elizabeth's Gluten-Free Flour Blend (see Index), plus 1 teaspoon baking powder or 1 cup The Pure Pantry Gluten-Free Organic All Purpose Baking Mix
- 1 cup The Pure Pantry Gluten-Free Organic Buckwheat-flax Pancake and Baking Mix
- 1 teaspoon vanilla
- ¾ cup chopped hazelnuts, toasted
- ¾ cup gluten-free, dairy-free chocolate chips, preferably Enjoy Life brand

1. Preheat oven to 350°F. Grease baking sheet, with cooking spray.

2. Using electric mixer with paddle attachment, cream butter with both sugars. Beat in egg whites and egg (or egg replacer). Add baking mix, and baking powder if using Elizabeth's Blend, and beat until combined. Add Buckwheat Flax baking mix and vanilla and continue blending on low until combined. Stir in chopped hazelnuts and chocolate chips.

3. Lightly dust a large wooden cutting board with rice flour. Dust hands with rice flour. Place biscotti dough on board and with your hands roll into a log, 3 inches wide and 15 inches long. Transfer log to baking sheet. Bake until golden brown, about 30 minutes.

4. Remove from oven and cool on baking sheet for 30 minutes. Gently place log on wooden cutting board. Using a serrated knife cut the log on the diagonal into ½-inch slices. Arrange biscotti cut-side down back on baking sheet. Bake 20 minutes. Let cool completely. Store in an airtight container.

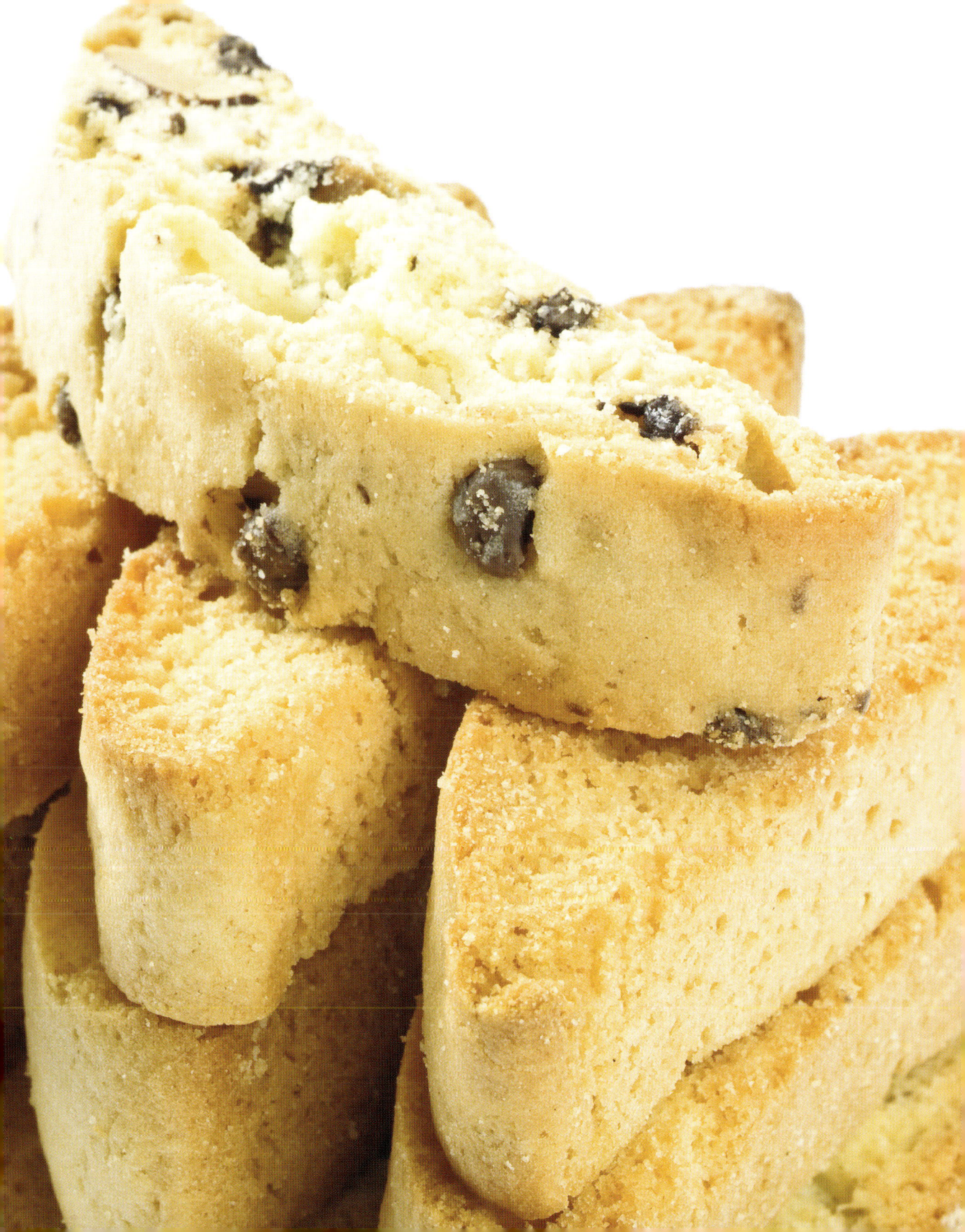

White Chocolate Mac-Toffee Cookies

Gluten-Free/Dairy-Free Option

Makes 3 dozen cookies

These are my husband's favorite cookies. They can be made either as drop cookies or as bars. Either way, everyone loves them!

1 cup (two sticks) butter or coconut oil

¾ cup light brown sugar, firmly packed

½ cup granulated sugar

2 teaspoons vanilla

2 eggs

2 ½ cups Elizabeth's Gluten-Free Flour Blend (see Index) plus 1 teaspoon baking soda, or 2½ cups plus 1 teaspoon The Pure Pantry Gluten-Free Organic All Purpose Baking Mix

½ teaspoon salt

¾ cup toffee bits

¾ cup white chocolate chips

1 cup macadamia nuts, chopped

1. Preheat oven to 350°F. Line baking sheet with parchment paper.

2. Using an electric mixer, cream butter or coconut oil. Add both sugars and mix on medium speed until well blended. Add vanilla. Beat in eggs one at a time.

3. Turn mixer on low setting and gradually add baking mix, and baking soda if using Elizabeth's Blend, and beat until combined. Add salt.

4. Fold in toffee bits, white chocolate chips and macadamia nuts.

5. Drop dough by tablespoon portions onto baking sheet at least 3 inches apart. Flatten slightly with palm of hand. Bake for 10 minutes or until golden brown. For bars, spread batter into a greased 8 x 8-inch baking pan and bake for 12-14 minutes. Cool before removing from baking sheet or pan.

Whole-Grain Graham Crackers

Gluten-Free/Casein-Free

Makes 14-18 graham crackers

"We can have s'mores again!" my kids exclaimed when they saw that I had made homemade gluten-free graham crackers. Not only do we make s'mores, we also create piecrusts, nut butter and jam "grahamwiches" and Almond-Joy Bars (see Index). Make a large batch and freeze them for convenience.

1¼ **cup The Pure Pantry Gluten-Free Organic All Purpose Baking Mix**

¾ **cup The Pure Pantry Gluten-Free Organic Buckwheat Flax Baking Mix**

½ **cup maple sugar or light brown sugar**

1¾ **teaspoon cinnamon**

½ **cup plus 1 tablespoon coconut oil or non-hydrogenated shortening, such as Spectrum brand**

3 **tablespoons cold water**

3 **tablespoons agave nectar, preferably Nature's Agave, Amber variety**

1 **teaspoon vanilla**

1. Preheat oven to 350°F. Line a cookie sheet with parchment paper.

2. In a large bowl, mix together baking mixes, sugar and cinnamon. Using your fingertips, work the coconut or shortening into the dry ingredients. Stir in cold water, agave nectar and vanilla. If the dough is too dry, add a little more cold water.

3. Gather dough into a ball and flatten into a disk. Wrap with plastic wrap and refrigerate for about 1 hour.

4. Roll half the dough between two pieces of waxed paper lightly floured with baking mix. Roll out to ⅛-inch thickness. Remove top layer of waxed paper. Trim edges to make a large square, removing scraps. Place baking sheet on top of dough and flip over onto baking sheet. Remove waxed paper. Cut into small 2 x 3-inch rectangles and prick all over with a fork. Bake for 30 minutes or until golden brown. Remove from baking sheet and let cool.

the cookie jar

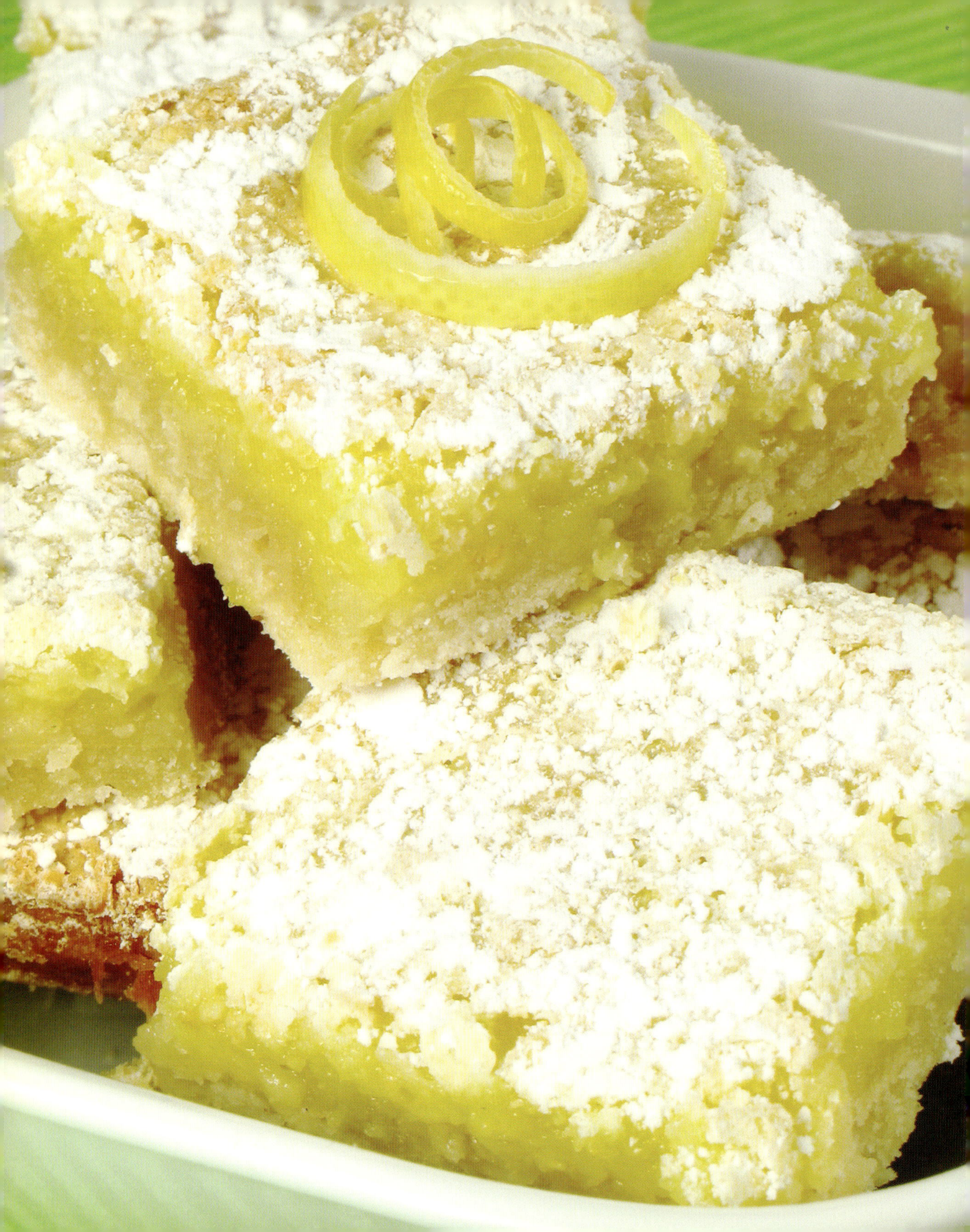

Coconut Lemon Curd Squares

Gluten-Free/Dairy-Free

Makes 16 squares

Crust

¾ cup Elizabeth's Gluten-Free Flour Blend (see Index), or ¾ cup The Pure Pantry Gluten-Free Organic All Purpose Baking Mix

½ cup butter or Earth Balance Buttery Spread

⅓ cup unsweetened flaked coconut, lightly toasted and cooled

½ cup maple sugar or regular sugar

Lemon Curd Filling

4 eggs

1¼ cups sugar

¼ cup Elizabeth's Gluten-Free Flour Blend (see Index), or ¼ cup The Pure Pantry Gluten-Free Organic All Purpose Baking Mix

¾ cup lemon juice (about 4 lemons)

3 tablespoons freshly grated lemon zest

Topping

⅓ cup unsweetened flaked coconut, toasted and cooled

1. To make crust: Preheat oven to 325°F and butter 9 x 12-inch baking pan.

2. In a bowl blend together baking mix, butter, coconut, and sugar with fingertips until butter has no lumps and mixture resembles coarse meal. Pat mixture into prepared pan and pierce with fork all over. Bake in middle of oven for 20 minutes or until golden brown. Remove from oven and reduce temperature to 300°F.

3. To make filling: In a medium bowl, whisk together eggs and sugar until combined. Whisk in baking mix, lemon juice and lemon zest until well combined.

4. Pour mixture over crust and bake in middle of oven 15 minutes. Top custard with toasted coconut and bake 5 minutes or until just set. Cool in pan, then chill 1 hour before cutting into squares.

the cookie jar

Dark Chocolate Brownies
Gluten-Free

Makes 12 brownies

1½ cups semi-sweet gluten-free, dairy-free chocolate chips, preferably Enjoy Life brand

2 ounces dark chocolate, chopped

½ cup coconut oil or non-hydrogenated shortening, such as Spectrum brand

3 eggs

1 cup sugar

2 teaspoons vanilla

1½ cups Elizabeth's Gluten-Free Flour Blend (see Index) plus 1 teaspoon baking powder, or 1½ cups plus 1 teaspoon The Pure Pantry Gluten-Free Organic All-Purpose Baking Mix

3 tablespoons cocoa powder

1. Preheat oven to 350°F. Grease a 9 x 12-inch baking pan.

2. Place semi-sweet and dark chocolates and butter or coconut oil in double boiler on medium heat and stir until melted. Remove from heat and set aside.

3. Using an electric mixer, beat eggs in a large mixing bowl. Add sugar and vanilla and continue beating until well blended. With mixer on low, add melted chocolate and blend.

4. In a medium bowl, add baking mix, and baking powder if using Elizabeth's Blend, and beat until combined. Sift cocoa powder into the bowl. Gradually add the dry ingredients to the wet ingredients with mixer on low setting.

5. Pour mixture into baking pan and bake for 30-35 minutes. Cool completely – this is very important otherwise they will crumble. Once cooled, cut into squares.

Options: Add 2 tablespoons instant espresso powder for an "adult" brownie; fold in ½ cup chopped nuts after adding dry ingredients

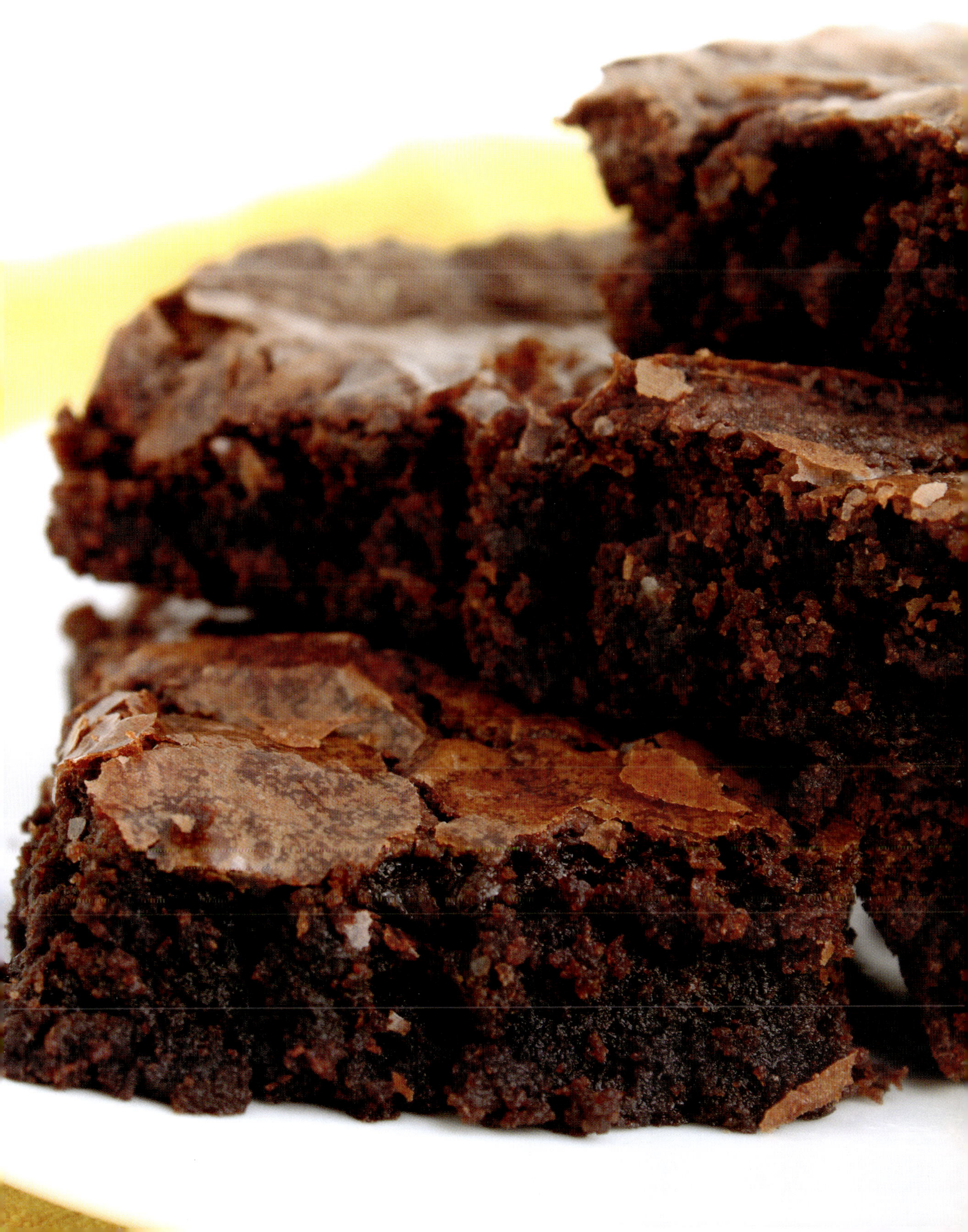

Almond-Joy Bars

Gluten-Free

Makes 16 bars

A quick and easy treat for Almond-Joy lovers.

10 gluten-free Whole-Grain Graham Crackers, (see Index) or store bought (approximately 1¾ cups when finely crushed)

½ cup butter or coconut oil, melted

1¼ cups shredded coconut

2 cups toasted slivered almonds

8 ounces semi-sweet chocolate, chopped

1- 14 ounce can sweetened condensed milk

1. Preheat oven to 350°F. Place graham crackers in food processor and pulse until fine crumbs. Add melted butter and pulse 2-3 times to combine.

2. Press crumbs into bottom of 9 x 13-inch pan. Sprinkle crust layer with coconut. Press gently. Sprinkle with toasted almond and press gently. Next sprinkle with chopped chocolate. Drizzle condensed milk all over the top of layers.

3. Bake 20 minutes or until golden brown. Cool before cutting into bars.

Mexican Wedding Cakes

Gluten-Free/Dairy-Free

Makes 40 cookies

½ **cup pecans**

1 cup powdered sugar

3/4 cup unsalted butter, softened, or Earth Balance Buttery Sticks

1 teaspoon vanilla

2 cups Elizabeth's Gluten-Free Baking Mix plus 1 teaspoon baking powder, or 2 cups The Pure Pantry Organic All Purpose Baking Mix

½ **teaspoon salt**

½ **cup powdered sugar, sifted, for finishing cookies**

1. Preheat oven to 350°F. Grease baking sheet with cooking spray.

2. On a separate baking sheet, toast pecans for 10 minutes. Cool completely. Using a food processor, grind the cooled pecans and powdered sugar to a fine powder. Set aside.

3. Cream the softened butter, or butter substitute, and vanilla in a mixer. Add the sugar-pecan mixture and mix well. Gradually add the baking mix, baking powder if using Elizabeth's baking mix, and salt. Mix until well combined. Cover tightly and refrigerate for 1 to 3 hours.

4. Roll the chilled dough into 1 inch balls. Place balls, 4 inches apart, on baking sheet. Bake cookies for 20 minutes. Cool on baking sheet for 3 minutes then transfer to a cooling rack. Sprinkle the cooled cookies with additional powdered sugar.

Fall Family Get Together

Gigi's French Onion Soup with Gruyere and Parmesan Cheeses

Cheddar Drop Biscuits

Pear, Persimmon & Fennel Salad

Apricot-Agave Glazed Meatloaf

Pumpkin-Agave Pie

Cozy Winter Supper

David's Carrot Ginger Soup
with Polenta Croutons

French Green Beans with
Sundried Tomatoes & Pine Nuts

Sweet Potato Gratin with
Pecan-Cinnamon Topping

Rosemary-Scented
Pork Tenderloin with
Cranberry-Cherry Chutney

Sticky Toffee Pudding with
Warm Caramel Sauce

menu ideas 167

Spring Celebration

Vegetable Saute in Lemon-Thyme-Basil Sauté Sauce

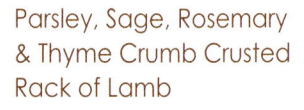

Parsley, Sage, Rosemary & Thyme Crumb Crusted Rack of Lamb

Asparagus and Leek Risotto

Key Lime Meringue Pie

Summer Family BBQ

Caesar Salad
with Polenta Croutons

Yukon Gold Potato
Goat Cheese Gratin

Chicken Grilled with
Pomegranate-Chipotle
BBQ sauce

Brownie Sundaes with
Coconut Ice Cream
and Chocolate Agave
Sauce

A

Agave nectar, 19
Allergy-Free Gingerbread Pals, 152
Almonds
    Almond-Encrusted Tilapia with Apricot-Orange Teriyaki Dipping Sauce, 99
    Almond-Joy Bars, 164
    Curried Quinoa Mango Salad, 88
Amaranth Muffins, Apricot, 51
Apple-Cinnamon Crêpes, 35
Apricots
    Apricot-Agave Glaze, 92
    Apricot-Agave Glazed Meatloaf, 92
    Apricot Amaranth Muffins, 51
    Apricot-Orange Teriyaki Dipping Sauce, 99
Asian Veggies in Tamari-Sesame-Ginger Stir-Fry Sauce, 104
Asparagus and Leek Risotto, 107
Avocados
    Caesar Salad with Polenta Croutons, 76
    Ensalada Verano (Summer Salad), 80

B

Bananas
    Banana Bread or Muffins, 52
    Banana Coconut Cream Pie, 122
Basic Chicken or Turkey Stock, 75
Basil
    Edamame Pesto Hummus, 84
    French Green Beans with Sundried Tomatoes and Pine Nuts, 113
    Lemon-Thyme-Basil Sauce, 116
    Spinach Pesto Sauce, 40
Beans, 17
    Edamame Pesto Hummus, 84
    French Green Beans with Sundried Tomatoes and Pine Nuts, 113
    White Bean Oregano Chili, 74
Beef
    Apricot-Agave Glazed Meatloaf, 92
Belgian endive
    Pear, Persimmon and Fennel Salad with Pear-Champagne Vinaigrette, 83
Bell peppers
    Ensalada Verano (Summer Salad), 80
    Mojito Chicken on Cilantro Rice, 96
    Quinoa with Roasted Eggplant Caponata, 112
    Veggie Frittata, 42
Biscotti, Hazelnut Chocolate Chip, 156
Biscuits, Cheddar Drop, 64
Blintzes, Ryan's Berry, 36
Blueberries
    Blueberry Cheesecake, 142
    Blueberry Millet Scones, 47
    Blueberry Oat Pancakes with Blueberry-Agave Syrup, 24
    Ryan's Berry Blintzes, 36
Bread. See also Biscuits; Muffins; Scones
    Banana Bread, 52
    Cornbread, 59
    Gigi's French Onion Soup, 73
    Gluten-Free Breadcrumbs, 93
    Lemon Tea Bread, 55
    Pumpkin Streusel Bread, 56
    Savory Polenta Bread, 63
    Tomato-Pesto Breakfast Strata, 40
Brownies
    Brownie Sundaes, 146
    Dark Chocolate Brownies, 162
Butter
    alternatives to, 19
    Pecan-Agave Butter, 28
    Strawberry-Agave Butter, 27
Butternut Squash and Pumpkin Risotto, 108

C

Caesar Salad with Polenta Croutons, 76
Cakes. See also Cheesecakes; Coffee cakes; Cupcakes
    Carrot Cake with Heavenly Cream Cheese Frosting, 132
    Cranberry Ginger Pound Cake, 134
    Flourless Chocolate Decadence, 138
    Sticky Toffee Pudding with Warm Caramel Sauce, 141
Caponata, Roasted Eggplant, Quinoa with, 112
Caramel Sauce, 141
Carrots
    Carrot Cake or Cupcakes with Heavenly Cream Cheese Frosting, 132
    David's Carrot Ginger Soup with Polenta Croutons, 69
    Easy Fried Rice, 109
    Lentil and Root Vegetable Soup, 70
    Spaghetti with Turkey Meatballs, 110
Cheese, 19
    Asparagus and Leek Risotto, 107
    Blueberry Cheesecake, 142
    Butternut Squash and Pumpkin Risotto, 108
    Cheddar Drop Biscuits, 64
    dairy-free alternatives to, 19
    Ensalada Verano (Summer Salad), 80
    Gigi's French Onion Soup, 73
    Greek Salad with Omega-Oregano Dressing, 79
    Heavenly Cream Cheese Frosting, 132
    Heirloom Tomato Mozzarella Stack with Edamame Pesto Hummus, 84
    Maui Onion and Chèvre Tart, 41
    Pear, Persimmon and Fennel Salad with Pear-Champagne Vinaigrette, 83
    Pumpkin Cheesecake, 145
    Quinoa with Roasted Eggplant Caponata, 112
    Ryan's Berry Blintzes, 36
    Spinach Pesto Sauce, 40
    Tomato-Pesto Breakfast Strata, 40
    Veggie Frittata, 42
    Yukon Gold Potato–Goat Cheese Gratin, 117
    Zucchini Goat Cheese Gratin, 119
Cheesecakes
    Blueberry Cheesecake, 142
    Pumpkin Cheesecake, 145
Cherry-Cranberry Chutney, 98
Chia gel egg replacer, 19
Chicken
    Basic Chicken Stock, 75
    Chicken Grilled with Pomegranate Chipotle BBQ Sauce, 95
    Mojito Chicken on Cilantro Rice, 96
    White Bean Oregano Chili, 74
Chili, White Bean Oregano, 74
Chocolate
    Almond-Joy Bars, 164
    Chocolate-Agave Frosting, 149
    Chocolate-Agave Sauce, 149
    Chocolate Bourbon Pecan Pie, 125

Chocolate Chip Espresso Coffee Cake, 38
Chocolate Chocolate-Chip Cupcakes, 137
Chocolate-Dipped Molasses Ginger Cookies, 155
Chocolate Peppermint Meringues, 154
Chocolate Swirl Meringues, 154
Dark Chocolate Brownies, 162
Flourless Chocolate Decadence, 138
Hazelnut Chocolate Chip Biscotti, 156
Raspberry Chocolate Crêpes, 35
Chutney, Cranberry-Cherry, 98
Cilantro Rice, 109
Cinnamon-Poached Pears, 31
Coconut
   Almond-Joy Bars, 164
   Banana Coconut Cream Pie, 122
   Coconut Crust, 129
   Coconut Lemon Curd Squares, 161
   milk, 19
   oil, 19
   sugar, 19
   yogurt, 19
Coffee cakes
   Chocolate Chip Espresso Coffee Cake, 38
   Quick Cranberry Nut Coffee Cake, 37
Cookies. See also Brownies
   Allergy-Free Gingerbread Pals, 152
   Almond-Joy Bars, 164
   Chocolate-Dipped Molasses Ginger Cookies, 155
   Chocolate Peppermint Meringues, 154
   Chocolate Swirl Meringues, 154
   Coconut Lemon Curd Squares, 161
   Hazelnut Chocolate Chip Biscotti, 156
   Mexican Wedding Cakes, 165
   Vanilla Icing for Decorating Cookies, 153
Cornmeal
   Cornbread or Cornbread Muffins, 59
   Polenta Croutons, 89
   Savory Polenta Bread, 63
Cranberries
   Cranberry-Cherry Chutney, 98
   Cranberry Ginger Pound Cake, 134
   Quick Cranberry Nut Coffee Cake, 37
   Rice and Lentils with Cranberries and Oranges, 87
Crêpes
   Apple-Cinnamon Crêpes, 35
   Homemade Gluten-Free Crêpes, 32
   Raspberry Chocolate Crêpes, 35
   Ryan's Berry Blintzes, 36
Croutons, Polenta, 89
Crumb Topping, 56
Crusts
   Coconut Crust, 129
   Gingersnap Crust, 129
   Pecan Crust, 129
   Pie Crust, 131
   Whole-Grain Graham Cracker Crust, 129
Cucumbers
   Greek Salad with Omega-Oregano Dressing, 79
   Quinoa Tabouli, 86
Cupcakes
   Carrot Cupcakes with Heavenly Cream Cheese Frosting, 132
   Chocolate Chocolate-Chip Cupcakes, 137
Curried Quinoa Mango Salad, 88

D
Dairy products. See also Butter; Cheese
   alternatives to, 19
   organic, 19
Dark Chocolate Brownies, 162
Dates
   High-Fiber Date Nut Scones, 48
   Sticky Toffee Pudding with Warm Caramel Sauce, 141
David's Carrot Ginger Soup with Polenta Croutons, 69
Desserts
   Allergy-Free Gingerbread Pals, 152
   Almond-Joy Bars, 164
   Banana Coconut Cream Pie, 122
   Blueberry Cheesecake, 142
   Brownie Sundaes, 146
   Carrot Cake or Cupcakes with Heavenly Cream Cheese Frosting, 132
   Chocolate Bourbon Pecan Pie, 125
   Chocolate Chocolate-Chip Cupcakes, 137
   Chocolate-Dipped Molasses Ginger Cookies, 155
   Chocolate Peppermint Meringues, 154
   Chocolate Swirl Meringues, 154
   Coconut Lemon Curd Squares, 161
   Cranberry Ginger Pound Cake, 134
   Dark Chocolate Brownies, 162
   Flourless Chocolate Decadence, 138
   Hazelnut Chocolate Chip Biscotti, 156
   Key Lime Meringue Pie, 128
   Meringue Nests, 154
   Mexican Wedding Cakes, 165
   Pumpkin-Agave Pie, 126
   Pumpkin Cheesecake, 145
   Sticky Toffee Pudding with Warm Caramel Sauce, 141
   White Chocolate Mac-Toffee Cookies, 158
Dilly-Lemony "Tartar" Sauce, 100

E
Easy Fried Rice, 109
Edamame Pesto Hummus, 84
Eggplant Caponata, Roasted, Quinoa with, 112
Eggs
   Chocolate Peppermint Meringues, 154
   Chocolate Swirl Meringues, 154
   Easy Fried Rice, 109
   Meringue Nests, 154
   replacers for, 19
   Tomato-Pesto Breakfast Strata, 40
   Veggie Frittata, 42
Elizabeth's Gluten-Free Flour Blend, 18
Ensalada Verano (Summer Salad), 80
Espresso
   Chocolate Chip Espresso Coffee Cake, 38
   Flourless Chocolate Decadence, 138

F
Fennel, Pear, and Persimmon Salad with Pear-Champagne Vinaigrette, 83
Fish
   Almond-Encrusted Tilapia with Apricot-Orange Teriyaki Dipping Sauce, 99
   Grilled Salmon on Edamame Pesto Hummus with Zucchini "Pasta," 103
   Grilled Salmon or Halibut with Dilly-Lemony "Tartar" Sauce, 100
Flax gel egg replacer, 19

index **171**

Flour
- Elizabeth's Gluten-Free Flour Blend, 18
- gluten-free, 17

Flourless Chocolate Decadence, 138
French Green Beans with Sundried Tomatoes and Pine Nuts, 113
Frittata, Veggie, 42
Frostings
- Chocolate-Agave Frosting, 149
- Heavenly Cream Cheese Frosting, 132

G

Gigi's French Onion Soup, 73
Gingerbread
- Allergy-Free Gingerbread Pals, 152
- Gingerbread Waffles with Pecan-Agave Butter and Cinnamon-Poached Pears, 31

Gingersnap Crust, 129
Glaze, Apricot-Agave, 92
Gluten-Free Breadcrumbs, 93
Graham crackers
- Almond-Joy Bars, 164
- Whole-Grain Graham Cracker Crust, 129
- Whole-Grain Graham Crackers, 159

Grains, gluten-free, 17
Gratins
- Sweet Potato Gratin with Pecan-Cinnamon Topping, 115
- Yukon Gold Potato–Goat Cheese Gratin, 117
- Zucchini Goat Cheese Gratin, 119

Greek Salad with Omega-Oregano Dressing, 79
Grilled Salmon on Edamame Pesto Hummus with Zucchini "Pasta," 103
Grilled Salmon or Halibut with Dilly-Lemony "Tartar" Sauce, 100

H

Halibut, Grilled, with Dilly-Lemony "Tartar" Sauce, 100
Hazelnut Chocolate Chip Biscotti, 156
Heavenly Cream Cheese Frosting, 132
Heirloom Tomato Mozzarella Stack with Edamame Pesto Hummus, 84
High-Fiber Date Nut Scones, 48
Homemade Gluten-Free Crêpes, 32
Homemade Gluten-Free Pancakes, 23
Hummus, Edamame Pesto, 84

I

Ice cream
- Brownie Sundaes, 146
- dairy-free, 19

Icing, Vanilla, for Decorating Cookies, 153
Isabelle's Strawberry-Pecan Pancakes with Strawberry-Agave Butter, 27

J

Jicama
- Ensalada Verano (Summer Salad), 80

K

Key Lime Meringue Pie, 128

L

Lamb, Parsley, Sage, Rosemary and Thyme Crumb Crusted Rack of, 93
Leek and Asparagus Risotto, 107

Lemons
- Coconut Lemon Curd Squares, 161
- Lemon Tea Bread, 55
- Lemon-Thyme-Basil Sauce, 116

Lentils, 17
- Lentil and Root Vegetable Soup, 70
- Rice and Lentils with Cranberries and Oranges, 87

Lettuce
- Caesar Salad with Polenta Croutons, 76
- Ensalada Verano (Summer Salad), 80
- Greek Salad with Omega-Oregano Dressing, 79

Limes
- Key Lime Meringue Pie, 128
- Mojito Chicken on Cilantro Rice, 96

M

Macadamia nuts
- Ensalada Verano (Summer Salad), 80
- White Chocolate Mac-Toffee Cookies, 158

Mangoes
- Curried Quinoa Mango Salad, 88
- Ensalada Verano (Summer Salad), 80

Maple Nut Scones, 50
Maple sugar, 19
Margarine, 19
Maui Onion and Chèvre Tart, 41
Meatballs, Turkey, Spaghetti with, 110
Meatloaf, Apricot-Agave Glazed, 92
Menus, seasonal, 166–69
Meringues
- Chocolate Peppermint Meringues, 154
- Chocolate Swirl Meringues, 154
- Meringue Nests, 154

Mexican Wedding Cakes, 165
Millet Scones, Blueberry, 47
Mojito Chicken on Cilantro Rice, 96
Muffins
- Apricot Amaranth Muffins, 51
- Banana Muffins, 52
- Cornbread Muffins, 59
- Peach Cobbler Muffins, 60

N

Nutmeg Pumpkin Pancakes with Pecan-Agave Butter, 28
Nuts, 17. See also individual nuts

O

Oats, 17
- Blueberry Oat Pancakes with Blueberry-Agave Syrup, 24
- Maple Nut Scones, 50

Olives
- Greek Salad with Omega-Oregano Dressing, 79
- Quinoa with Roasted Eggplant Caponata, 112

Omega-Oregano Dressing, 79
Onions
- Gigi's French Onion Soup, 73
- Lentil and Root Vegetable Soup, 70
- Maui Onion and Chèvre Tart, 41
- Veggie Frittata, 42

Oranges
- Apricot-Orange Teriyaki Dipping Sauce, 99
- David's Carrot Ginger Soup with Polenta Croutons, 69
- Mojito Chicken on Cilantro Rice, 96
- Rice and Lentils with Cranberries and Oranges, 87

P

Palm, hearts of
  Ensalada Verano (Summer Salad), 80
Pancakes
  Blueberry Oat Pancakes with Blueberry-Agave Syrup, 24
  Homemade Gluten-Free Pancakes, 23
  Isabelle's Strawberry-Pecan Pancakes with Strawberry-Agave Butter, 27
  Nutmeg Pumpkin Pancakes with Pecan-Agave Butter, 28
Pantry, stocking, 16–19
Parsley
  Parsley, Sage, Rosemary and Thyme Crumb Crusted Rack of Lamb, 93
  Quinoa Tabouli, 86
  Rice and Lentils with Cranberries and Oranges, 87
  Spinach Pesto Sauce, 40
Pasta
  gluten-free, 17
  Grilled Salmon on Edamame Pesto Hummus with Zucchini "Pasta," 103
  Spaghetti with Turkey Meatballs, 110-111
Pastry Cream, 128
Peach Cobbler Muffins, 60
Pears
  Cinnamon-Poached Pears, 31
  Pear, Persimmon and Fennel Salad with Pear-Champagne Vinaigrette, 83
Peas
  Easy Fried Rice, 109
Pecans
  Carrot Cake or Cupcakes with Heavenly Cream Cheese Frosting, 132
  Chocolate Bourbon Pecan Pie, 125
  High-Fiber Date Nut Scones, 48
  Isabelle's Strawberry-Pecan Pancakes with Strawberry-Agave Butter, 27
  Maple Nut Scones, 50
  Mexican Wedding Cakes, 165
  Pecan-Agave Butter, 28
  Pecan Crust, 129
  Pumpkin Streusel Bread, 56
  Quick Cranberry Nut Coffee Cake, 37
  Sweet Potato Gratin with Pecan-Cinnamon Topping, 115
Peppermint Meringues, Chocolate, 154
Persimmon, Pear, and Fennel Salad with Pear-Champagne Vinaigrette, 83
Pesto
  Edamame Pesto Hummus, 84
  Spinach Pesto Sauce, 40
  Tomato-Pesto Breakfast Strata, 40
Pies. See also Crusts
  Banana Coconut Cream Pie, 122
  Chocolate Bourbon Pecan Pie, 125
  Key Lime Meringue Pie, 128
  Pie Crust, 131
  Pumpkin-Agave Pie, 126
Pine nuts
  French Green Beans with Sundried Tomatoes and Pine Nuts, 113
  Spinach Pesto Sauce, 40
Polenta. See Cornmeal
Pomegranate Chipotle BBQ Sauce, 95
Pork Tenderloin, Rosemary-Scented, with Cranberry-Cherry Chutney, 98

Potatoes
  Lentil and Root Vegetable Soup, 70
  Yukon Gold Potato–Goat Cheese Gratin, 117
Pound Cake, Cranberry Ginger, 134
Pumpkin
  Butternut Squash and Pumpkin Risotto, 108
  Nutmeg Pumpkin Pancakes with Pecan-Agave Butter, 28
  Pumpkin-Agave Pie, 126
  Pumpkin Cheesecake, 145
  Pumpkin Streusel Bread, 56

Q

Quick Cranberry Nut Coffee Cake, 37
Quinoa, 17
  Curried Quinoa Mango Salad, 88
  Quinoa Tabouli, 86
  Quinoa with Roasted Eggplant Caponata, 112

R

Raspberries
  Flourless Chocolate Decadence, 138
  Raspberry Chocolate Crêpes, 35
  Sticky Toffee Pudding with Warm Caramel Sauce, 141
Rice, 17
  Asparagus and Leek Risotto, 107
  Butternut Squash and Pumpkin Risotto, 108
  Cilantro Rice, 109
  Easy Fried Rice, 109
  Mojito Chicken on Cilantro Rice, 96
  Rice and Lentils with Cranberries and Oranges, 87
Risotto
  Asparagus and Leek Risotto, 107
  Butternut Squash and Pumpkin Risotto, 108
Rosemary-Scented Pork Tenderloin with Cranberry-Cherry Chutney, 98
Ryan's Berry Blintzes, 36

S

Salad dressings
  Caesar Salad Dressing, 76
  Omega-Oregano Dressing, 79
  Pear-Champagne Vinaigrette, 83
Salads
  Caesar Salad with Polenta Croutons, 76
  Curried Quinoa Mango Salad, 88
  Greek Salad with Omega-Oregano Dressing, 79
  Heirloom Tomato Mozzarella Stack with Edamame Pesto Hummus, 84
  Pear, Persimmon and Fennel Salad with Pear-Champagne Vinaigrette, 83
  Quinoa Tabouli, 86
  Rice and Lentils with Cranberries and Oranges, 87
Salmon
  Grilled Salmon on Edamame Pesto Hummus with Zucchini "Pasta," 103
  Grilled Salmon with Dilly-Lemony "Tartar" Sauce, 100
Sauces
  Apricot-Orange Teriyaki Dipping Sauce, 99
  Caramel Sauce, 141
  Chocolate-Agave Sauce, 149
  Dilly-Lemony "Tartar" Sauce, 100
  Lemon-Thyme-Basil Sauce, 116
  Pomegranate Chipotle BBQ Sauce, 95
  Spinach Pesto Sauce, 40
  Tamari-Sesame-Ginger Stir-Fry Sauce, 104

index **173**

Sausage
    Apricot-Agave Glazed Meatloaf, 92
Savory Polenta Bread, 63
Scones
    Blueberry Millet Scones, 47
    High-Fiber Date Nut Scones, 48
    Maple Nut Scones, 50
Seeds, 17
Soups
    David's Carrot Ginger Soup with Polenta Croutons, 69
    Gigi's French Onion Soup, 73
    Lentil and Root Vegetable Soup, 70
Sour cream alternative, 19
Spaghetti with Turkey Meatballs, 110-111
Spinach
    Edamame Pesto Hummus, 84
    Spinach Pesto Sauce, 40
    Tomato-Pesto Breakfast Strata, 40
    Veggie Frittata, 42
Squash. See also Zucchini
    Butternut Squash and Pumpkin Risotto, 108
Sticky Toffee Pudding with Warm Caramel Sauce, 141
Stock, Basic Chicken or Turkey, 75
Strata, Tomato-Pesto Breakfast, 40
Strawberries
    Isabelle's Strawberry-Pecan Pancakes with Strawberry-Agave Butter, 27
    Ryan's Berry Blintzes, 36
Streusel Topping, 38
Sundaes, Brownie, 146
Sweeteners, 19
Sweet Potato Gratin with Pecan-Cinnamon Topping, 115
Syrup, Blueberry-Agave, 24

T
Tabouli, Quinoa, 86
Tamari-Sesame-Ginger Stir-Fry Sauce, 104
Tart, Maui Onion and Chèvre, 41
Tilapia, Almond-Encrusted, with Apricot-Orange Teriyaki Dipping Sauce, 99
Toffee
    Sticky Toffee Pudding with Warm Caramel Sauce, 141
    White Chocolate Mac-Toffee Cookies, 158
Tomatoes
    French Green Beans with Sundried Tomatoes and Pine Nuts, 113
    Greek Salad with Omega-Oregano Dressing, 79
    Heirloom Tomato Mozzarella Stack with Edamame Pesto Hummus, 84
    Lentil and Root Vegetable Soup, 70
    Pomegranate Chipotle BBQ Sauce, 95
    Quinoa Tabouli, 86
    Savory Polenta Bread, 63
    Spaghetti with Turkey Meatballs, 110
    Tomato-Pesto Breakfast Strata, 40
    Veggie Frittata, 42
    White Bean Oregano Chili, 74
    Zucchini Goat Cheese Gratin, 119
Turkey
    Apricot-Agave Glazed Meatloaf, 92
    Basic Turkey Stock, 75
    Gigi's French Onion Soup, 73
    Spaghetti with Turkey Meatballs, 110-111

V
Vanilla Icing for Decorating Cookies, 153
Vegetables. See also individual vegetables
    Asian Veggies in Tamari-Sesame-Ginger Stir-Fry Sauce, 104
    Lentil and Root Vegetable Soup, 70
    Vegetable Sauté in Lemon-Thyme-Basil Sauce, 116
    Veggie Frittata, 42
Vinaigrettes. See Salad dressings

W
Waffles, Gingerbread, with Pecan-Agave Butter and Cinnamon-Poached Pears, 31
Walnuts
    Apricot Amaranth Muffins, 51
    Brownie Sundaes, 146
    Carrot Cake or Cupcakes with Heavenly Cream Cheese Frosting, 132
    High-Fiber Date Nut Scones, 48
    Lemon Tea Bread, 55
    Pear, Persimmon and Fennel Salad with Pear-Champagne Vinaigrette, 83
    Quick Cranberry Nut Coffee Cake, 37
    Spinach Pesto Sauce, 40
White Bean Oregano Chili, 74
White Chocolate Mac-Toffee Cookies, 158
Whole-Grain Graham Cracker Crust, 129
Whole-Grain Graham Crackers, 159

Y
Yukon Gold Potato–Goat Cheese Gratin, 117

Z
Zucchini
    Apricot-Agave Glazed Meatloaf, 92
    Grilled Salmon on Edamame Pesto Hummus with Zucchini "Pasta," 103
    Quinoa with Roasted Eggplant Caponata, 112
    Spaghetti with Turkey Meatballs, 110
    Veggie Frittata, 42
    Zucchini Goat Cheese Gratin, 119